Homeschooling in the 21st Century

Education began on the most intimate levels: the family and the community. With industrialization, education became professionalized and bureaucratized, typically conducted in schools rather than homes. Over the past half century, however, schooling has increasingly returned home, both in the United States and across the globe. This reflects several trends, including greater affluence and smaller family size leading parents to focus more on child well-being; declining faith in professionals (including educators); and the Internet, whose resources facilitate home education. In the United States, students who are homeschooled for at least part of their childhood outnumber those in charter schools. Yet remarkably little research addresses homeschooling.

This book brings together work from 20 researchers, addressing a range of homeschooling topics, including the evolving legal and institutional frameworks behind home education; why some parents make this choice; home education educational environments; special education; and outcomes regarding both academic achievement and political tolerance. In short, this book offers the most up-to-date research to guide policy makers and home educators, a matter of great importance given the agenda of the current presidential administration.

The chapters in this book were originally published as articles in the *Journal of School Choice*.

Robert Maranto is the Twenty-First-Century Chair in Leadership in the Department of Education Reform at the University of Arkansas, USA. He also serves on the boards of the Fayetteville Public Schools and Achievement House Cyber Charter School. He is the editor of the *Journal of School Choice*.

Debra A. Bell is Executive Director of AIM Academy, which provides college-prep classes online for homeschool students. After homeschooling her four children K–12, she completed a PhD in Educational Psychology at Temple University, USA. She is the Vice-Chair of the Global Home Education Conference.

T0347564

Homeschooling in the 21st Century

Research and Prospects

Edited by
Robert Maranto and Debra A. Bell

Routledge
Taylor & Francis Group

LONDON AND NEW YORK

First published 2018 by Routledge

2 Park Square, Milton Park, Abingdon, Oxfordshire OX14 4RN
52 Vanderbilt Avenue, New York, NY 10017

Routledge is an imprint of the Taylor & Francis Group, an informa business

First issued in paperback 2019

British Library Cataloguing in Publication Data
A catalogue record for this book is available from the British Library

ISBN 13: 978-1-138-50140-9 (hbk)
ISBN 13: 978-0-367-89175-6 (pbk)

Typeset in Minion Pro
by diacriTech, Chennai

Publisher's Note
The publisher accepts responsibility for any inconsistencies that may have arisen
during the conversion of this book from journal articles to book chapters, namely
the possible inclusion of journal terminology.

Disclaimer
Every effort has been made to contact copyright holders for their permission to
reprint material in this book. The publishers would be grateful to hear from any
copyright holder who is not here acknowledged and will undertake to rectify any
errors or omissions in future editions of this book.

Contents

Citation Information   vii
Notes on Contributors   ix

SECTION I
Legal and Social Foundations of Home Education

1 The Fall and Rise of Home Education   1
   Angela Watson, Robert Maranto and Debra A. Bell

2 The Human Right of Home Education   19
   Michael P. Donnelly

3 Homeschooling, Virtual Learning, and the
   Eroding Public/Private Binary   33
   Aaron Saiger

SECTION II
Why Parents Homeschool

4 Types of Homeschool Environments and Need
   Support for Children's Achievement Motivation   56
   Debra A. Bell, Avi Kaplan, and S. Kenneth Thurman

5 A Descriptive Survey of Why Parents Choose
   Hybrid Homeschools   81
   Eric Wearne

6 African American Homeschool Parents' Motivations
   for Homeschooling and Their Black Children's
   Academic Achievement   98
   Brian Ray

CONTENTS

7 Homeschooling Is Not Just About Education: Focuses of Meaning 124
Ari Neuman and Oz Guterman

SECTION III
Homeschooling Outcomes

8 Homeschool Parents and Satisfaction with Special Education Services 144
Albert Cheng, Sivan Tuchman, and Patrick J. Wolf

9 Are Homeschoolers Prepared for College Calculus? 162
*Christian P. Wilkens, Carol H. Wade, Gerhard Sonnert,
and Philip M. Sadler*

10 Does Homeschooling or Private Schooling Promote Political
Intolerance? Evidence From a Christian University 181
Albert Cheng

Index 201

Citation Information

The following chapters were originally published in the *Journal of School Choice*. When citing this material, please use the original volume number, issue number, date of publication, and page numbering for each article, as follows:

Chapter 2
The Human Right of Home Education
Michael P. Donnelly
Journal of School Choice, volume 10, issue 3 (July 2016) pp. 283–296

Chapter 3
Homeschooling, Virtual Learning, and the Eroding Public/Private Binary
Aaron Saiger
Journal of School Choice, volume 10, issue 3 (July 2016) pp. 297–319

Chapter 4
Types of Homeschool Environments and Need Support for Children's Achievement Motivation
Debra A. Bell, Avi Kaplan, and S. Kenneth Thurman
Journal of School Choice, volume 10, issue 3 (July 2016) pp. 330–354

Chapter 5
A Descriptive Survey of Why Parents Choose Hybrid Homeschools
Eric Wearne
Journal of School Choice, volume 10, issue 3 (July 2016) pp. 364–380

Chapter 6
African American Homeschool Parents' Motivations for Homeschooling and Their Black Children's Academic Achievement
Brian Ray
Journal of School Choice, volume 9, issue 1 (January 2015) pp. 71–96

Chapter 7

Homeschooling Is Not Just About Education: Focuses of Meaning
Ari Neuman and Oz Guterman
Journal of School Choice, volume 11, issue 1 (January 2017) pp. 148–167

Chapter 8

Homeschool Parents and Satisfaction with Special Education Services
Albert Cheng, Sivan Tuchman, and Patrick J. Wolf
Journal of School Choice, volume 10, issue 3 (July 2016) pp. 381–398

Chapter 9

Are Homeschoolers Prepared for College Calculus?
Christian P. Wilkens, Carol H. Wade, Gerhard Sonnert, and Philip M. Sadler
Journal of School Choice, volume 9, issue 1 (January 2015) pp. 30–48

Chapter 10

Does Homeschooling or Private Schooling Promote Political Intolerance? Evidence From a Christian University
Albert Cheng
Journal of School Choice, volume 8, issue 4 (November 2014) pp. 49–68

For any permission-related enquiries please visit:
http://www.tandfonline.com/page/help/permissions

Notes on Contributors

Debra A. Bell is Executive Director of AIM Academy, which provides college-prep classes online for homeschool students. After homeschooling her four children K–12, she completed a PhD in Educational Psychology at Temple University, USA. She is the Vice-Chair of the Global Home Education Conference.

Albert Cheng is a postdoctoral researcher in the Program on Education Policy and Governance at Harvard University, USA. His research interests include school choice, religious schools, and civic values.

Michael P. Donnelly is Director of Global Outreach at Home School Legal Defence Association (HSLDA), USA. He coordinates HSLDA's support of homeschooling freedom all over the world. He is also Adjunct Professor of Government at Patrick Henry College, USA.

Oz Guterman is a Senior Lecturer and heads the Department of Human Resource at Western Galilee College in Israel. His interests include homeschooling, factors of academic excellence among students, and nonverbal perception of emotion.

Avi Kaplan is Associate Professor of Psychological Studies in Education at Temple University, USA. His research looks into student motivation and self-regulation, learning environments, and self and identity development.

Robert Maranto is the Twenty-First-Century Chair in Leadership in the Department of Education Reform at the University of Arkansas, USA. He also serves on the boards of the Fayetteville Public Schools and Achievement House Cyber Charter School. He is the editor of the *Journal of School Choice*.

Ari Neuman is Senior Lecturer and Chair at the Department of Education, Western Galilee College, Israel. His research interests include homeschooling and program evaluation.

Brian Ray is President of the National Home Education Research Institute (NHERI), USA. He has been investigating the homeschool movement for over 30 years.

Philip M. Sadler is Senior Lecturer in the Department of Astronomy and Director of the Science Education Department, Harvard University, USA. His research interests include developing graduate students' teaching skills, the STEM career pipeline, assessment in science, and the enhancement of the skills of teachers of science.

Aaron Saiger is Professor of Law at Fordham University, USA. He writes and teaches in the areas of administrative law and regulation, education law, legislation, and property.

Gerhard Sonnert is a Research Associate at the Harvard-Smithsonian Center for Astrophysics, Harvard University, USA. He works on large-scale survey studies in the area of science and mathematics education and is particularly interested in the gender aspects of science careers.

S. Kenneth Thurman is Professor of Special Education in Teaching and Learning at Temple University, USA. His areas of professional interest include ecological models of service delivery, infant and preschool development, and families.

Sivan Tuchman is a Research Analyst at the Center on Reinventing Public Education, where she studies how educators and families experience the implementation of innovative policies and programs in K-12 schools and the systems that support them. Her work spans school choice policies (private schools, charters, virtual schooling, and homeschooling), as well as outcomes for students in special education (academic achievement, identification changes, school discipline, and satisfaction). Sivan holds a PhD in Education Policy from the University of Arkansas' Department of Education Reform, a BA in Sociology from the University of California, Berkeley, and holds a California Educational Specialist credential in mild/moderate disabilities.

Carol H. Wade is Assistant Professor of Education at The College at Brockport, USA. Her research concerns secondary mathematical preparation for college calculus success and student motivation to learn STEM content.

Angela Watson is Distinguished Doctoral Fellow at the University of Arkansas, USA. She is pursuing a PhD in Education Policy in the Department of Education Reform. Her research interests include school choice, STEM education, informal education, and the impact of religion on educational outcomes.

Eric Wearne is Associate Professor of Education at Georgia Gwinnett College, USA. His academic interests include education policy, history of American education, and school choice.

Christian P. Wilkens is Assistant Professor of Education at The College at Brockport, USA. His research interests include school choice, charter schools, homeschooling, and students with disabilities.

Patrick J. Wolf is Distinguished Professor of Education Policy and Twenty-First-Century Endowed Chair in School Choice in the Department of Education Reform at the University of Arkansas, USA. As principal investigator of the School Choice Demonstration Project, he has led or is leading major studies of school choice initiatives including longitudinal evaluations of school voucher programs in Washington, DC, Milwaukee, WI, and the state of Louisiana.

The Fall and Rise of Home Education

Angela Watson, Robert Maranto and Debra A. Bell

Introduction

Originally, schooling occurred chiefly in the home, within families or, for the relatively wealthy, through paid tutors. Gradually, American schooling came to take place largely in the dominant local religious congregations, reflecting that churches were the primary local institutions and that learning to read the Protestant Bible was then the key goal of schooling (Berner, 2017; Glenn, 2012; Peterson, 2010; Ravitch, 2000). From these highly personal, parent-controlled beginnings, over the past century and a half, formal schooling in the United States grew in size and magnitude, with ever-expanding public bureaucracies educating and caring for more children for increasing portions of their lives. Compulsory attendance laws and education by certified professionals gradually became the norm in the United States (Dumas, Gates, & Schwarzer, 2010), and the West generally (Dixon, 2014). Although most Western nations had mixed educational systems, in which public schools operated alongside publicly subsidized faith-based schools of various kinds, in the United States, traditional public schools became the dominant mode of schooling in most localities attaining near-monopoly status (Berner, 2017; Glenn, 2012). This bureaucratization of education reflected trust in Progressive era ideals, which from clean water and sanitation to civil service systems, certainly offered more than a few victories for humankind. Yet by the late twentieth century, the industrial model of schooling reached its zenith (Hess, 2010). Smaller family size and greater wealth led parents, particularly the better educated, to invest more in each child, creating demand for *individualized* instruction that traditional public bureaucracies were and are ill-suited to provide (Lareau, 2003; Petrilli, 2012; Stevens, 2001). Declining trust in experts and in authority generally led some parents to conclude that they could educate their own children as competently as credentialed instructors. Home education entrepreneurs, often themselves homeschoolers, arose to meet the curricular and social needs of homeschooled students and their parents. Concurrently, organized political groups arose to safeguard homeschooling (Stevens, 2001). By the early twenty-first century, burgeoning information technologies enabled these parent-educators to receive help as needed to teach their children a wide range of courses (Hanna, 2012; Martin-Chang, Gould, & Meuse, 2011; Vander Ark, 2012).

Outlawed in many states until the middle 1990s, homeschooling, the original American method of schooling, has made a comeback in the past four decades (Lines, 2000a; see the Aaron Saiger chapter and the Bell, Kaplan and Thurman chapter in this volume). In the 1960s, a growing, individualistic counterculture proved fertile ground for writers such as Ivan Illich, John Taylor Gatto, and John Holt to develop conceptual terms like *deschooling* and *unschooling*, justifying a return to homeschooling. By the late 1980s, homeschooling had grown from the fringe to a significant social and political movement (Knowles, Marlow, & Muchmore, 1992; Kunzman & Gaither, 2013; Stevens, 2001). By 2000, homeschooling had by and large gained political and social acceptance (Anthony & Burroughs, 2010) and a certain diversity, practiced by traditional Christian parents, counterculture parents, and parents (including parents of special education students, as shown in Cheng, Tuchman and Wolf chapter in this volume) seeking to shelter their children from concerns ranging from bullying to bureaucratic standardization and testing. As noted below, though traditional public schools are on the whole quite safe physically (e.g., Petrilli, 2012), bullying is not uncommon, and rare but widely publicized incidents of violence seemingly led some parents to seek the safety of home education. Whatever their distinct motives, one thing nearly all homeschool parents have in common is prioritizing their children's educational needs over their own material gain, as noted in the title of Mitchell Stevens' (2001) pioneering study *Kingdom of Children*. As we discuss below at length, homeschooling parents sacrifice considerable income for the well-being of their children. For the most part, they are very dedicated parents. Though systematic research has not addressed the question, we suspect that many homeschool parents themselves had less than satisfactory experiences in traditional public schools, in sharp contrast to traditional public school educators, most of whom loved their schooling enough to choose careers in public education (Maranto, 2017).

How Many Homeschoolers?

The National Center for Education Statistics (NCES) estimated 1.1 million homeschool students in 2003 and nearly 1.8 million (3.4% of school-aged children) in 2012 (Jeffrey, 2015; Redford, Battle, & Bielick, 2016). Similarly, the National Home Education Research Institute (NHERI), a homeschool advocacy group, estimated nearly 2 million homeschoolers in spring 2010 (Ray, 2011; see Figure 1.1). These are single point-in-time estimates, and some children may be homeschooled for limited portions of their childhood; thus some estimate that 6%–12% of American school-aged children will be homeschooled for one or more grades (Isenberg, 2007; Lines, 1999). No doubt many others considered the option. Early research indicated that most homeschool families do not persist into a second year (Isenberg, 2007). Homeschooling likely has a constant churn with new families choosing homeschooling as others drop out, alongside a stable core group of home educators, as may also characterize cyber charter student populations (Beck, Egalite, & Maranto, 2014; Watson, Beck, & Maranto, 2017). Many homeschool families shift in and out of homeschooling depending on the needs of their children, sometimes to avoid a particular school, grade, or even teacher. Commonly, a family will homeschool some children while sending others to more traditional schooling options (Isenberg, 2007).

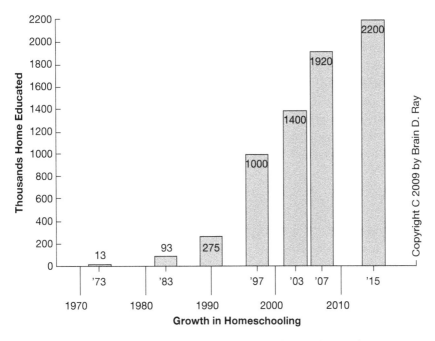

Figure 1.1. Estimated growth of homeschooling in the United States (NHERI).

Some estimate that homeschooling grew 74% from 1999 to 2007 (Basham, Merrifield, & Hepburn, 2007; Grady & Bielick, 2010; Ray, 2005, 2009, 2011). As of 2007, this explosive growth appears to have slowed, with some estimates indicating stasis. Notably, NCES cautions against comparing later figures with those from 2007 or before, owing to changes in its methodology (Redford *et al.*, 2016). Generally, the broad range of estimates in and of itself suggests how very little we know about this dynamic population, a point we develop later.

As homeschooling has expanded, it has also become more diverse. As many as 15% of homeschool families are from nonwhite, non-Hispanic minority groups (Ray, 2016). The reasons for choosing homeschooling have also grown more diverse (Lubienski, Puckett, & Brewer, 2013; see Bell *et al.* in this volume). Further, as the Aaron Saiger essay and the Eric Wearne study of hybrid home-schooling in this volume show, the very types of homeschooling and range of homeschooling options have grown over time. Increasingly, children may homeschool part-time, while also taking occasional classes at online schools (of all kinds, charter, private, and traditional public), colleges, blended charter schools, private schools, and even traditional public schools. Within home edu-cation even more than school choice generally, no one size fits all. Increasingly, traditional public schools allow homeschool children to take part in extracur-ricular activities and even take individual classes. Sometimes this occurs via state mandates or extra funding for courses taken by homeschoolers, some-times when traditional public schools attempt to win back homeschoolers, and often for reasons of mutual advantage. As one public school superintendent we know quipped in a public meeting, traditional public schools eagerly welcome to their extracurricular activities any homeschooler who can dunk a basketball. More seriously, our fieldwork indicates that one Arkansas school district under threat of consolidation due to low enrollment now actively recruits homeschool families for its own hybrid program, paying for and helping with their home education curricula; in exchange parents formally enroll their children in the school district and agree to state-mandated testing. This provides resources for homeschool families, and additional enrollment and concomitant state funding for the school district.

Empirical Limitations of Home Education Research

With increased homeschooling has come increased research on homeschooling in all its forms. Yet as Hess (2017) notes of educational research generally, we experts probably know less than we think we know. A major limitation to research on the effects of homeschooling is that homeschoolers self-select into these education models for a variety of durations and reasons. Those might make homeschooled children different from their traditional public school peers in ways eluding large-scale measurement, making comparisons between the two populations problematic. The selection bias inherent to homeschooling makes empirical analyses seeking causal relationships difficult (Lubienski *et al.*, 2013). The very thing that makes a family choose to homeschool could also be the thing that causes homeschool students to outperform their traditional public school peers. Relatedly, some parents choose homeschooling from a desire for less education and less oversight for their children: such parents may not voluntarily submit to reporting, testing, or surveys, and are thus likely under-represented in homeschool data. In short, much homeschool research is methodologically weak, undermining efforts to demonstrate causation (Kunzman & Gaither, 2013). Even more than for educational research generally, we should consider research findings tentative. To be clear, this includes the findings reported in this volume.

Further exacerbating this empirical dilemma is the combative political history of homeschooling (Dumas *et al.*, 2010). Again, many homeschooling parents resist attempts to measure their children, including testing or reporting, thus complicating the efforts of empirical researchers (Collum, 2005; Kunzman, 2005; Kunzman & Gaither, 2013). Some families prefer to educate their children *off the grid*. Known as "homeschooling under your constitutional rights," undeclared or underground homeschooling is legally considered truancy (Isenberg, 2007). Even calculating the actual numbers of homeschoolers in the United States is difficult because many states do not require homeschool parents to register, as we discuss later (Reich, 2005). Accordingly, available data on homeschool students come from parents who volunteer information, students who switch between homeschooling and public schooling for whom data are captured in public school settings, or students who later enter college and declare that they were homeschooled. None of these methods fully represent the population of homeschoolers, again complicating comparisons with brick-and-mortar school students.

As noted, even determining the numbers of homeschool students is difficult. Although homeschooling is legal in all states, state policies intended to track homeschool students vary widely. Some states require parents to register students as homeschooled with the state, through local districts, or through private umbrella schools (Kunzman & Gaither, 2013). We cannot know the percentage of parents who comply with those requirements. As noted earlier, since 1991 the NCES has issued the National Household Education Surveys (NHES) program to survey a representative sample of American households (Bielick, Chandler, & Broughman, 2001). This dataset provides the official federal estimate of homeschool students (NCES, 2009), but some homeschool advocates view the estimate as low in part due to perceived survey question bias and low response rates (Ray, 2005). Even so, the 2.9% homeschool market share estimated for 2007 by Redford *et al.* (2016) equaled the number of students in charter schools and voucher programs at that time (Apple, 2007; Isenberg, 2007). Isenberg (2007) estimated approximately one homeschooled student for every five students enrolled in private schools.

Some researchers use data from Wisconsin as a potential higher bounds estimate of the homeschool population. Wisconsin has the least restrictive laws regarding parent registration of homeschool students, requiring only the completion of a simple one-page document informing the state that a student is homeschooled. Because of the ease of the process, Wisconsin may have the most accurate estimation of homeschool market share (Isenberg, 2007). Recent data representing all registered homeschoolers in Wisconsin indicate a drop in homeschool numbers around 2007, in accord with NCES findings (see Figure 1.2). However, Wisconsin homeschool numbers appear to rebound post-2012. Clearly, this deserves a deeper, multi-state inquiry.

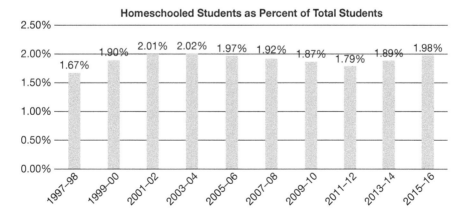

Figure 1.2. Wisconsin homeschool data (Wisconsin Department of Public Instruction).

Similarly, the American Community Survey collects data for homeschool status, but some feel that the emotional affect of the questions employed leads parents to under-report homeschooling; thus the results of this survey are considered a lower bound estimate of the homeschool market share (Isenberg, 2007). The true number of homeschooling families likely falls in the middle of these various estimates.

Further, as noted earlier and shown below in the chapters in this volume by Saiger and Wearne, respectively, homeschooling is not an all-or-nothing proposition. Many, if not most, homeschooling families, particularly those not stating their main impetus for homeschool choice as religious, move freely in and out of traditional schooling and homeschooling to meet the varying needs of their children over time, and occasionally even to avoid individual teachers seen as arrogant or ineffective (Isenberg, 2007; Lines, 1999; Stevens, 2001). Again, this increases the percentage of students who have ever been homeschooled over point-in-time estimates.

Who Homeschools?

Parents who choose to homeschool their children are diverse, but not representative of parents generally (Lines, 2000b; Ray, 2010). In 2009, the Homeschool Legal Defense Association (HSLDA) offered data indicating that 98% of homeschool parents graduated from high school, compared to 82% nationally. Half hold a bachelor's degree or more, compared to 42% of K-12 parents generally (Kunzman & Gaither, 2013). Between 89% and 97.9% of homeschool parents report being married, with 62.1% having three or more children (Basham *et al.*, 2007; Bielick *et al.*, 2001; HSLDA, 2009; Kunzman & Gaither, 2013). Nationally, only 73% of parents are married and in two-parent households, and families have a mean of 2.1 children (Kunzman & Gaither, 2013). Median family income for homeschool families resembled the national mean of $79,000 in 2009, though with relatively fewer rich and poor (Murphy, 2012). Possibly, low-income families lack the resources to homeschool, whereas the wealthy can afford premium private schools. Conversely, the wealthy may be less willing than middle-class families to suffer the economic costs of home education, a matter we discuss at length later. Relatedly, only 19.4% of homeschool mothers reported working for pay, with 85% only working part time (HSLDA, 2009). According to the NCES's homeschooling in the United States 2012 report, 41% of homeschool students live in rural areas, 83% are white, with genders equally represented.

Advocacy Efforts

As noted earlier, legal threats led homeschoolers to organize on the state and national levels (Stevens, 2001). With home education's legal status established, certain homeschool organizations and state conferences have closed or merged, though Florida and Virginia still have strong state organizations. Two key national homeschool advocates remain. The HSLDA founded in 1983 in Virginia by Michael Farris, lobbies for homeschooling, offers legal assistance to homeschool parents, and organizes the periodic Global Home Education Conference as a forum for research from around the world. (Some of the chapters in this volume were originally presented there; all have since gone through an additional round of double-blind peer review.) The entrepreneurial Farris also founded Patrick Henry College, a small Christian college 50 miles from Washington, DC, meant to appeal to homeschoolers, with institutional aspirations to become "God's Harvard," and with some clout in government (Rosin, 2007). The NHERI, headed by Dr. Brian D. Ray, provides research and advocacy information to policy makers and homeschool parents. In part due to the efforts of these and other organized interest groups, homeschooling is legal in every state (Isenberg, 2007; Murphy, 2012). The homeschool lobby had sufficient power to ensure that homeschoolers were excluded from the chief requirements of No Child Left Behind (NCLB), and the more recent Every Student Succeeds Act (ESSA) (Estrada, 2015; Gloeckner & Jones, 2013; Isenberg, 2007). Our fieldwork suggests that in the absence of existential legal threats, homeschool families are now less apt to organize politically and more likely to identify with a particular curricula, blogger or Facebook group. For example, Hip Homeschool Moms has 116,000 Facebook subscribers. More than 100,000 belong to Classical Conversations, a Christian hybrid homeschool model in which children study a range of subjects including Latin at home, attending a co-op several days a week.

Why Homeschool?

In her 1991 seminal *Ideologues and Pedagogues*, Jane Van Galen categorized homeschool parents into those acting out of religion or ideology, and those seeking more individualized, child-centered education (Knowles *et al.*, 1992; see also Stevens, 2001; Taylor-Hough, 2010). The Neuman and Guterman study of Israeli homeschoolers included in this volume generally suggests the latter motivation, as does the American study in this volume by Bell *et al.* Yet the NCES 2012 homeschool report finds 91% of parents reporting concerns about "safety, drugs, or negative peer pressure" as a motivation for homeschooling, followed by 77% reporting concerns with "providing moral instruction," 74% reporting "dissatisfaction with academic instruction," and 64% wanting "religious instruction." Thus, safety seemingly plays a greater role in aggregate than moral and religious instruction, perhaps reflecting changing public school climates, or at least changed perceptions of those climates. Summarizing various small surveys, Ray (2016) identifies these motivations, but also the desire to improve family relationships between parents and with peers, a finding largely in accord with that reported in the study by Stevens (2001) and also with the Neuman and Guterman Israeli study and the Bell *et al.* American study in this volume.

Academic Outcomes

Even critics of school choice (e.g., Berliner & Glass, 2014) admit that most homeschoolers seem to do well academically and socially. However, comparing the academic achievement of homeschool students to that of other students is difficult, in part because of missing demographic, income, and test score data from homeschool populations, and the inability of such data to fully account for differences with traditional public school students. Still, researchers have attempted comparisons of homeschool and traditional public school student academic outcomes by using Scholastic Aptitude Test (SAT) and similar data (Carpenter, 2012; Kunzman & Gaither, 2013). Although biased by self-selection, these studies may offer some insight.

Generally, studies examining SAT data show that homeschool students outperform traditional public school students. Findings are suspect, however, since the differences are robust no matter how long a child was homeschooled, whether for a single year or far longer (Carpenter, 2012; Ray, 2010). Accordingly, some view parent involvement, income, race, and marital status (rather than homeschooling) as the real determinants of increased test scores (Green, 2008; Lubienski *et al.*, 2013). Viewed from another angle, perhaps untrained, but highly engaged parents are as effective as certified professional educators. The NHES Parent and Family Involvement in Education (PFI) survey, as implied, measures levels of family involvement. PFI data indicate that traditional public school students whose parents are highly involved in their education do about as well as homeschooled students, who by definition likely have highly involved parents (Barwegen, Falciani, Putnam, Reamer, & Stair, 2004). Again, this leads critical scholars to cite parental involvement as the moderator of academic outcomes regardless of education model (Lubienski *et al.*, 2013).

Nontest score measures of academic outcomes show that homeschool students outperform all other students on college grade point average (GPA), both cumulative and first year. Similarly, homeschool students are more likely to persist in college at both two- and four-year institutions, and thus graduate at higher percentages (Carpenter, 2012; Ray, 2016). The Wilkens, Wade, Sonnert, and Sadler chapter in this volume finds that relative to students with more traditional preparation former homeschoolers earn higher grades in higher education calculus classes, even though one might expect traditional public school options to have advantages teaching technical subjects such as mathematics.

The limited research on student satisfaction suggests that homeschoolers are satisfied with their homeschool environments. As the Cheng *et al.* chapter in this volume reports, this seems particularly true of special education parents and students, who eschew the contrasting large size and relatively impersonal character of many traditional public schools. Interestingly, the same results are obtained for general and particularly special education students and parents in cyber charter schools, who express far more satisfaction than in their prior traditional public schools (Beck *et al.*, 2014). Apple (2007), Reich (2005), and Lines (2000a,b), among others, fear that homeschooling may undermine democratic values, producing more atomized young people. The current evidence, though limited, suggests otherwise, perhaps since home-schoolers have postmaterialistic motives, a point discussed further below. Albert Cheng's chapter in this volume reports evidence that among Christian college students, former homeschoolers show greater political tolerance than either public or privately educated peers. This aligns with prior research suggesting that traditional public schools offer no advantages in inculcating key democratic values (Berner, 2017). Summarizing smaller surveys, Ray (2016) reports that compared to traditional public school peers homeschool students are more likely to volunteer for community service as adults, to vote, and to attend public meetings, again suggesting that homeschooling helps build support for civic values.

Critics of homeschooling have proposed legislation requiring parents seeking to homeschool their children to first obtain teacher certification. Yet research finds little to no difference between the scores of homeschool students with parents who have teacher certifications and those who do not (Ray, 2016). These results align with similar findings that compare the academic outcomes of traditional public school students and those of private school students, who are far less likely to have teachers who are certified or licensed. Indeed elite private schools (including those educating Barack Obama, Al Gore, John Kerry, John McCain, and the Bushes) seldom employ certified teachers, yet seem to have good academic records. Further, survey research does not suggest that teachers see their traditional training regimes as useful (Jenkins & Grigg, 2006; Maranto & McShane, 2012).

Race and Gender

As homeschooling has expanded; it has grown more diverse (Gaither, 2008). Estimates indicate that approximately 10% of current homeschoolers are African American. Like their white counterparts, African American home-school parents have relatively high levels of education and income, as Brian Ray shows in his chapter in this volume. Also like white parents, African American parents often cite safety as a key reason to homeschool. Particularly in urban areas, many African Americans report choosing homeschooling to keep their children physically and emotionally safe from violence and racism. Via "racial protectionism," many African American parents report homeschooling to protect their children from Eurocentric curricula, prejudiced white teachers with low expectations for black students, and the violence of urban schools (Lundy & Mazama, 2014; Mazama & Lundy, 2012; Musumunu & Mazama, 2014).

Research finds few, if any, gender differences in homeschooling academic outcomes, nor in the likelihood of being homeschooled (Carpenter, 2012; Ray, 2010). Some homeschooling critics hypothesize that religious conservative home-school families discriminate against their female children by preparing daughters for traditional roles in the home, while preparing sons for work outside the home; indeed certain homeschool curricula suggest as much (Carpenter, 2012). Yet available data do not show notable differences in homeschool standardized test scores by gender; indeed as in educational research generally, those differences found show females slightly outperforming males (Carpenter, 2012; Ray, 2010).

A Costly Choice

Any discussion about the economic motivation of families who choose home-schooling must include principal agent theory, which addresses relationships between principals and the agents they employ to achieve their goals. In an educational context, principals such as parents, taxpayers, and elected officials have diverse goals that they expect their agents, educators, to realize (Chubb & Moe, 1990). As Van Galen (1991) famously noted, many homeschoolers are categorized as "ideologues and pedagogues," those choosing to homeschool for religious or ideological reasons and those seeking pedagogical freedom (Knowles *et al.*, 1992; Taylor-Hough, 2010). Naturally, diverse goals create conflicts between parents (who are among the principals) and educators (their agents). Homeschooling reduces the roles of elected officials and other prin-cipals, while enlarging the role of parents. Homeschooling also allows its key principals (parents) to act as agents, further simplifying often complex relation-ships. Yet this comes at a high cost.

For future gains of homeschooling to outweigh present sacrifices of time and money, homeschooling parents must place a high utility on their long-term schooling goals; thus, homeschooling can be considered an extreme choice due to its high cost. As noted below, this may make homeschooling sensitive to the provision of alternative school choices such as charter schools and vouchers to private schools, which could quickly erode the homeschool market share, or to public subsidies of home education, which might quickly increase market share (Gaither, 2008; Murphy, 1996). Pure homeschooling might also lose market share to hybrid homeschooling options (typically 2–3 days a week in a private school and 2–3 days homeschooled) like the Classical Conversations coops or other innovative schooling arrangements, as Wearne's chapter in this volume details.

Families who choose to homeschool their children do so at a considerable cost, because the parent-educator likely must curtail paid employment. Further, these parents pay for their children's education at least twice, once through taxes collected to fund public education, and again through opportunity cost of lost wages and time invested. While a few states currently have voucher programs to help with homeschool costs, most parents bear complete out-of-pocket expenses for curriculum materials and educational services for homeschooling. In short, homeschool parents must have extreme motivations.

Calculating the cost of homeschooling depends on the counterfactual of what the parent, usually the mother, who stays home, would do instead. If the parent were marginally educated or skilled and unlikely to garner high wages, then the opportunity cost of lost wages and time might be low. However, average homeschool parents are highly educated and, therefore, would be more likely to earn high wages (and to add to retirement accounts). Add to this opportunity cost consideration not only the loss in potential wages earned, but also the loss of workforce experience and actual losses could be considerable. A highly educated and skilled woman who quits a good job to educate her children for several years may later have difficulty reentering her field at the same level. She may have to retool her education or skills, or at the least will have missed additional years of work experience and the financial returns to that experience in increased wages and status (Stevens, 2001). Further, age-earnings profiles suggest that human capital acquisition decreases and stock depreciates with age; thus a mother leaving the workforce to school her children may suffer more loss of human capital than she would have otherwise. Given their higher precareer schooling, these mothers have higher human capital depreciation than their age peers with less education. Arguably, mothers staying home to school their children are adding to their human capital; however, labor markets undervalue this brand of human capital. Quite literally adding insult to economic injury, upper income women making the choice to homeschool may face moral sanctions from their counterparts who remain in the paid workplace, and view homeschooling mothers and full-time homemakers generally as antifeminist (e.g., Hirshman, 2006).

Slowing Growth in a School Choice Market With More Options

Increased access to school choice would decrease participation in homeschooling by home educators with marginal preferences to homeschool, while likely having little effect on the participation of relatively extreme pedagogues and ideologues, who would be willing to pay the high costs. Policy changes such as increased access to vouchers or education savings accounts (ESAs) will incentivize utility-maximizing individuals on the margins to choose a safe private school via voucher funding, or a free charter school rather than the more costly homeschool option. Indeed the spread of school choice may well have muted the growth of homeschooling in recent years.

Yet policy changes, perhaps driven by homeschool advocates, could insulate homeschooling from such competition. Vouchers and ECAs could extend benefits to homeschool families. Indeed, Arizona, Illinois, Indiana, Minnesota, and New Hampshire (*The ABC's of School Choice*, 2016) already offer such financial support for homeschool families. Although current state programs offer low benefits with corresponding low incentives, higher benefit vouchers and ESAs would offer stronger positive incentives for homeschool families. Even modest incentives may have impacts. As homeschooler Melissa Cogan (Cato. Org) explained:

> Without the scholarship, homeschool would not have been an option for us … We are a large family with very limited resources … The generosity of (scholarship organization) has made it possible for us to purchase everything we need to become a successful homeschool family.

Yet homeschool advocates fear that increased public funding would lead to increased public oversight and accountability, restrictions ideologically, or pedagogically extreme homeschoolers disdain (Estrada, 2017). Second, public funding could weaken the social bonds holding homeschoolers together, lessening their need for self-organization. Finally, one source of its public legitimacy is that homeschooling costs the public nothing and indeed saves public dollars, since homeschoolers pay taxes used to educate the children of others (Ray, 2016). Public funding would alter this, possibly undermining public support for homeschooling. Still, one cannot discount the power of homeschool advocacy groups in ameliorating these threats.

Conclusion and the Plan for This Book

Home education has grown rapidly and sometimes off the grid, rendering generalizations difficult. Given the limitations of existing empirical research, findings regarding homeschooling outcomes compared to those in traditional public schools must be considered tentative. That said, the evidence so far is mainly positive. By most accounts, homeschooled students test above the national mean of their age peers and seem to do somewhat better in college. Further, the limited evidence extant, some of it in this volume, indicates that homeschooled students and parents, particularly special education families, show somewhat more satisfaction with their homeschool settings than their school settings. Homeschool parents and students who switch sectors, at least those who continue to homeschool, seem more satisfied with their homeschooling than with traditional education models. There is some evidence that they are also more politically tolerant. Further, home educators are pioneering innovative modes of schooling, some of which may over the long-term influence traditional public and private schools.

In short, homeschooling has considerable promise, and needs more research. Yet conventional education researchers, most of whom reside in schools of education, have done relatively little to explore homeschooling in part due to the methodological challenges noted earlier, but also since most researchers seem wedded to traditional school systems, and uncomfortable exploring alternatives

(Hess, 2017; Maranto, 2017). This makes a volume of this kind essential. In this book, we combine the most influential homeschooling research from the *Journal of School Choice*, particularly (most) manuscripts from a special issue of the journal offering the best work from the 2016 Global Home Education Conference held in Rio de Janeiro. All the papers survived double-blind peer review. We intend to increase scholarly understanding of this dynamic, but little studied social and educational movement. The diverse offerings following present some of the best research on homeschooling.

We start with the legal and social foundations of home education. HSLDA attorney and Director of Global Outreach Michael Donnelly's opening essay critiques legal analyses from the European Court of Human Rights permitting Germany to prohibit homeschooling. Donnelly argues that both in an American context as in the case of *Pierce v. Society of Sisters* and also in international law under the framework of the Universal Declaration of Human Rights, the child is more than the mere creature of the state; hence home education should have legal status, albeit subject to reasonable regulations. In Chapter 3, Homeschooling, Virtual Learning, and the Eroding Public/Private Binary, Fordham University Law Professor Aaron Saiger notes that the distinction between public and private is a deeply rooted legal and regulatory concept. Yet the spread of charter schools, virtual schools, blended schools, and the bundling of educational options, all of these often coming in tandem with homeschooling, are eroding localism and public–private distinctions. Whatever their value educationally, these evolutionary and in some chases revolutionary changes are remaking educational law, politics, and policy.

The four chapters of Section 2 address why parents homeschool, a vital topic too seldom explored by researchers, who often disdain the perspectives of parents. Coeditor Debra Bell of Aim Academy and Avi Kaplan and S. Kenneth Thurman of Temple University use self-determination theory to classify homeschool learning environments. Surveying a sample of parents recruited from a nonsectarian homeschool organization ($n = 457$), the authors use cluster analyses, finding that home educators are very goal oriented and endorse a highly autonomous, child-centered motivational orientation. Autonomy, relatedness, and competence all correlate with each other, and with student academic engagement. Interestingly, the longer a child homeschools, the greater their academic engagement, in contrast to children in traditional public schools.

In Chapter 5, Eric Wearne of Georgia Gwinnett College offers an exploratory descriptive analysis of why parents choose hybrid homeschools in Georgia. As noted earlier, students attend such schools with other students 2 or 3 days a week while being homeschooled the balance of the time. Such options typically provide a greater variety of courses, socialization options, and extra-curricular activities than pure home education, while costing far less than private schools.

Findings indicate that parents using these options are relatively wealthy and suburban, and seek information on accreditation, curricula, and religion when choosing schools. This is among the first published pieces on a rapidly growing school sector, one that might grow still more rapidly as ECAs reduce costs for parents (Malkus, Peshek, & Robinson, 2017).

Chapter 6, by Brian Ray of the NHERI, explores the motivations of 81 African American families for choosing homeschooling, and the academic achievement of their students. As noted earlier, African American reasons for homeschooling resemble those of homeschool parents in general; although some use homeschooling to help their children understand black culture and history and escape perceived racism in traditional public schools. The mean reading, language, and math test scores of these black homeschool students are significantly higher than those of black public school students (with effect sizes of 0.60 to 1.13) and equal to or higher than all public school students as a group in this exploratory, cross-sectional, and explanatory nonexperimental study. While these findings are fascinating and in accord with other work suggesting that marginalized populations are net winners when educational options expand (Maranto, 2017; Maranto & McShane, 2012, 34, 96 for summaries), clearly, more research is needed.

Chapter 7, by Ari Neuman and Oz Guterman of Western Galilee College, employs qualitative methodologies to explore the motivations of 30 Israeli homeschool mothers. Although the subjects attributed diverse meanings to homeschooling, the dominant themes centered on controlling their children, having close personal relationships with their children, and inculcating nonmaterialistic, communal values. These motives played far greater roles than such oft-cited outcomes as test scores and work readiness, suggesting the complexity inherent to schooling outcomes. This largely accords with American findings in this volume (Ray, Bell *et al.*) and elsewhere.

The final section of the book explores homeschooling outcomes, including outcomes beyond test scores. Chapter 8, by Albert Cheng of Harvard University, Sivan Tuchman of the University of Washington, and Patrick Wolf of the University of Arkansas, explores homeschool parent satisfaction with special education services, a matter of considerable concern since home educators might lack the skills to serve students with disabilities. Using a nationally representative sample of 17,000 households from the NHES, the authors find that parents who homeschool are more satisfied than parents of children in traditional public schools and a variety of private schools with their special education services. Results suggest that homeschooling may benefit certain students with disabilities, though additional research examining other student outcomes would be invaluable, particularly since parents choosing to homeschool their special needs children are likely atypical.

In Chapter 9, Christian P. Wilkens (College at Brockport, State University of New York), Carol H. Wade (College at Brockport, State University of New York), Gerhard Sonnert (Harvard), and Philip M. Sadler (Harvard), explore whether homeschooled students are sufficiently prepared to succeed in college level higher mathematics classes, a matter of concern given that home educators might lack the skills to teach advanced mathematics. Many find this a particular concern given the increased emphasis on science, technology, engineering, and mathematics (STEM) fields of study. The authors present findings from the Factors Influencing College Success in Mathematics (FICSMath) survey, a national study of 10,492 students enrolled in calculus, including 190 students who reported homeschooling for most of their high school years. Compared with students receiving other types of secondary schooling, homeschooled students were demographically similar and earned similar SAT Math scores, but earned higher calculus grades in college.

Finally, in Chapter 10, Albert Cheng of Harvard University explores political tolerance and homeschooling. Political tolerance is the willingness to extend civil liberties to people who hold views with which one disagrees, and is thus a vital democratic value. Some fear that homeschooling propagates political intolerance by fostering separatism, and an unwillingness to consider alternative viewpoints. Cheng empirically tests this claim by measuring the political tolerance levels of undergraduate students attending an evangelical Christian university. Ordinary least squares regression analysis indicate that greater exposure to private schooling instead of traditional public schooling is not associated with any more or less political tolerance, and greater exposure to homeschooling is associated with more political tolerance.

Taken together, these papers break new ground, and suggest that home education, at least for those families choosing it, does more good than harm. Yet this leaves any number of questions unanswered. Will relatively positive results continue as homeschooling grows, if it grows? Will short-term positive results mask long-term deficiencies as homeschoolers age into adulthood, and in some cases produce second- or even third-generation homeschoolers? Over the long term, will homeschooling in an increasingly diverse America tend to defuse, or inflame culture wars? What sorts of public policies can assure parental freedom to homeschool, while also protecting children? Will innovations from the homeschool sectors, such as hybrid homeschooling, spread to traditional public schools? As the movement grows globally (e.g., Barbosa, 2016; Bongrand, 2016), will the mainly positive results from American home education occur elsewhere? On a more microlevel, how does homeschooling affect psychological well-being for students and parents? How do homeschool students interpret their homeschooling experience in hindsight? How is homeschooling affected by the growing array of publicly funded options such as cyber charters, vouchers, or educational savings accounts? What best homeschool methodological practices can be identified, or, as Hess (2017) argues, will it all depend on the students served and their parent educators? These and other questions will, one hopes, engage a new generation of home education researchers.

History rarely moves in straight lines. We can posit that as distance learning technology develops and family size remains low by historic standards, homeschooling will continue to grow in America and across an increasingly postindustrial world. Possibly, future historians will trace the evolution of education from the home to institutional schooling back to the home, from personalization to bureaucratization back to the personal. This is one of those social movements which social science exists to study.

References

The ABC's of School Choice (2016). The comprehensive guide to every private school choice program in America. Friedman Foundation for Educational Choice.

Anthony, K.V., & Burroughs, S. (2010). Making the transition from traditional to home schooling: Home school family motivations. *Current Issues in Education*, 13(4), 1–33.

Apple, M.W. (2007). Who needs teacher education? Gender, technology and the work of home schooling. *Teacher Education Quarterly*, 34(2), 111–130.

Barbosa, L.M.R. (2016). Homeschooling in Brazil: A matter of rights or a political debate? *Journal of School Choice*, 10(3), 355–363.

Barwegen, L.M., Falciani, N.K., Putman, S.J., Reamer, M.B., & Stair, E.E. (2004). Academic achievement of homeschool and public school students and student perception of parent involvement. *School Community Journal*, 14(1), 39–58.

Basham, P., Merrifield, J., & Hepburn, C. (2007). *Home Schooling: From the Extreme to the Mainstream*. Vancouver, Canada: Fraser Institute.

Beck, D., Egalite, A., & Maranto, R. (2014). Why they choose and how it goes: Comparing special education and general education cyber student perceptions. *Computers and Education*, 76, 70–79.

Berner, A.R. (2017). *No One Way to School: Pluralism and American Public Education*. New York, NY: Macmillan/Palgrave.

Berliner, D.C., & Glass, G.V. (2014). *50 Myths and Lies That Threaten America's Public Schools*. New York, NY: Teachers College Press.

Bielick, S., Chandler, K., & Broughman, S. (2001). Homeschooling in the United States: 1999. *Education Statistics Quarterly*, 3(3), 1–13.

Bongrand, P. (2016). "Compulsory schooling" despite the law: How education policy underpins the widespread ignorance of the right to home educate in France. *Journal of School Choice*, 10(3), 297–320.

Carpenter, D.M. (2012). Mom likes you best: Do homeschool parents discriminate against their daughters. *University of St. Thomas Journal of Law and Public Policy*, 7(1), 24–50.

Chubb, J.E., & Moe, T.M. (1990). *Politics, Markets, and America's Schools*. Washington, DC: Brookings Institution.

Collom, E. (2005). The ins and out of homeschooling: The determinants of parental motivations and student achievement. *Education and Urban Society*, 37, 307–335.

Dixon, P. (2014). International Aid and Private Schools for the Poor: Smiles, Miracles and Markets, Worldwide. Northampton, MA and Gloucestershire, UK: Edward Elgar.

Dumas, T.K., Gates, S., & Schwarzer, D.R. (2010). Evidence for homeschooling: Constitutional analysis in light of social science research. *Widener Law Review*, 16(1), 63–87.

Estrada, W.A. (2015). *Homeschool Freedom Protected in ESEA rewrite, but concerns remain. Homeschool Legal Defense Association* (HSLDA). www.hslda.org/docs/news/2015/201512020.asp. Accessed June 9, 2017.

Estrada, W.A. (2017). *4 Ways that HR 610 will threaten your rights*. Homeschool Legal Defense Association (HSLDA). https://nche.hslda.org/docs/news. Accessed June 9, 2017.

Gaither, M. (2008). *Homeschool: An American history*. New York, NY: Palgrave MacMillan.

Galen, J.V., & Pitman, M.A. (1991). *Homeschooling: Political, Historical, and Pedagogical Perspectives*. Norwood, NJ: Alex Publication Corporation.

Glenn, C.L. (2012). *The American Model of State and School*. New York, NY: Continuum.

Gloeckner, G.W., & Jones, P. (2013). Reflections on a decade of changes in homeschooling and homeschooled into higher education. *Peabody Journal of Education*, 88(3), 309–323.

Grady, S., & Bielick, S. (2010). *Trends in the Use of School Choice: 1993 to 2007* (NCES 2010–004). Washington, DC: National Center for Education Statistics, Institute of Education Sciences, U.S. Department of Education.

Green, C.L. (2008). Linking parental motivations for involvement and student proximal achievement outcomes in home-schooling and public-schooling settings. Dissertation, Vanderbilt University, May, 2008, Nashville, TN.

Hanna, L. (2012). Homeschooling education: Longitudinal study of methods, materials, and curricula. *Education and Urban Society*, 44(5), 609–631.

Hess, F.M. (2017). *Letters to a Young Education Reformer*. Cambridge, MA: Harvard Education Press.

Hess, F.M. (2010). *The Same Thing Over and Over*. Cambridge, MA: Harvard Education Press.

Hirshman, L.R. (2006). *Get To Work: A Manifesto for Women of the World*. New York, NY: Viking.

HSLDA (2009). Homeschool Progress Report 2009: Academic achievement and demographics.

Isenberg, E.J. (2007). What have we learned about homeschooling? *Peabody Journal of Education*, 82(2–3), 387–409. www.tandfonline.com/doi/pdf/10.1080/01619560701312996. Accessed March 23, 2017.

Jeffrey, T.P. (2015). 1,773,000 homeschooled children Up 61.8% in 10 years. CNS News.com. http://cnsnews.com/news/article/terence-p-jeffrey/1773000-homeschooled-children-618-10-years. Accessed June 9, 2016.

Jenkins, B.H., & Grigg, W. (2006). *Comparing Private Schools and Public Schools Using Hierarchical Linear Modeling* (NCES 2006–461). Washington, DC: U.S. Department of Education, National Center for Education Statistics, Institute of Education Sciences.

Knowles, J.G., Marlow, S.E., & Muchmore, J.A. (1992). From pedagogy to ideology: Origins and phases of home education in the United States, 1970–1990. *American Journal of Education*, 100(2), 195–235.

Kunzman, R. (2005). Homeschooling in Indiana: A closer look. Education Policy Brief, 3(7). Bloomington, IN: Indiana University, Center for Evaluation and Education Policy.

Kunzman, R., & Gaither, M. (2013).Homeschooling: A comprehensive survey of the research. *Other Education: The Journal of Educational Alternatives*, 2(1), 4–59.

Lareau, A. (2003). *Unequal Childhoods*. Berkeley, CL: University of California Press.

Lines, P.M. (1999). *Homeschoolers: Estimating Numbers and Growth*. Washington, DC: U.S. Department of Education, National Institute on Student Achievement, Curriculum, and Assessment.

Lines, P.M. (2000a). Homeschooling comes of age. *The Public Interest*, 140, 74–85.

Lines, P.M. (2000b). When home schoolers go back to school: A partnership between families and schools. *Peabody Journal of Education*, 75, 159–186.

Lubienski, C., Puckett, T., & Brewer, T.J. (2013). Does homeschooling "work"? A critique of the empirical claims and agenda of advocacy organizations. *Peabody Journal of Education*, 88, 378–392. www.tandfonline.com/doi/full/10.1080/0161956X.2013.798516. Accessed June 9, 2017.

Lundy, G., & Mazama, A. (2014). "I'm keeping my son home": African American males and the motivation to homeschool. *Journal of African American Males in Education*, 5(1), 53–74.

Malkus, N., Peshek, A., & Robinson, G. (2017). *Education Savings Accounts: The New Frontier in School Choice*. Lanham, MD: Rowman & Littlefield.

Maranto, R. (2017). In the school choice debate, both sides are right. School reformers and backers of traditional public schools are talking past each other. *Education Week*. www.edweek.org/ew/articles/2017/05/19/in-the-school-choice-debate-both-sides.html. Accessed May 19, 2017.

Maranto, R., & McShane, M.Q. (2012). *President Obama and Education Reform*. New York, NY: Palgrave/Macmillan.

Martin-Chang, S., Gould, O.N., & Meuse, R.E. (2011). The impact of schooling on academic achievement: Evidence from homeschooled and traditionally schooled students. *Canadian Journal of Behavioural Science/Revue canadienne des sciences du comportement*, 43(3), 195.

Mazama, A., & Lundy, G. (2012). African American homeschooling and racial protectionism. *Journal of Black Studies*, 43(7), 723–748.

Murphy, J. (1996). *The Privatization of Schooling: Problems and Possibilities*. Newbury Park, CA: Corwin.

Murphy, J. (2012). *Homeschooling in America: Capturing and Assessing the Movement*. Thousand Oaks, CA: Corwin.

Musumunu, G., & Mazama, A. (2014). The search for school safety and the African American homeschooling experience. *Journal of Contemporary Issues in Education*, 9(2), 24–38.

National Center for Education Statistics (NCES) (2009). 1.5 Million Homeschool Students in the United States in 2007. *Issue Brief NCES 2209–030*.

Peterson, P.E. (2010). *Saving Schools: From Horace Mann to Virtual Learning*. Cambridge, MA: Harvard University Press.

Petrilli, M.J. (2012). *The Diverse Schools Dilemma*. Washington, DC: Thomas B. Fordham Institute.

Ravitch, D. (2000). *Left Back: A Century of Battles Over School Reform*. New York, NY: Simon and Schuster.

Ray, B.D. (2005). A homeschool research story. in B.S. Cooper (Ed.), *Home Schooling in Full View* (1–19). Greenwich, CT: Information Age.

Ray, B.D. (2009). *Home Education Reason and Research: Common Questions and Research-based Answers about Homeschooling*. Salem, OR: National Home Education Research Institute.

Ray, B.D. (2010). Academic achievement and demographic traits of homeschool students: A nationwide study. *National Home Research Institute*, 8(1), 1–32.

Ray, B.D. (2011). 2.04 Million homeschool students in the United States in 2010. National Home Education Research Institute. www.nheri.org/HomeschoolPopulationReport2010.pdf. Accessed March 24, 2017.

Ray, B.D. (2016). Research facts on homeschooling. National Home Research Institute.

Redford, J., Battle, D., & Bielick, S. (2016). Homeschooling in the United States: 2012. NCES., American Institute for Research.

Reich, R. (2005). Why homeschooling should be regulated. in B.S. Cooper (Ed.), *Home Schooling in Full View* (109–1120). Greenwich, CT: Information Age.

Rosin, H. (2007). *God's Harvard: A Christian College on a Mission to Save America*. Orlando, FL: Harcourt.

Stevens, M. (2001). *Kingdom of Children: Culture and Controversy in the Homeschooling Movement*. Princeton, NJ: Princeton University Press.

Taylor-Hough, D. (2010). Are all homeschooling methods created equal? www.inreachinc.org/are_all_homeschooling_methods_created_equal.pdf. Accessed June 9, 2017.

Vander Ark, T. (2012). *Getting Smarter*. San Francisco, CL: Jossey-Bass.

Van Galen, J.A. (1991). Ideologues and pedagogues: Parents who teach their children at home. *Home Schooling: Political, Historical, and Pedagogical Perspectives*. Norwood, NJ: Ablex Publishing.

Watson, A., Beck, D., & Maranto, R. (2017). Do testing conditions explain cyber charter schools' failing grades? Presented at the Annual Journal of School Choice Conference, Honolulu, HI., January 5, 2017.

The Human Right of Home Education

Michael P. Donnelly

ABSTRACT

Homeschooling is legal and growing in many countries but is virtually forbidden by law in Germany and a few others. The European Court of Human Rights (ECtHR) has reviewed and upheld this ban. Is home education a human right? How do these courts employ their jurisprudence of proportionality to find banning home education does not violate relevant constitutional or human rights norms? Why does Germany forbid home education? Why does the ECtHR uphold Germany's position? What does this divergence imply about the right of home education and the jurisprudence of these courts? If the promise of human rights is individual liberty then a system that justifies or endorses state control of education for the purpose of cultural conformity can be said to be far too statist for a free and democratic society. In this article, I argue that both the German Constitutional Court (FCC) and the ECtHR have adopted an approach to education rights that is profoundly mistaken. I conclude that home education is a right of parents and children that must be protected by every state. Nations that respect and protect the right of parents and children to home educate demonstrate a commitment to respecting human rights; nations that do not, such as Germany and Sweden need to take steps to correct their failure to protect this important human right.

Introduction

I find that [the Romeikes] belong to a particular social group of homeschoolers who, for some reason, the [German] government chooses to treat as a rebel organization, a parallel society, for reasons of its own. As I stated above, this is not traditional German doctrine, this is Nazi doctrine, and it is, in this Court's mind, utterly repellant to everything that we believe in as Americans. ... [I]f Germany is not willing to let them follow their religion, not willing to let them raise their children, then the United States should serve as a place of refuge for the applicants. (Burman, 2010; Immigration Judge Lawrence O. Burman, granting political asylum to the Romeike family because of Germany's antihomeschooling policy.[1])

Reflecting a striking international contrast, homeschooling is a legal and flourishing form of education in the United States but is forbidden in Germany and effectively banned in Sweden; this total prohibition on home education has been upheld by the European Court of Human Rights

(ECtHR). This contrast reflects a curious divergence between countries that are otherwise seen as similar in their protections of most other basic human rights. If the promise of human rights is individual liberty then a system that justifies or endorses state control of education for the purpose of cultural conformity can be said to be far too statist for a free and democratic society. In this article, I will articulate the case for home education as a human right, a subject I have written on in more detail elsewhere (Donnelly, 2016), and critically assess the proportionality model of rights review used by Germany and the ECtHR to arrive at the conclusion that banning home education does violate accepted constitutional and human rights norms.[2]

With over 2 million children, the United States has by far the largest and fastest-growing homeschooling population. Murphy (2012) describes home education as much as a social movement as a form of education. He writes that it is effective and delivers no less on academic and social outcomes than other forms of education. Although parents give many reasons for choosing home education, including concern about the environment in schools, quality of academic instruction, or the desire to give instruction in morality or religion (U.S. Department of Education, 2012), homeschooling is a legal form of education in all of the states and territories of the United States and in most western democratic countries.

This is not the case in Germany, however. Spiegler (2015) observes that "home education is not allowed in Germany as an alternative to public schooling." He affirms that fines, criminal prosecution, and loss of custody of children are possible state actions against families who persist in home-schooling. It is widely reported that many families who wish to home educate their children have felt they had no choice but to emigrate. This cultural hostility in Germany, and similarly in Sweden, have contributed to the bulk of international human rights case law on the issue. We will focus on the German cases because they are the most recent and well documented, and because Germany has a highly regarded constitutional court.

Why doesn't Germany, a highly regarded democracy with a strong human rights record, protect this right? Why it that while Germany accepts hundreds of thousands of refugees fleeing from war in the Middle East, it creates its own exodus (admittedly in smaller numbers) of parents who wish to homeschool their children? What does this divergence imply about the right of home education and the jurisprudence of the court's ruling on the issue? In this article I argue that both the German Constitutional Court (FCC) and the ECtHR have adopted an approach to education rights that is profoundly mistaken.

Home education as a right

Some countries and some international human rights treaties explicitly identify education as a right—although most also explicitly recognize the rights of parents to make decisions about the education of their children.

And while home education is not mentioned by name in international human rights treaties, it can be identified as a specific nexus of other explicit human rights such that it demands respect and protection by the state (Donnelly, 2016). The human right of home education emanates out of the demands of other explicitly identified rights including the right to education, the rights of parents to make decisions for and about their children's education, the rights to freedom of conscience and religion and the recognition of the family as the fundamental group unit of society.

Although the United States Supreme Court has declined to recognize "education" itself as a constitutionally protected right, virtually every state has recognized education as a right. In 1925, the U.S. Supreme Court ruled that the liberty protected by the 14th Amendment included the substantive rights of parents to direct the education of their children. This was one of the main justifications the court gave in *Pierce v. Society of Sisters*, when it struck down an Oregon statute that would have eradicated all private education (*Pierce, Governor of Oregon, et al. v. Society of the Sisters of the Holy Names of Jesus and Mary*, 1925).

In *Pierce*, the U.S. Supreme Court overturned the Oregon law and declared that although the state may reasonably regulate education to ensure minimum standards,

> The fundamental theory of liberty upon which all governments in this Union repose excludes any general power of the State to standardize its children by forcing them to accept instruction from public teachers only. The child is not the mere creature of the State; those who nurture him and direct his destiny have the right, coupled with the high duty, to recognize and prepare him for additional obligations.

The international human rights framework is founded on the Universal Declaration of Human Rights (UDHR; United Nations, 1948). In response to the atrocities committed during the Second World War, the UDHR recognizes education as both an individual and a parental right. Article 26.1 establishes the right to education, and Article 26.3 establishes that "parents have the prior right to decide what kind of education their children shall receive" (United Nations, 1948). The parental right includes both the right to provide for and also the right to exempt a child from any particular instruction in religious or moral subjects.[3] The International Covenant of Economic Social and Cultural Rights (ICESCR) specifically recognizes that "individuals" as well as "bodies" may form educational institutions (United Nations, 1966a). The International Covenant of Civil and Political Rights (ICCPR) recognizes that the right of parents to ensure the education of their children in conformity with their religious and philosophical convictions is non-derogable (United Nations, 1966b, Article 18 and Article 4.2). Article 2 of Protocol 1 of the European Convention on Human Rights and Fundamental Freedoms (ECHR) strongly enjoins the state in "all areas of education" to respect the convictions of parents (Council of Europe, 1950).

However, in contrast to the United States, where homeschooling is legal in every state and territory, and in spite of these internationally recognized rights of parents in education, the FCC has applied the jurisprudential model of proportionality to totally ban home education. The court ruled that it was not a disproportionate interference with the constitutional rights of parents to direct the education of their children, because "the state's educational mandate has equal ranking with the parents' right to educate [Article 6 of the basic law] as derived from Art. 7 Sec 1 of the Basic Law" (*In the matter of Konrad*, 2003). This reasoning was upheld by the ECtHR (Konrad, 2006). The ECtHR built on previous cases on the issue of home education (*Family H. v. United Kingdom*, 1984; *Leuffen v. Germany*, 1992; *B.N. and S.N. v. Sweden*, 1993) to uphold a state "right" to compel public school attendance. It ruled that Germany's ban on home education was within Germany's "margin of appreciation"[4] and thus not a violation of the treaty.

In 2014, both courts had the opportunity to reconsider these findings, but declined to do so. In *Schaum v. Germany* (2014), a family who homeschooled their nine children were criminally fined for not sending their children to school.[5] These fines were distinct from the Konrad's, who received civil fines, not criminal fines; nevertheless, the FCC refused to revisit its ban on home education and the ECtHR denied the family's application. For the time being, both courts appear fixed in their determination to deny that home education is a right that should be recognized and protected. How does Germany and the ECtHR arrive at such a disparate outcome from other democratic countries that permit homeschooling?

Between a rock and a rights place: Proportionality

Critics argue that balancing may not be appropriate when talking about rights. They use the analogy that balancing rights is like balancing the length of a line with the weight of a rock (Tsakyrakis, 2009). European rights jurisprudence, however, is characterized by the application of balancing rights and interests. This is generally described as the proportionality model of rights analysis. Under the proportionality review model, virtually any course of action is considered a "right"—the question is whether the government has interfered in a way that is disproportionate.

Kai Moller says that the "doctrine of balancing holds the central position in the global model of constitutional rights … the final and often decisive stage of the proportionality test, where it is used to resolve a conflict between a right and a competing right or public interest" (2012, p. 134). Proportionality review involves a four-step court analysis to determine whether or not government interference may be justified as "proportional." The ECtHR has explicitly adopted a review of proportionality in its case law (Council of Europe/European Court of Human Rights, 2015).

First, the court assesses whether the alleged interference pursues a *legitimate* goal. For example, is it a *legitimate* policy goal to sanction certain behavior, such as speeding? Second, the court evaluates whether the inter- ference is *suitable*, or rationally connected to achieving (even if only to a small extent) that goal. For example, is it *suitable* to achieve the goal of prohibiting speeding to permit the use of photo enforced speed limits? Third, the court must determine whether the interference is *necessary*. Here the court must ask whether there is any less intrusive but equally effective alternative to the government's infringing action. Finally, the law must not impose a *disproportionate* burden on the right-holder—this is the *proportion- ality/balancing* stage. Here the court will balance the value of the right versus the public interest to determine whether the interference is in fact proportional.

In *Konrad*, religious parents sought to home school their children. They were fined by the local authorities for not sending their children to school. The parents appealed to the German courts all the way to the FCC, arguing they had a right under Article 6 of the German Basic Law, which says, "The care and upbringing of children is the natural right of parents and a duty primarily incumbent upon them."[6] In 2003, the FCC denied their claim, arguing that a ban on home education in the Federal Republic of Germany was consistent with the Basic Law because "society has an interest in counter- acting the development of parallel societies and integrating minorities" (*In the matter of Konrad*, 2003; *Schaum v. Germany*, 2014). The FCC interpreted the states' Article 7 duty to supervise the "entire school system" to mean that the state was endowed with an *equal* interest in the education of children, and could thus prevent a parent from home educating their children.

The FCC reasoned that even if home education could meet the academic needs of students, the social integration required for a "tolerant" society could not be achieved in any other way than attending the closely supervised and controlled system of state and private schools (*In the matter of Konrad*, 2003). The FCC further reasoned that because children were unable to foresee the long-term consequences of home education (presumably harmful in the court's mind), the court had an obligation to protect children from such potential consequences. Spiegler (2015) questions this concern, suggest- ing that German education policy may be more focused on the overarching goal of maintaining cultural homogeneity—a view which underscores the FCC's concern about the development of "parallel societies" as a major reason for their willingness to ban home education.

Is the challenged policy legitimate?

Applying the first stage of proportionality review, we inquire whether coun- teracting the development of parallel societies is a *legitimate* goal of the state. This appears to have been the primary policy goal advanced by the government and evaluated by the court. The German court explicitly indicated that the educational needs of children were a secondary consideration.

Regrettably, the FCC does not explain what is meant by parallel societies. Elsewhere, I have suggested that a parallel society is a group of people who live inside or within another society, but who do not share a minimum set of common characteristics (Donnelly, 2007). I define these *commons* as a common boundary, common language, common economic system, common legal system, and common political authority that reflects the will of the people with respect to laws that apply equally to all.

A parallel society would be one that seeks to effectively eliminate its connection with the larger society. It would seek to operate its own civic institutions and judiciary, reject using a common language, maintain a separate economic system, and apply its own political will through its own political institutions. It might even dispute the boundary authority of the larger society (e.g., the Kurds in Iraq).

It is a well-established principle in a liberal democracy that the state must protect the rights of its citizens and apply the law equally to all people who live within its jurisdiction. On that basis, perhaps one may accept that parallel societies could be dangerous in a democratic nation. Such societies might deny to some citizens the equal protection of the laws. For example, some have expressed concern that sharia courts do not treat women equally (Friedland, 2014). But even if parallel societies are contrary to the principles underlying the liberal democratic state, isn't a kind of coerced uniformity (of education) contrary to pluralism, which is another of those crucial underlying principles? When we look at the context of a complete ban on home education, we are left to wonder if such a strict view of parallel societies is really consistent with the idea of pluralism.

Pluralism is an important principle for liberal democracies where people with significant religious, cultural, linguistic, philosophical (even pedagogical) differences are able to live together peacefully pursuing their own concepts of the good life. Are Belgium's French, Fleming, and Walloon populations, who each maintain their own parliaments, parallel societies? What about German, Italian, and French cantons in Switzerland? The Amish in the United States are very different from the general population but are not a true parallel society, because they speak English and do not seek total isolation from the larger society.

At what point does a cultural difference become the kind of rebellion that leads to a parallel society, and thus deserve to be completely banned? Critics of home education in the United States have argued that home education should be severely limited through greater regulation (Ross, 2010; West, 2009; Yuracko, 2008) or even completely banned (Albertson-Fineman & Worthington, 2009). This approach has caused concern for advocates of liberal policy in education.

Glanzer (2013) says home education is *needed* in a liberal society. "Although a concern with the political dimension of our human personhood is understandable and necessary in education, we are more than political citizens." The "beauty of a liberal democracy" is that it allows pluralism to flourish. The political dimension of education in liberal democracies, however, endangers pluralism when it becomes an "all encompassing, exclusive life philosophy or functional religion." This "increasing tendency of educational philosophers" appears to be the trend, as "leaders and practitioners think about education primarily in terms of our political identity," and it signals a potential danger. Glanzer criticizes scholars such as Amy Gutmann (1999) who write about the "primacy of political education." Instead, Glanzer proposes that "leaders of liberal democracies, including educational leaders, need reminders of liberal democracy's limits and the fact that the child is not the mere creature of the state." He says that homeschooling and a meaningful protection of parental decision making in education provide these needed reminders to policymakers and citizens (see also Eichner, 2005; Farris, 2013).

At this stage of proportionality jurisprudence, however, the court must determine whether the government is pursuing a *legitimate* goal. Defined in this way, parallel societies could be seen as threatening. Thus, counteracting parallel societies may constitute a *legitimate* goal of state action.

Is the policy suitable?

In step two, the court assesses the policy for *suitability*, asking whether banning home education will achieve the sought-after goal—in this case, counteracting the development of parallel societies. The policy need not be perfect to survive; it must only contribute to the legitimate goal, even if only a little.

In *Konrad*, the FCC asserts that inculcating the value of "lived tolerance" is also needed to counteract the development of parallel societies, and can only be obtained by exposing children to others who have different beliefs—and, importantly, this necessary exposure can only be achieved by requiring children to attend a public school or a state-approved private school. Regrettably, the FCC doesn't reason its way to this conclusion with facts and evidence, but asserts it as an obvious truth. Neither does the court examine any evidence to supports the claim that homeschooling contributes to a lack of tolerance, an allegation that recent research suggests may be questionable.

Cheng (2014) has shown that political tolerance is actually positively correlated with more exposure to home education—exactly the opposite of the FCC's presumption. Both Wolf (2007) and Campbell (2001) have also shown that in the American context, private schools are better at inculcating tolerance and good citizenship than public schools. Both of these strands of research contradict the German court s presumption, albeit in an American context. It does not appear that the German court made any effort at comparative jurisprudence. Instead, it relied solely on its own inherent presuppositional bias that only public schools are an acceptable way to help children be tolerant of the differences in others.

Still, the metric for the court at this stage is that the state action only has to justify contributing to the *legitimate* goal "a little bit." Requiring all children to attend school may be said to logically increase the chances of interaction with others. Does this mere fact make them more tolerant? Does this contribute to the policy of counteracting the development of "parallel societies?" The hurdle is not very high to overcome at this stage; thus, the policy might be seen as suitable.

Is the interference necessary?

The third step in proportionality analysis is to determine whether the policy is *necessary*. As Moller (2014) puts it, the "principle of necessity requires that there must be no other, least restrictive policy that achieves the legitimate goal equally well." In the U.S. constitutional jurisprudence this would be the "least restrictive means" test. At this stage, the court should determine if there are any other ways the state can achieve its goal without interfering with the parents' rights.

A comparative assessment of other countries where homeschooling is tolerated clearly shows that homeschooling does not contribute to parallel societies. Murphy (2012, p. 151) cites numerous researchers who found that home-schooled adults were "indeed heavily involved in community life at the local and national levels and were more civically involved than the general population of adults." Furthermore, in countries where home education is regulated, authorities have not found the need to impose significant regulation to address tolerance or the development of parallel societies (Donnelly, 2012). It would seem even from this cursory examination that a *complete ban* on homeschooling is not *necessary*, at least not in a *judicial* sense. Even taking the United States out of the set of comparators would show that most European countries allow for home education, and that they are not concerned about parallel societies arising as a result. On the contrary, Beck, a Norwegian professor of education (2015, p. 96), observes that "home educated students appear to be well socialized" and that home schooling is "essential for maintaining social integration and social and knowledge diversification in postmodern societies."

Neither the FCC or the ECtHR conducted any rigorous comparative analysis. In fact, the FCC does not reference any comparative law at all in Konrad. The ECtHR goes along with the FCC, stating that it:

observes in this respect that there appears to be no consensus among the Contracting States with regard to compulsory attendance of primary schools. While some countries permit home education, other States provide for compulsory attendance of its State or private schools. (Konrad, 2006, p. 7)

The idea of consensus is related to the court's use of the margin of appreciation. In some cases, the court has reasoned that where some large number of states allows for a practice, then the court will find that a consensus exists, and it may then narrow the "margin of appreciation" that a nation may be afforded with respect to a particular policy. However, I have personally reviewed the laws of the states in Europe and have demonstrated that most states allow for home education, even as they also universally have compulsory attendance laws (Donnelly, 2012). The fact that a majority of European nations explicitly permit home education proves that there is a less restrictive way to counteract the development of parallel societies. Such assumptive reasoning has been criticized as undermining the court's credibility (Dzehtsiarou, 2015).

A total ban on home education is NOT *necessary* to achieve the state's "legitimate goal" of promoting tolerance and counteracting the development of parallel societies. Both the FCC and ECtHR would have been able to find a violation of the parental constitutional rights or the treaty rights under this analysis. But even if the decision regarding the necessity of the policy was protected within Germany's margin of appreciation, is the interference a proportionate interference?

On balance, is the interference proportional?

In the fourth stage of *proportionality* review, the court *balances* or weighs the rights and interests to find whether "on balance" the interference was proportional or not. In evaluating the Konrad's claims that Germany violated their treaty rights, the ECtHR had to determine whether Germany's interference with homeschooling violated its treaty obligations. The family's primary claim was that Germany's antihomeschooling policy violated Article 2 of Protocol 1 of the ECtHR. Article 2 of Protocol 1 is considered the *lex specialis* of education rights by the ECtHR (COE/ECHR, 2015).

Article 2 of Protocol No. 1 says:

No person shall be denied the right to education. In the exercise of any functions which it assumes in relation to education and to teaching, the State shall respect the right of parents to ensure such education and teaching in conformity with their own religious and philosophical convictions.

The Konrads also made claims under Articles 8 (right to respect for private and family life) and 9 (freedom of thought, conscience, and religion), which allow the state to interfere with these rights but only if the interference is "prescribed by law," is "necessary in a democratic society" and "in the interests" of *inter alia* public safety, for the protection of public order, health, or morals, or for the protection of the rights and freedoms of others. Article 2 of Protocol 1 does not contain these same exceptions. However, the court only addressed the other claims in a perfunctory manner, focusing primarily on the Article 2 of Protocol 1 claim. I have analyzed the court's legal reasoning at more length elsewhere (Donnelly, 2016), and I encourage interested readers to look there for more detail on why I believe the court misapplied its own precedent in upholding Germany's ban on home education.

In addition to balancing the state's interest (in counteracting parallel societies), the FCC also sought to balance the interests of the parents and their (potentially) homeschooled children. The FCC determined that it had to protect the children from their parents' decision to homeschool because the children could not foresee the long term consequences of such a decision, since they were too young. The ECtHR stated Germany's reasoning this way:

> The [German] court noted that the State's obligation to educate would also further the children's interests and served the protection of their personal rights. Because of their young age, the applicant children were unable to foresee the consequences of their parents' decision for home education.

This is a curious argument that is at some odds with a well-known legal understanding that minors lack capacity to make decisions for themselves. Even the child-centered view contemplated by the United Nations Convention on the Rights of the Child requires those responsible for a child to provide guidance and direction consistent with the evolving capacities of the child (UNCRC; United Nations, 1989, Article 5). For the state to intervene in such a clearly protected realm of decision making and uphold a total ban without strong evidence of actual harm is striking; yet this is exactly what the FCC did.

In exercising review of the FCC in light of Germany's treaty obligations, the ECtHR essentially *deferred* to the findings of the FCC as "not being erroneous and falling within its margin of appreciation" as a contracting party to manage its internal educational matters in this way. Put another way, the FCC and the ECtHR upheld the total prohibition on a form of education that is widely acknowledged to serve the interests of children and society in most jurisdictions within Europe and other liberal democracies. That they would make such a sweeping determination with so little support is also striking.

Regrettably, neither court engages in any real balancing—either in the previous stages or at the fourth stage. They did not rigorously examine the weights of the interest, the severity of the restrictions, or evidentiary support for their conclusions. Some commentators have criticized the ECHR for taking this kind of approach because it is de-legitimizing. Dzehtsiarou

(2015, Kindle Locations 2905–2906) recommends that by showing its reasoning openly to the public that the ECtHR explain its balancing test openly as a way to enhance the court's legitimacy.

"It is suggested that the Court should not clearly indicate how it has arrived at a particular solution," Dzehtsiarou writes:

> but provide a smokescreen to cover its motives. It is very doubtful that such a strategy can be sustainable in the long run. Such reasoning is open for criticism from a wide range of stakeholders, for not presenting clear evidence supporting the judgment. One can argue that transparent and fair examination of comprehensive comparative data would increase trust in the Court's rulings.

I argue here, and in more detail elsewhere (Donnelly, 2016), that both courts' reasoning suffers from serious defects. They assumed facts not in evidence, failed to properly analyze the comparative jurisprudence and legislative status of home education in relevant jurisdictions, and essentially *presumed* that the challenged public policy—a complete ban on home education—was the only way to achieve the desired outcome. But this was a total ban on an activity that other reputable nations who respect human rights allow under their laws. Such a ban demands a higher-quality judicial response and ought to be viewed with suspicion.

Conclusion

Herein I have proposed that home education is a human right which emanates from, or can be properly understood as a synthesis of, other important rights that are clearly articulated in the modern international human rights framework. As such, home education is itself worthy of status as a human right which should be protected. The outcomes of proportionality review for home education as a right in its specific application in the FCC and the ECtHR cast doubt on proportionality as a judicial technique that is able to protect, at least some, human rights.

Spiegler (2015) suggests that the FCC's failure to seriously grapple with the right of parents to choose home education may result from bias and cultural preferences for homogeneity. The ECtHR's failure to intervene and address these rights in a transparent and evidentiary manner detracts from its credibility and fails to adhere to the purpose of a human rights review court—to protect individual rights from the state, not the other way around. Moreover, these failures have resulted in the dislocation of families and in a form of persecution, as Judge Burman found, on those who are excessively fined and prosecuted over their desire to home educate their children.

I maintain that home education is a right of parents and children that must be protected by every state. Nations that respect and protect the right of parents and children to home educate demonstrate a commitment to respecting human rights; nations that do not, such as Germany and Sweden, should be encouraged to reexamine their effective bans on homeschooling, and to take steps to correct their failure to protect this important human right.

Notes

1. Ultimately the Romeikes claim for asylum was rejected by the U.S. Supreme Court although the family remain in the United States subject to an order of removal that has been indefinitely deferred. The author was an attorney representing the family.
2. By home education I mean elective home education where a parent for religious, philosophical, or pedagogical reasons prefers home education to education at a state or private institutional school. The FCC and the ECHR have made technical distinctions between parents who are motivated by reasons of conscience from those motivated by "practical" reasons of children's medical conditions or parental job requirements.
3. Human Rights Committee, General Comment 22 (September 27, 1993). Para. 4 and 6.
4. For a more detailed and technical critique of the ECtHR use of the margin of appreciation in this context see: http://www.ghec2016.org/sites/default/files/thursday_farris_home_education_its_a_right_1.pdf. The presentation can be watched at: https://www.youtube.com/watch?v=FdZOqTnRdKo&index=19&list=PLlnNEcPjg5O6xvSd8FZD6KauzONXfSKE3 beginning at 25:44.
5. By way of disclosure, the author was an attorney in the case. The case was denied review by the FCC in 2013 and by the ECtHR in 2014. However, a second case challenging the removal of children from the Wunderlich family because of homeschooling is still pending at the court.
6. German Basic Law Article 6 §2. https://www.btg-bestellservice.de/pdf/80201000.pdf at 16.

References

Albertson-Fineman, M., & Worthington, K. (2009). *What is right for children? The competing paradigms of religion and human rights*. Burlington, VT: Ashgate Publishing Company.

Beck, C. (2015). Home education and social integration. In P. Rothermel (Ed.), *International perspectives on home education: Do we still need schools?* (pp. 87–98). UK: Palgrave Macmillan.

B.N. and S.N. v. Sweden. no. 17678/91. European Court of Human Rights. (Commission decision of June 30, 1993).

Burman, L. (2010). *Oral decision of immigration judge. In asylum proceedings, in the matter of Uwe Andreas Josef Romeike et. al.* Retrieved from http://www.hslda.org/hs/international/Germany/Romeike_Official_Decision_Transcript_1-26-10.pdf

Campbell, D. E. (2001, Fall). Bowling together: Private schools, public ends. *Education Next*. Retrieved from http://educationnext.org/files/ednext20013_55.pdf

Cheng, A. (2014). Does homeschooling or private schooling promote political intolerance? Evidence from a Christian university. *Journal of School Choice*, 8, 49–68. doi:10.1080/15582159.2014.875411

Council of Europe. (1950). *European Convention for the Protection of Human Rights and Fundamental Freedoms*. Retrieved from http://www.echr.coe.int/Documents/Convention_ENG.pdf

Council of Europe/European Court of Human Rights. (2015). *Guide on Article 2 of Protocol no. 1 to the European Convention on Human Rights: Right to Education*. Retrieved from http://www.echr.coe.int/Documents/Guide_Art_2_Protocol_1_ENG.pdf

Donnelly, M. (2007). *Homeschooling: Pluralistic freedom, not parallel society*. Retrieved from http://www.hslda.org/hs/international/Germany/200709190.asp

Donnelly, M. (2012). Homeschooling. In C. Glenn, & J. De Groof (Eds.), *Balancing freedom, autonomy and accountability in education* (pp. 199–220). Nijmegan, Netherlands: Wolf Legal Publishers.

Donnelly, M. (2016). State power vs. parental rights: An international human rights perspective on home education. In B. Cooper, F. Spielhagen, & C. Ricci (Eds.), *Homeschooling in new view* (pp. 65–82). Charlotte, NC: Information Age Publishing.

Dzehtsiarou, K. (2015). *European consensus and the legitimacy of the European court of human rights*. Cambridge, UK: Cambridge University Press. Retrieved from http://www.law.uchicago.edu/files/file/358-sd-judicial.pdf

Eichner, M. (2005). Dependency and the liberal polity: On Martha Fineman's the autonomy myth. *California Law Review*, 93(4), 1285–1322. Retrieved from http://scholarship.law.berkeley.edu/californialawreview/vol93/iss4/6

Family H. v/the United Kingdom, no. 10233/83, commission decision March 6, 1984.

Farris, M. (2013). Tolerance and liberty: Answering the academic left's challenge to homeschooling freedom. *Peabody Journal of Education*, 88(3), 393–406. doi:10.1080/0161956X.2013.798520

Friedland, E. (2014, February 19). *Women's rights under Sharia: An overview of the lack of equality and oppression of women under Sharia—The position of women in Muslim majority societies*. The Clarion Project. Retrieved from http://www.clarionproject.org/understanding-islamism/womens-rights-under-sharia

Glanzer, P. L. (2013). Saving democratic education from itself: Why we need homeschooling. *Peabody Journal of Education*, 88(3), 342–354. doi:10.1080/0161956X.2013.798509

Gutmann, A. (1999). *Democratic education*. Princeton, NJ: Princeton University Press.

In the matter of Konrad. 1 BvR 436/03 (F.R.G.). Bundesverfassungsgericht [BVerfG] [Federal Constitutional Court]. (2003, April 29).

Konrad v. Germany. no. 35504/03. European Court of Human Rights. (Denied September 11, 2006).

Leuffen v. Germany. no. 19844/92. European Court of Human Rights. (Commission decision of July 9, 1992).

Moller, K. (2012). *The global model of constitutional rights*. Oxford, UK: Oxford University Press.

Moller, K. (2014). Balancing as reasoning and the problems of legally unaided adjudication: A rejoinder to Francisco Urbina. *International Journal of Constitutional Law*, 12(1), 222–225. doi:10.1093/icon/mou002

Murphy, J. (2012). *Homeschooling in America: Capturing and assessing the movement*. Thousand Oaks, CA: Corwin Press.

Pierce, Governor of Oregon, et al. v. Society of the Sisters of the Holy Names of Jesus and Mary, 268 U.S. 510. United States Supreme Court. (1925).

Ross, C. (2010). Fundamentalist challenges to core democratic values: Exit and homeschooling. *William and Mary Bill of Rights Journal*, 18, 991–1014.

Schaum v. Germany, 2 BvR 920/14 (F.R.G.). Bundesverfassungsgericht [BVerfG] [Federal Constitutional Court]. (2014, October 15).

Spiegler, T. (2015). Home education versus compulsory schooling in Germany: The contribution of Robert K. Merton's typology of adaption to an understanding of the movement and the debate about its legitimacy. In P. Rothermel (Ed.), *International perspectives* on home education: Do we still need schools? (pp. 151–164). United Kingdom: Palgrave Macmillan.

Tsakyrakis, S. (2009). Proportionality: An assault on human rights? *International Journal of Constitutional Law, 7*(3), 468–493. doi:10.1093/icon/mop011

U.S. Department of Education, National Center for Education Statistics. (2012). *Parent and family involvement in education survey of the national household education surveys program* (PFI-NHES:2003, 2007, and 2012). (This table was prepared November 2014). Retrieved from https://nces.ed.gov/programs/digest/d13/tables/dt13_206.10.asp?current=yes

United Nations. (1948). *Universal Declaration of Human Rights*, 10 December 1948, 217 A (III). Available at http://www.refworld.org/docid/3ae6b3712c.html

United Nations. (1966a). *International Covenant on Economic, Social and Cultural Rights*, 16 December 1966, United Nations, Treaty Series, vol. 993, p. 3. Available at http://www.refworld.org/docid/3ae6b36c0.html

United Nations. (1966b). *International Covenant on Civil and Political Rights*, 16 December 1966, United Nations, Treaty Series, vol. 999, p. 171. Available at http://www.refworld.org/docid/3ae6b3aa0.html

United Nations. (1989). *Convention on the Rights of the Child*, 20 November 1989, United Nations, Treaty Series, vol. 1577, p. 3. Available at http://www.refworld.org/docid/3ae6b38f0.html

West, R. (2009). The harms of homeschooling. *Philosophy & Public Policy Quarterly, 29*(3–4, Summer/Fall). University of Maryland.

Wolf, P. J. (2007, Summer). Civics exam. Schools of choice boost civic values. *Education Next*. Retrieved from http://educationnext.org/files/ednext_20073_66.pdf

Yuracko, K. (2008) Education off the grid: Constitutional constraints on homeschooling. *California Law Review, 96*(1), 123–184. Retrieved from http://scholarship.law.berkeley.edu/californialawreview/vol96/iss1/3

Homeschooling, Virtual Learning, and the Eroding Public/Private Binary

ABSTRACT

Regulators ubiquitously dichotomize schooling into two discrete sectors: *public* and *private*. Although homeschooling is regulated in some contexts as a third sector, the general approach is to treat it as a species of private education by subjecting it to public regulation while simultaneously denying it public funds. But the public/private binary is increasingly difficult to sustain as charter schools multiply and, especially, as virtual schooling increasingly penetrates primary and secondary education. Public school systems are deploying virtual education in ways that erode once impermeable walls between public and private. Many obstacles to homeschooling will fall with those walls—particularly obstacles related to government financing of homeschooling activities.

The hegemonic public/private binary

A legal and regulatory binary, deeply rooted in many legal systems, demands that every school be either *public* or *private*. Under this binary, regulators understand home schools as a particular genus of the phylum, "private schools." This taxonomy is unsurprising. There is an undeniable and strong analogy between home and private schooling: both involve parents opting out of state-provided education. The United States guarantees the right to homeschool as it does the right to private school, and for many of the same reasons (*Pierce v. Society of Sisters*, 1925). Concomitantly, it requires families who elect homeschooling, like those who choose private school, to forfeit all but *de minimis* entitlements to state educational subsidies for their children.

To be sure, regulatory regimes for homeschools with respect to issues like curriculum, teacher qualifications, and the school day are, in many jurisdictions in the United States at least, considerably less demanding than those faced by institutional private schools (McMullen, 2002, pp. 87–88; Waddell, 2010, pp. 547–548; Yuracko, 2008, pp. 151 & n. 138, 169). This can make homeschools appear to be a *sui generis*, third regulatory category. But these differences ultimately represent particular adaptations of regulatory approaches used for private schooling. They should not obscure the fundamental regulatory categorization of homeschools as "private."

Important comparative legal scholarship demonstrates that the categories of "public" and "private," as applied to schools, bear vastly different meanings in different systems (Glenn & DeGroof, 2005). In the United States, moreover, the meaning of the terms developed "late in time," through a process both "slow and uneven" (Reese, 2007, p. 100).[1] Prior to the 20th century, in the United States "[t]he terms 'public' and 'private' did not have their present connotations, and most schools did not fit neatly into either of our modern categories" (Kaestle, 1983, p. 13; see also, Green, 2010, p. 253; Tyack, 1974, p. 57). In the 1800s, American schools were arranged by cooperatives of neighbors. Schools' organizers understood their institutions to serve a "public" function, and some even received taxpayer subsidies. Nevertheless, "contemporary standards" of the time deemed these schools "private institutions" (Reuben, 2005, p. 5). Attacks by progressive-era reformers on "private" schools targeted institutions quite different than those Americans would reflexively call "private schools" in, say, the 1960s or 1990s (Kaestle, 1983, p. 116; Reese, 2007, pp. 99–102).

Today's American idea of what makes a school public or private is, in other words, highly contingent. Nevertheless, by the latter half of the 20th century, the contemporary concepts of "public" and "private" had achieved ideological "hegemony" in America. A particular sort of "public" school, founded and managed along progressive lines, had become the "taken-for-granted educative institution for most Americans" (Jones, 2008, pp. 2–4). It was education's "one best system" (Tyack, 1974), a "natural state of affairs" (Hess, 2010, pp. 163–64). Like the free press, it was a fundamental "institution of American constitutional democracy," although nowhere mentioned in the United States Constitution (Pelikan, 2005, p. xiii). Its exemplary characteristics, and their combination within a single institution, have been a fixed point in public understanding for decades.

That understanding designates public schools as those that are free of charge to parents. It understands them to be governed by a local school government, a "board of education" that monopolizes the provision of public schooling within its jurisdiction. That board is popularly elected within that jurisdiction. The board imposes taxes on property to support its activities. (Later in time, state and federal monies came substantially to supplement the local financing of public schools.) Public school systems must educate all pupils within the jurisdiction—although certain categories of children, notably racial minorities, the disabled, and noncitizens, only came to be included within this stricture over time. Public schools are and must be secular.

Private schools are understood to have a very different characteristic vector of institutional features. Private schools are privately managed and run. They have no obligation to educate any particular child beyond duties created by the civil rights laws prohibiting discrimination, by enrollment contracts, and by the dictates of their own mission or conscience. They may select their students from any geographic location. They are regulated by the state, but the scope of that regulation is considerably less than that affecting public schools. They receive no or minimal government monies. Instead, they charge tuition, rely upon charitable contributions, or otherwise support themselves. And private schools may be religious. Indeed, religious institutions today account for approximately 75% of private school enrollment (Kena et al., 2015, p. 75).

Because private schools are, by definition, not *public*, parents and schools that wish to forgo public management or pervasive regulation must also forfeit public subsidy and pay their own way. Thus, the famous observation that those who opt out of public schooling in the United States pay twice, although, as some have noted, it is more accurate to say that they pay *three* times (Sugarman, 1991, p. 181). They pay taxes to support the public schools, like every other taxpayer; they do not send their children to the public schools, relieving the public fisc of the duty to expend resources to educate those children; and then, under compulsory schooling laws, they must utilize their own resources to provide that education.

Homeschoolers are like private school parents in this respect, except that they pay with their time the bulk of the expenses that other private school parents pay also for in cash. There remain some items for which home-schoolers also in cash, of course, such as materials and sometimes special instruction. Homeschoolers, like private schools, are also eligible for certain minimal subsidies, as, for example, when they are allowed to use public school facilities or transportation without charge.

As noted previously, from the legal and regulatory perspective, a great deal hinges on whether a home school, or for that matter any other school or school system, is deemed to be "public" or "private." Its categorization determines whether it can receive public monies, teach religion, or deny admission to a student it does not desire to teach. But, precisely because the public/private binary is "taken for granted," categorization has not histori-cally depended upon precise definitions. "Public" and "private" are descriptions of the two clusters of school types that existed in the United States for most of the 20th century. In a world where the types' classic exemplars—the neighborhood, district-run public school, the Catholic school, the tony private academy—were ubiquitous, the need for definitions was not felt. It was generally clear to everyone, including lawyers, legislators, bureaucrats, and parents, which schools were which. It was, therefore, easy to determine which set of regulatory requirements applied to any given school. For this reason, I have purposely described the key features of "public" and "private" schools as constituting "understandings" or "vectors of characteristics" rather than definitions.

The absence of formal definition permits some departures from ideal types, and, as is to be expected in a country as diverse as the United States, a field as complex as education, and a binary that substantially postdates the development of formal schooling, such departures have a long history. The United States is far from the only country that has preserved specialized academies for blind, deaf, disabled, and academically talented students inside its "public" school system, notwithstanding that such institutions have admissions criteria, which means that they are *not* open to all children within a jurisdiction. During the civil rights era, the set of "public" schools not available to all children grew, as school systems and their judicial supervisors sought to create and maintain racially integrated schools by the use of zoning, magnet programs, racial quotas, and other devices.

Likewise, there has long been variation in the institutions of governance. The progressive era largely homogenized a pre-existing diversity of governance arrangements, but did not eradicate all variation (Cronin, 1973, Chapter 6). The standard progressive arrangement, a school board directly elected by voters and given the power to manage the schools and tax on their behalf, is called in the United States an "independent school district." This well-worn phrase reveals a long history of "dependent" school districts; these relatively unusual school systems are administrative arms of general-purpose city or state governments. Recently, additional kinds of dependency have become more common. On the one hand, there has been a recent revival of interest in mayoral control, which has displaced independently elected school boards in many of America's largest cities (Cronin, 1973, Chapter 7; Wong, 2007). On the other, states have asserted the authority to impose "substitute administration" upon school districts whose performance, in their view, is inadequate. This involves the disempowerment or even ousting of locally elected school boards in favor of state-appointed bureaucrats (Anderson, 2012; Saiger, 1999). Notwithstanding these arrangements, nobody doubts that the school system of New York City, run by the City's mayor, or that of Newark, New Jersey, run by appointees of the state's Governor, remain "public."

A paradigmatic legal example of the fuzziness of the line between "public" and "private" schools arose in a case heard by the United States Supreme Court in 1982, *Rendell-Baker v. Kohn*. *Rendell-Baker* involved a school organized as a private corporation, but that received nearly all of its income by contracting with the state to meet the state's obligation to educate special-needs children. Those children attended the school free of charge; the State of Massachusetts paid their fees. The school was sued by teachers who argued that they had been unfairly dismissed. Notwithstanding that the school's only function was to provide classically "public" services to nonpaying students using public monies, the Court held that the school was a "private" entity. But this holding was limited to the question of which rules of employment law governed the dispute between the school and the teachers. The Court was not called upon to, and did not, define "public" and "private" schools more generally.

For a long time, these kinds of variations, although present, were marginal. Lately, however, they have moved to center stage, substantially eroding the public/private binary and its hegemony. This change was catalyzed by movements for parental choice in education, and especially by the rise of charter schools. Going forward, the most important influence destabilizing the public/private binary will be virtual education.

Charters as desectorizing

The idea of school choice, implemented through any number of modalities, challenges the foundations of the public/private binary. A government-issued school voucher, usable at a public or private school at a parent's election, is publicly funded, but the school that cashes it is privately run (*Zelman v. Simmons-Harris*, 2002). Is the school "public" or "private"? Or, rather than issuing vouchers, a state offers tax credits or tax-advantaged savings accounts to parents who incur private-school costs (Garnett, 2016). Is a tuition-dependent school whose fees can be higher because parental payments are untaxed "public" or "private"?

These issues are raised especially by charter schools. A charter is a school created by some group of stakeholders that receives public funds to provide education on a nondiscriminatory basis to students who choose to enroll. Charters are important to the argument here for two reasons. First, the charter sector is growing explosively. In 2012–2013, 2.3 million children were enrolled in over 6,000 charter schools. By comparison, 450,000 children were enrolled in 1,993 charters in 2000–2001, and there were no charter schools in 1990 (U.S. Department of Education, National Center for Education Statistics, 2015, tbl. 216.20). Nearly all government-funded schools in New Orleans are now charter schools; other large districts, including Los Angeles, Chicago, Houston, Philadelphia, and Miami-Dade, enroll more than 10% of their students in charters (Saiger, 2013). The possibility that chartering will fizzle out seems remote.

Second, the challenge that chartering poses to the public/private binary is particularly sharp. Charter schools share many important features with traditional public schools. Charter schools are publicly funded and require a government permit to operate (the "charter"). They do not admit privately paying students and may not charge tuition (Mead, 2003, p. 367). Only in some states are charters exempt from the collective bargaining agreements reached by their local school districts with teachers and other staff (Godwin & Kemerer, 2010, p. 6). Charters are also prohibited from discriminating among students in admission. Oversubscribed charters must admit students by lottery, although there is perennial concern that they use strategies such as location, targeted advertising, and counseling students at enrollment and re-enrollment to shape their student bodies to their liking (Lubienski & Weitzel, 2009, p. 361; Sugarman & Kuboyama, 2001, p. 873).

In other, equally important respects, charters are classically private. They can be established by any group of people or institution that can meet the regulatory requirements and attract students. This group might be made up of teachers, parents, not-for-profit, or for-profit actors. They are thus private, incorporated entities; in some ways the government-issued charter is more like the corporate "charter" issued to all private companies than the organizational documents of a public school or school district. Charters are privately managed and regulated much less heavily than archetypical public schools.

And families choose charters; no child is forced to attend. Charters, like private schools, therefore face market discipline. Within whatever regulatory strictures are imposed, charters compete for students with other charters and with other types of schools. If students enroll, a charter thrives. Otherwise it disappears (Sugarman & Kuboyama, 2001, p. 876; Vergari, 2003, p. 500).

Charter schools, therefore, pose a clear challenge to the binary. The only fair description of charter schools, given their characteristics, is that they are public/private hybrids. Nor are they a single type; charters occupy various intermediate midpoints along the spectrum between entirely public to entirely private, varying from state to state and school to school.

By opening up the space between the poles of that spectrum, charters make the task of categorizing schools as "public" and "private"—still so necessary under our regulatory regime—especially difficult. The field is full of competing definitions and descriptions, with both descriptive and pre-scriptive agendas, that emphasize one or another element of the classic vectors of publicness and privateness. The charter school industry and its customer base, on the one hand, insist that charters are "public," as do nearly all states' charter school statutes (Saiger, 2013). Aware of the finan-cial and political benefits of that categorization, charter proponents empha-size that charters receive public money and are subject to public oversight. Teachers' unions, for exactly the same reasons, declare that only traditional, district-managed schools are genuinely "public" schools.

The debate in the field is paralleled in the literature. Hill (2001, p. 316), for example, argues that "[p]ublic education is a set of goals," not "a fixed set of institutions"; he would apparently categorize even a privately managed and funded religious academy as a "public" school. His interlocutors insist that a school is only truly "public" if it is constituted as a government, so that its decisions are the conclusions of processes of "public" deliberation among citizens rather than the outcome of market-based processes among consu-mers (e.g., Gutmann, 1987).

Descriptively, the only fair conclusion seems to be that the popular and political decision to define charters and other choice arrangements as "public" or "private" is an attempt to place a square peg in one of two round holes. No element of the vector of publicness does or should be singled out as the critical one. Moreover, a school that is public for one set of purposes can be private for another (Green, Baker, & Oluwole, 2015).

These observations, moreover, indicate both the continuing hold of the binary and its ultimate unsustainability. Calling charters "public" when they have so many "private" features has already begun to raise all manner of legal problems, chief among them whether they may constitutionally accept public funding. As Garnett (2016) argues, these problems clearly portend the continuing erosion of the binary itself.

Virtuality as desectorizing

Virtual education is a less mature reform than charters, but, like charters, its diffusion seems inexorable. Compared to higher education in particular, broad public awareness of e-delivery of primary and secondary education is fairly low (Barbour et al., 2011, p. 18). But big changes are happening despite—or, perhaps, because of—there not being much of a spotlight. And the potential of virtuality to disrupt the public/private binary is even greater than that of charter schools.

Today's virtual education sector can be divided into three broad categories. The first involves virtual tools used to supplement existing in-person education. Educators and entrepreneurs are busily rolling out a gallimaufry of school technology (Selwyn, 2011, pp. 23–24). Schools are buying computers, wiring for high-speed Internet, and instructing their students to "bring your own device." They are rolling out online platforms that allow students and teachers to communicate, to post and respond to homework assignments, to take quizzes, and to monitor student progress. They are "flipping" classrooms (Khan, 2012, pp. 115–118; Murphy et al., 2014b). They are building "completely realized, networked digital environment[s]" that will integrate in-school pedagogy, learning, and assessment into single, seamless "digital teaching platforms" (Dede & Richards, 2012, p. 1). Various current iterations of these platforms allow teachers electronically to analyze student work for plagiarism, individualize assessment, and even track student behavior (Singer, 2014).

Ultimately, those building these tools envision them as seeds for a new "blended" or "personalized" model of schooling. "Blended learning" can be described as "splitting up the work of teaching between man and machine [by] combining teacher-led lessons with computer-based lectures and exercises" (Sengupta, 2011). Educators who study the technique define it as instruction some of which takes place "at a supervised brick-and-mortar location away from home"—school, in other words—while at the same time "a student learns at least in part through online delivery of content and instruction with some element of student control over time, place, path, and/or pace" (Staker & Horn, 2012, p. 3). In a 2015 survey, 45% of school-district administrators reported that they were using blended learning "with positive results." (Project Tomorrow, 2015, p. 6). A 2014 report from the Michael and Susan Dell Foundation expects blended learning to become "standard practice in many classrooms in the future" (Murphy et al., 2014a, p. 3).

Another possibility, however, is that information technology will come to *supplant* some or all traditional classroom instruction. The proliferation of online courses, especially at the middle- and high-school levels, is the clearest example. All over the country, schools are using online courses to provide instruction that they cannot, or no longer want to, provide in person (Clements, Stafford, Pazzaglia, & Jacobs, 2015, p. 9; Queen, Lewis, & Coopersmith, 2011, p. 3). The foreign language that the school does not offer, the advanced science or math course, or the advanced placement course not in the curriculum can all be taken online instead. As of August 2014, high school students in Alabama, Arkansas, Florida, Michigan, and Virginia were required by law to take at least one online course to be graduated. Other states have passed legislation that facilitates online instruction (Layton & Brown, 2011; Watson, Pape, Murin, Gemin, & Vashaw, 2014, p. 64).

Local school districts also create incentives for their students to move their learning online. Districts like those in Fairfax, Virginia and Houston, Texas, maintain an "online campus" through which high school students can register for online versions of standard high school courses. "These courses," according to the "Frequently Asked Questions" list on the Fairfax campus's Web site, are intended "for students who have scheduling conflicts, special medical needs requiring a home or hospital setting, special needs requiring a flexible schedule, or, are seeking to complete high school graduation requirements" (Fairfax County Public Schools, n.d.). That last category, of course, applies to almost every student enrolled in high school.

Just as supplementation can shade into substitution, online courses can be combined to the point that school itself becomes online. In a 2010 survey of public school districts, 22% reported that high school students "could take a full course load in an academic term using only distance education courses," and another 12% reported that students "could fulfill all high school graduation requirements using only distance education courses" (Queen et al., 2011, p. 3). By simply combining online courses, students can turn themselves into online students, even as they are matriculants of traditional schools.

Specific legislation in the states has also enabled the creation of fully online schools, or even "virtual school districts," designed purposefully to operate exclusively online.[2] These districts, which exist in at least 17 states, including Florida, Massachusetts, and Virginia, are distinct from any of the state's brick-and-mortar public school districts. Students anywhere in the state may enroll in these schools; they are not students in any other school, as are many students who take online classes.

Many other online schools, not part of virtual districts, have been organized as *cybercharter schools*. These schools use the charter school form discussed previously, which of course was developed for, and is still mostly used by, in-person schools. In recent years, several states have adapted their regulatory regimes to permit charter schools that operate exclusively online (Clark, 2008, p. 57). Cybercharters operate at every educational level, from kindergarten through high school. Students of virtual school districts and cybercharter schools do their coursework entirely in the cloud.

These forms of online learning—the online supplement, blended learning, the online course, the state virtual school district, and the cybercharter school—represent the very earliest forms of online K–12 education. They will certainly grow and change. But they are already a significant phenomenon. Consistent data are hard to obtain, "because there currently is no single entity that tracks students, and because of the wide variety of ways in which students can engage in this form of schooling" (Waters, Barbour, & Menchaca, 2014, p. 380). But, in the 2013–2014 school year, one census counted 400 full-time virtual schools with an estimated enrollment of 263,705 students (Molnar et al., 2015, p. 2). A different study in the same year counted 316,320 pupils, about one half of 1% of all students, receiving all of their K–12 education online. Fully online schools were operating in 30 different states (Watson et al., 2014, p. 53).

Meanwhile, by the 2007–2008 school year, 70% of school districts that offered online learning were reporting that at least one of their students was taking an online course (Picciano & Seaman, 2009). In the 2009–2010 school year, there were more than 1.8 million enrollments in online courses (some students may have taken more than one course). Most, but not all, online learning that supplanted in-person learning was at the high-school level. In the 2009–2010 school year, "[s]eventy-four percent of the distance education enrollments were in high schools, [nine] percent were in middle or junior high schools, and [four] percent were in elementary schools" (Queen et al., 2011, p. 3).

These are not amazingly high numbers, but neither are they insubstantial. More important, their trajectory is steep. The 1.8 million online enrollments in 2009–2010 can be compared to the estimated 506,950 registrations in technology-based distance education courses during the 2004–2005 school year and the 317,070 in 2002–2003 (Zandberg, Lewis, & Greene, 2008, p. 15). Compare these numbers to a small scale survey that suggests that, in the 2001–2002 academic year, only 40,000 to 50,000 students took an online course (Clark, 2001, p. i). In some states, growth has been even more explosive. For example, state virtual schools in Georgia and North Carolina have seen double-digit growth in course enrollments in each of the last 2 years. During the 2013–2014 school year, state virtual schools reported 741,516 supplemental online course enrollments (Hall, 2011; Watson et al., 2014, p. 27).

In full-time virtual schools, enrollment increased by a factor of 10 between 2002 (25,000 students) and 2010 (250,000 students) (Miron & Urschel, 2012, p. 2).[3] Cyber-charters, similarly, grew in both number and size over a span of 5 years during the same time period. A 2014 report found that the number of cybercharter schools increased from 147 cybercharters with 65,000 students in 2006 to 220 cybercharters with 217,000 students in 2011 (Waters et al., 2014, p. 381). It is hard to imagine that in the mid-1990s, when postsecondary institutions helmed the distance-education movement, these enrollment numbers for K–12 education were anything other than close to zero (Sikora & Carroll, 2002, p. iii). Before the Office of Educational Technology in the U.S. Department of Education commissioned a survey of the distance education courses for public elementary and secondary students during the 2002–2003 school year, there was "no nationally representative study [that] examined technology-based distance education availability, course offerings, and enrollments in the nation's elementary and secondary schools" (Setzer, Lewis, & Greene, 2005, p. 1).

Virtual education is a foundational challenge to the public/private binary because it abolishes several key features that are core characteristics of the traditional "public" school, without replacing them with corresponding features of a "private" school. In particular, virtual education need not be bundled, need not be organized into traditional communities, and need not be localist in orientation.

Bundling

Traditional schooling is a package deal. The constraints of buildings and transportation mean that, with very rare exceptions, a given child must attend one school during school hours. That school sets a curriculum which its students consume. This curriculum may, especially as children get older, allow them a measure of choice in some areas; in many other respects, however, even older students have no choice at all. A school or school district might decide, for example, that every student should take calculus, or not to offer calculus to anyone. Both of these options might be available to it from the perspective of district policy and state law; but once the school has made its election, its students are bound by it. Such school choices, moreover, might be driven by pedagogical considerations, but they might also be made based upon actual or perceived demand, resource constraints (teachers, space, money), and other nonpedagogical factors.

Virtual education radically unbundles schooling. No matter if one school does not offer calculus; surely some other provider does. Indeed, access to arcane and advanced course offerings is routinely touted as one of the more obvious benefits of virtual schooling. But unbundling has other effects whose normative implications are less clear. Today, if a school teaches about family structure, evolution, or history in ways a family does not like, its options are to complain or to depart for a different school. The first of these options is often ineffective and the other frequently expensive. The option merely to move to a different online module for social studies or biology, one more sympatico with a family's tastes, saves it, to use Hirschman's classic categories (1970), the uncertainties associated with voice and the expense otherwise associated with full exit.

Bundling is not a new issue. In one sense, many middle- and upper-class parents already unbundle when they supplement public education with after-school lessons. A robust market for such services supports not only extra-curricular karate, ballet, and piano lessons but enrichment or drill in academic subjects as well. Parents who supplement choose how to do so, so that many children's total package of educational activities differ one from another. Home schooling, as noted below, often involves radical unbundling.

Virtuality dramatically expands the range of unbundling and makes it relevant to a much larger group than was interested in partial exit from public schooling under the bricks-and-mortar technological paradigm. If virtuality invites all students to search for and enroll in the particular courses that meet their needs, everyone becomes an unbundler. In such an environment, an all-or-nothing view is untenable. This is so even if religion is a motivator for choices among commodities; it will be but one among many.

Community

One objection to allowing unbundling of the public school programs is that it undermines the school as a learning community. Since the consolidation of informal schooling at the dawn of the common-school and progressive eras, it has seemed obvious and necessary to most public school people that schools are and must be *communities*. As discrete places where students, teachers, and staff gather together at set times in set places in order to teach and learn, what else could they be? Many educators have made virtue of necessity, understanding community to be at the core of civically informed pedagogy.

Community clearly plays a central role in bricks-and-mortar schools. For teachers and staff, they are workplaces. For neighborhoods, they are local institutions. For students, they are complex sites of aggregation: to a greater or lesser extent involuntary, organized around learning, but also, because of the nature of children and the amount of time for which they are required to be in school, very often the locus of children s social and political as well as intellectual life.

Community seems less necessary in a world where individual students can log on asynchronously to a variety of providers to consume commodified courses. But it is not true that virtuality avoids community. It involves different kinds of communities than those we are used to, but, their participants insist, they are no less vital for that. Virtual users do not merely consume virtual experience. They also assist in shaping it. As the late Greg Lastowska put it (2010, p. 10):

> The most compelling element of virtual worlds, it turns out, is not the powerful graphic technologies they employ but the very real social interactions that occur through that technology. Virtual worlds are fundamentally new sorts of places. ... As books by journalists, anthropologists, sociologists, and others have explained, because virtual worlds are places, they are also sites of culture.

Balkin and Noveck (2006, p. 3), along with others, make a similar point: Virtual worlds "stimulate social experimentation" and "are full of social cooperation and social conflict."

At the same time, virtual worlds are clearly not the sort of communities that traditional public schools are. They are more atomistic, their membership is more fluid, and they do not have any natural geographic base. They are a different kind of community than the kind we are used to.

Localism

Geography is particularly important because localism is a foundational principle of American public school governance. *Brown v. Board* itself mentions localities. "Today," *Brown* states, "education is perhaps the most important function of state and local governments" (*Brown v. Board of Educ. of Topeka*, 1954, p. 493). The contemporary rule is best articulated in a later Supreme Court case, *Milliken v. Bradley* (1974, pp. 741–742):

> [T]he notion that school district lines may be casually ignored or treated as a mere administrative convenience is contrary to the history of public education in our country. No single tradition in public education is more deeply rooted than local control over the operation of schools; local autonomy has long been thought essential both to the maintenance of community concern and support for public schools and to quality of the educational process.

Localism has been a basic premise of schooling for a long time. School districts are, therefore, entrenched institutions. They have officeholders, staffs, budgets, and property. They have voters, constituencies, and interest groups. They have political capital and social meanings. They own buildings, grounds, and equipment. They are parties to labor contracts and insurance policies. These facts on the ground are among the many reasons districts have been so strong notwithstanding their inequity-promoting effects.

Districts will not disappear, therefore, at the first hint of digital learning. But the challenges that virtuality poses to localism will accelerate over time. The past few years, in which early digital education alternatives have begun to roll out, have made it already possible to see the shape of the coming challenge to the district's privileged position. Every single digital education effort, from the most local to the least, reflects the aterritorial nature of information technology. And newer initiatives seem to depart further and further from the localist paradigm.

Since the implementing agencies of public education in this country are school districts, many efforts have begun there. These are structured to be the most local of efforts. Consider again the online campuses like those managed by the school district of Fairfax, Virginia. Once something like an online campus is up and running, one would expect for its proprietors to find it nearly irresistible to fill available spaces with paying customers, should space remain available after district children fill their spots. Indeed, it ought to prove deeply tempting to increase capacity to accommodate such paying customers. Online learning of this kind, much more than in-person classes, has high start-up costs but low marginal costs. Once the infrastructure is established, adding more participants is fairly straightforward and relatively cheap.

Unsurprisingly, this is indeed the policy of the Fairfax Campus: district children attend for free—unless they are taking more than the seven-course load the district permits—but out-of-district students pay a few hundred dollars a course. Nor is this unique to Fairfax. The Houston (Texas) Independent School District runs a "Virtual School Tuition based Program"; its Web site, in conjunction with a price list, explains that its "unique program allows for any student from any district in any part of the world to complete courses online with the approval of their school guidance counselor." The Madison (Wisconsin) Virtual High School offers similar arrangements.

It must be emphasized how striking this policy is. In the context of bricks-and-mortar education, districts, especially affluent ones like Fairfax, have mightily resisted admitting or registering students from out of district. Options for interdistrict transfers that have been a part of education reform packages have generally withered. Such programs generally provide that receiving, wealthy districts must certify that there is space for additional students; and such districts rarely do so.

This has been the case, for example, in the Cleveland school voucher program. This program permitted parents of Cleveland public school chil-dren to receive vouchers for use outside the district. That program, and the Supreme Court case upholding it, was famous because it allowed the vou-chers to be used at private religious schools (*Zelman v. Simmons-Harris*,

2002). But the voucher law also provided that vouchers could be cashed at public schools in neighboring, whiter, wealthier districts. This part of the program was *not* famous. This is because no vouchers moved across district lines. Receiving districts had to agree to accept the vouchers, and none would.

Similarly, until a legislative reauthorization in late 2015, the federal No Child Left Behind Act provided that children in what the Act called "failing" schools be permitted to transfer to other, more effective school districts. Again, this required that nonfailing districts accept such students. Unsurprisingly, almost none were willing. Most cited space constraints (Aikens, 2005). It should surprise no one that interdistrict transfer was the least utilized plank of the Act.

And then you find rich, successful Fairfax, not just accepting paying customers from anywhere in the country, but soliciting business on the Internet. Fairfax online is not the same as Fairfax on the ground, in part, because the students it accepts in this way are disembodied. No strangers, no out-of-towners, actually show up to your local school. Students from beyond the boundary don't pose the kind of challenges, real, symbolic, and imagined, when they are virtual as they do when they appear in person. In addition, they have low marginal cost. Not to solicit such students must seem to Fairfax like leaving money on the table. (There are relatively rare provisions by which traditional high schools in some sparsely populated states, especially in Northern New England, register students from neighboring districts without high schools of their own.)

Other challenges to localism are more direct. The cybercharter schools discussed previously are not necessarily tied to any school district. Like charter schools generally, cybercharters may be started and managed by a wide variety of organizations; the statutory lists generally include school districts, but also create options for chartering by nonprofits, groups of parents and teachers, or for-profit corporations. Similarly, charter statutes authorize a range of institutions to review charter applications, grant charters, and monitor the charter schools. Again, school districts are among the institutions that can do so; but so are state departments of education and state universities.

This means that many cybercharters are detached from the localist school district structure. They are present statewide, solicit customers statewide, and are regulated by state-level actors; for-profit entities must also respond to investors who live anywhere and everywhere. Because cybercharters are not local school districts, they have no local boundary which entitles them to favor children from a certain area over others. All comers within the state are treated equally. And this is what they want. They have no more interest than local efforts like that of Fairfax in leaving money on the table.

Still other cyberschools do not use the cybercharter form per se but nevertheless are organized as public schools that are independent of the local school district structure. Several states have now established schools known as Virtual Academies. Some of these, like the Texas Virtual Academy, are cybercharters. Others, however, are formally organized as institutions that serve students under the umbrella of particular school districts. But they are not really local projects. The schools are established under state legislation that invites districts—but not only districts—to plan and implement such schools, often in collaboration with an outside provider or contractor.

For example, the Massachusetts legislature passed an act in 2012 providing for the establishment of "one or more" "Commonwealth virtual schools." The statute allows various actors to apply to the state for permission to establish such a school. They could be institutions of higher education, nonprofits, or groups of parents or teachers, although private schools were prohibited from applying. But school districts were also invited to apply (Mass. Acts, 2012, Chapter 379; Mass. General Laws Chap. 71, § 94(b), 2013). The district of Greenfield won that competition; indeed, it was with a partnership with Greenfield in mind that the contractor lobbied for the state legislation in the first instance. The resulting school, the Massachusetts Virtual Academy, is available to any Massachusetts student tuition free, but preference is given to students in its "home" district of Greenfield (Layton & Brown, 2011; Massachusetts Virtual Academy at Greenfield, 2015).

Or consider the Virginia Virtual Academy, a full-time, all-virtual K–6 school. It was established under a state law, similar to Massachusetts', that allows school districts to cooperate with providers to provide online schools, and exempts such contracts from some rules that otherwise govern public contracts (Va. Code Ann., 2015). At the start of its life, the Virginia Academy was sponsored by the Carroll County School Board. Carroll County then withdrew and at the Academy became a joint project of the King and Queen County Public School District and the Patrick County Public Schools. Although students within the sponsoring districts attend for free, during the Carroll County period, fewer than 2% of its students were district residents. The rest lived elsewhere in the state. Indeed, this was one of the reasons that Carroll County withdrew its support (Chandler, 2013; Klein, 2013).

Although schools like the Massachusetts and Virginia academies are district-private partnerships, from the point of view of enrollment, they are statewide schools. From the perspective of parents and students, they are indistinguishable from cybercharters. Although the legal forms differ, both are government-established, publicly funded virtual schools, access to which does not depend, or depends only at the margins, on one's district of residence.

Other states have chosen to cut out the middleman. Florida is a case in point. Florida allows its school districts to establish their own virtual education programs. It also authorizes the creation of virtual charter schools. But at the same time, the state directly created the Florida Virtual School as a free-standing, nongeographically based school district. This entity is not a school district but a state-level government agency. Its Board of Trustees is appointed by the governor, not by the electorate of any jurisdiction. School districts, notably, are forbidden by law from "limit[ing] student access to courses offered through the Florida Virtual School," although they can contract with the school to provide local services (Fla. Stat. Ann. §§ 1002.37, 1002.45, 2015).

Perhaps the most critical aspect of the Florida Virtual School is its funding, which is based nearly entirely upon the number of enrolled students and the number of courses for which they enroll, and, potentially under the law, from general appropriations and philanthropy. This framework—an entirely nonlocal, nonproperty-tax based mechanism for student funding—was for many years, and continues to be, the impossible dream of state school finance reformers working in the context of bricks and mortar. Yet it not only appears, but does so in Florida, hardly a dark-blue, liberal state. Once the school is virtual, local funding simply does not make sense.

The Florida Virtual School shows no trace of the localism which, even 10 years ago, most scholars and reformers considered the foundation, the linchpin, of the institutional structure of American educational inequality. The virtual academies and other cybercharters, even those whose charter is granted by a school district, show little. Inequality, many scholars argued, was a permanent part of the landscape. But in the new and growing virtual sector, one sees almost no localism at all. Only the locally managed cyber-schools plausibly can be described as local institutions. This is a direct consequence of the aterritorial nature of the technology.

It is not that virtual schools are *non*local, but that they compete with local schools and localist districts. At the economic level, they compete for customers: will a child, and his associated entitlement to state funding, enroll in his or her local district, or in the charter? And at the conceptual level, they offer a competing model. Their aterritoriality is an alternative to the district's localism.

Given the central roles of bundling, community, and localism in sustaining and entrenching the standard public/private binary, their undermining by virtual schooling is a clear threat to that binary.

Impacts upon home schooling

The impact of virtual education upon home schooling is potentially very great. There are three categories of effects. First, homeschool families can use virtual education to meet their educational needs and desires. Second, virtuality facilitates unbundling, which has long been a principle and an activity important to home schoolers. Finally, and perhaps most important in the long run, virtuality, like charters, undermines the public/private binary that excludes homeschoolers from things like public subsidy and access to public facilities. A more polyphonic categorization of schools will confer upon homeschooling, with other nontraditional varieties of educational provision, greater fiscal and political resources and greater legitimacy.

The first category is straightforward. For some homeschoolers, virtual education will not respond to the motives for homeschooling. For example, parents concerned about the content of curriculum, those interested in unschooling, and those who object for principled reasons to governmental involvement in instruction will find virtual classes prepared or sanctioned by government unsatisfactory. But for many others, virtual education can be a means or even a substitute for classical homeschooling. If the goal is to keep children at home, to allow them to pace themselves, or to design curricula that meet their particular interests, virtual schooling fits the bill. It is a very attractive way to provide materials and expertise to students who remain at home. And online resources, of course, have already penetrated the homeschooling sector very dramatically.

Second, the acceleration of virtual schooling ought to make it easier for homeschooling families to navigate their contact with the public education system to their own advantage and the advantage of their children. Consider the cases, like those described in Mawdsley (1999, pp. 317–319), of students not enrolled in the full public school program by virtue of their attendance at homeschools (or private schools) who seek to avail themselves of particular portions of the public school program in which they are interested. Thus, a homeschooled child wants to join the public school band, or the varsity football squad. Or a student wishes to enroll in advanced chemistry, because the public school has the necessary labs and teachers, while taking her other coursework at home. When schools object, plaintiffs' arguments are straightforward. They have the legal right to enjoy the entirety of a public school program, and also the right to seek private alternatives to public school; surely they, therefore, are entitled to *part* of the public school curriculum. School and school districts object that selective disenrollment undermines schools' efforts to create coherent instructional programs and learning communities that have pedagogic, civic, and disciplinary coherence—not to mention school rules that can be fairly and easily administered.

In a variation on these cases, parents have also sought the right to withdraw their children piecemeal from the public school program in order to shield them from materials that they viewed as objectionable (Hirschoff, 1977, pp. 873–874 & nn. 3–7). These requests are generally motivated by religious objections to sex education, and to teaching about evolution and homosexuality, although other topics also arise (*Leebaert v. Harrington*, 2003;

Parker v. Hurley, 2008). These cases are conceptually of a piece with requests for selective enrollment public schools courses and activities; all that differs is the magnitude of the partial public school program parents seek for their children. The selective enrollment cases, like the selective withdrawal cases, also often but not always involve religious motivation, given the large proportion of private and home schooling that is religious in nature.

When these cases are litigated, courts have been unfriendly to selective enrollment, taking the view that that public school is an all-or-nothing proposition. They have been somewhat more friendly to selective withdrawal, although the more overtly religious cast of exemption requests has tempered judicial enthusiasm (Yudof, Levin, Moran, Ryan, & Bowman, 2012, p. 184 n. 4). Courts, in other words, generally though not universally enforce the prohibition on unbundling. Legislatures and education officials, however, have been less negative. In 23 states, homeschoolers by state statute or league rules have access to extracurricular sports, while the same number of states denies them access (Batista & Hatfield, 2005, pp. 224–252). Some of these statutes allow curricular access as well (Fuller, 1998, p. 1615 n. 73). Local regulation is similarly diverse.

The most important long-run effect of virtuality, however, is to defeat the public/private binary and make room in the public discourse and in its institutions for homeschooling generally. What, after all, is the formal difference between a cyber-charter school student and a homeschooled student who uses online courses? Both students are learning at home (or somewhere other than a school). The difference is only that in the cyber-charter case, it is the charter that has aggregated the online courses and produced a program of study, while in the latter case, the parent aggregates the educational resources. But the parent, of course, chooses the charter provider; and homeschoolers have long used off-the-shelf products as components of their instructional program. Suddenly, therefore, a homeschooled child looks quite similar to a "public," charter-school child.

In what sense, then, is an online public school different from a loose aggregation of homeschoolers? Online school districts are often managed by private providers. Both are regulated, though not to the same degree. As online education becomes a second wedge (after charter schools) that creates a strong incentive to define privately provided educational experiences as "public," the distinction between public, private, and home blurs further.

Virtuality also undermines the idea that only "public" schools can provide the kind of community necessary to democratic education. The question of community and socialization has also been central to many critiques of homeschooling. Homeschoolers have long rejoined that educating children at home is entirely consistent with both socialization and the training of democratic citizens (Medlin, 2000, 2013). This response is considerably strengthened by the governmental embrace of full-time virtual schooling, whose students also lack the kind of social community that accompanies traditional, bricks-and-mortar schools. Virtuality signals an acceptance that the classic, in-person full-time model of community associated with the traditional public school is not the only possible model of a democratic learning community. It will be harder to reject homeschools as a legitimate, alternative models.

There remains the difference that the government pays for cybercharter schools, but not for home schools. But state financial support is a consequence, not a cause, of whether a school is "public" or "private." The blurring is important because it offers a different answer to whether government *should* pay.

Finally, the modularity of online courses might help to deal with the problem of state support for religious education, which is an oversized presence in the American private and home sectors. The off-the-shelf nature of publicly-offered online courses substantially reduces the First Amendment entanglement concern that has been associated with public subsidy for the secular portions of a religiously inflected curriculum since at least the 1970s (*Lemon v. Kurtzman*, 1971). Virtuality neatly squares the circle that long blocked state support for the secular component of education: it requires neither cash grants, which are fungible in a religious school's budget, nor the sending of state personnel into religious institutions, which many courts held can signal government endorsement of religion. From an entanglement perspectives, virtual courses are more like secular books, filmstrips, or globes. It is now routine in some states for cyber-charter schools to recruit religious home educators and thus to provide, using government support, secular components of the total education designed by parents. Because entanglement has been a major motivator for the strength of the public/private divide, its mitigation is likely to reduce its vigor.

In short, the introduction of virtual education at a replicable scale is very likely to make the distinction between public and private schools—a divide long so obvious to Americans that the terms required no definition—increasingly anachronistic. Homeschools will then have a strong case for the claim that they should be regulated on their merits, and, in particular, that their use of state-sanctioned virtual tools should be regulated and supported no differently than that of any other school.

Notes

1. This discussion, along with other charter school materials in this article, relies heavily on the discussion and citations in Saiger (2013).

2. Ariz. Rev. Stat. Ann. § 15-808 (2014 & Supp. 2015); Fla. Stat. Ann. §§ 1002.37, 1002.45 (West 2012 & Supp. 2015); Ga. Code Ann. § 20-2-319.1 (2012 & Supp. 2015); Idaho Code Ann. § 33-5504A (2008 & Supp. 2015); Iowa Code Ann. § 256.42 (West 2012 & Supp. 2015); Me. Rev. Stat. Ann. tit. 20-A, § 19152 (Supp. 2015); Mass. Gen. Laws Ann. Ch. 71, § 94 (LexisNexis 2013); Miss. Code. Ann. § 37-161-3 (West 2009 & Supp. 2015); Mo. Ann. Stat. § 161.670 (West 2010); Mont. Code Ann. § 20-7-1201 (West 2009 & Supp. 2015); N.M. Stat. Ann. § 22-30-3 (West 2011); S.C. Code Ann. § 59-16-15 (2004 & Supp. 2015); S.D. Codified Laws § 13-33-24 (Supp. 2015); Tex. Educ. Code Ann. § 30A (West 2012 &Supp. 2015); Utah Code Ann. § 53A-15-1002.5 (LexisNexis 2013 & Supp. 2015); Va. Code Ann. § 22.1-212.24 (2011 & Supp. 2015); W. Va. Code Ann. § 18-2E-9 (LexisNexis 2012).

3. Online schools run by education management organizations (EMOs) saw the same rate of growth during the time period. For-profit and nonprofit EMO-operated schools enrolled 11,500 students during the 2003–2004 school year and almost 115,000 students in 2010–2011 (Miron, Urschel, Aguilar, Mayra, & Dailey, 2012, p. 18).

References

Act Establishing Commonwealth Virtual Schools, ch. 379, 2012 Mass. Acts 1594.

Aikens, A. (2005). Being choosy: An analysis of public school choice under No Child Left Behind. *West Virginia Law Review, 108,* 233.

Anderson, M. W. (2012). Democratic dissolution: Radical experimentation in state takeovers of local governments. *Fordham Urban Law Review, 39,* 577.

Balkin, J. M., & Noveck, S. B. (2006). Introduction. In J. M. Balkin & S. B. Noveck (Eds.), *The state of play: Law, games, and virtual worlds.* New York, NY: New York University Press.

Barbour, M., Brown, R., Waters, L. H., Hoey, R., Hunt, J. L., Kennedy, K., ... Trimm, T. (2011). *Online and blended learning: A survey of policy and practice of K–12 schools around the world.* International Association for K–12 Online Learning. Retrieved from http://files. eric.ed.gov/fulltext/ED537334.pdf

Batista, P. J., & Hatfield, L. C. (2005). Learn at home, play at school: A state-by-state examination of legislation, litigation and athletic association rules governing public school athletic participation by homeschool students. *Journal of Legal Aspects Sport, 15,* 213.

Brown v. Board of Educ. of Topeka, 347 U.S. 483 (1954).

Chandler, M. A. (2013, May 1). Virginia's first, largest statewide virtual school is likely to close. *Washington Post.*

Clark, T. (2001). *Virtual schools: Trends and issues.* Distance Learning Resource Network. Retrieved from https://www.wested.org/online_pubs/virtualschools.pdf

Clark, T. (2008). Virtual schooling and basic education. In W. J. Bramble & S. Panda (Eds.), *Economics of distance and online learning: Theory, practice and research* (pp. 52–71). New York, NY: Routledge.

Clements, M., Stafford, E., Pazzaglia, A. M., & Jacobs, P. (2015). *Online course use in Iowa and Wisconsin public high schools: The results of two statewide surveys.* Washington, DC: National Center for Education Evaluation and Regional Assistance.

Cronin, J. M. (1973). *The control of urban schools: Perspective on the power of educational reformers.* New York, NY: Free Press.

Dede, C., & Richards, J. (Eds.) (2012). *Digital teaching platforms.* New York, NY: Teachers College Press.

Fairfax County Public Schools. (n.d.). *Online campus frequently asked questions.* Retrieved from http://www.fcps.edu/is/onlinecampus/faq.shtml#Anchor-Wha-42320.

Fla. Stat. Ann. §§ 1002.37, 1002.45 (West 2012 & Supp. 2015).

Fuller, D. W. (1998). Public school access: The constitutional right of home-schoolers to "opt in" to public schools. *Minnesota Law Review, 82,* 1599.

Garnett, N. S. (2016, forthcoming). Sector agnosticism and the coming transformation of education law. *Vanderbilt Law Review,* forthcoming.

Glenn, C. L., & DeGroof, J. (2005). *Balancing freedom, autonomy and accountability in education* (Vol. 1). Nijmegen, The Netherlands: Wolf Legal Publishers.

Godwin, R. K., & Kemerer, F. R. (2010). *School choice tradeoffs: Liberty, equity, and diversity.* Austin, TX: University of Texas Press.

Green, P. C., Baker, B. D., & Oluwole, J. (2015). The legal status of charter schools in state statutory law. *University of Massachusetts Law Review, 10,* 240.

Green, S. (2010). *The second disestablishment: Church and state in nineteenth-century America.* New York, NY: Oxford University Press.

Gutmann, A. (1987). *Democratic education.* Princeton, NJ: Princeton University Press.

Hall, S. H. (2011, October 16). Enrollment in cyberschools soars in NEPA. *The Times-Tribune.*

Hess, F. M. (2010). *The same thing over and over: How school reformers get stuck in yesterday's ideas.* Cambridge, MA: Harvard University Press.

Hill, P. T. (2001). What is public about public education? In T. M. Moe (Ed.), *A primer on America's schools* (pp. 285–316). United States of America: Hoover Institution Press.

Hirschman, A. O. (1970). *Exit, voice, and loyalty: Responses to decline in firms, organizations, and states.* Cambridge, MA: Harvard University Press.

Hirschoff, M. M. U. (1977). Parents and the public school curriculum: Is there a right to have one's child excused from objectionable instruction. *Southern California Law Review, 50,* 871.

Jones, S. L. (2008). *Religious schooling in America: Private education and public life.* Westport, CT: Praeger Publishers.

Kaestle, C. (1983). *Pillars of the republic: Common schools and American society, 1780–1860.* New York, NY: Macmillan.

Kena, G., Musu-Gillette, L., Robinson, J., Wang, X., Rathbun, A., Zhang, J., ... Velez, E. D. (2015). *The condition of education 2015* (Report No. NCES 2015–144). Retrieved from http://nces.ed.gov/pubs2015/2015144.pdf

Khan, S. (2012). *The one world schoolhouse: Education reimagined.* London, UK: Hachette Book Group.

Klein, R. (2013, May 2, 6:42 p.m. EDT). Virginia's first statewide virtual school may be closing. *Huffington Post.*

Lastowka, G. (2010). *Virtual justice: The new laws of online worlds.* New Haven, CT: Yale University Press.

Layton, L., & Brown, E. (2011, November 26). Virtual schools are multiplying, but some question their educational value. *Washington Post.*

Leebaert v. Harrington, 332 F.3d 134 (CA2) (2003).

Lemon v. Kurtzman, 403 U.S. 602 (1971).

Lubienski, C., & Weitzel, P. (2009). Choice, integration, and educational opportunity: Evidence on competitive incentives for student sorting in charter schools. *Journal of Gender Race & Justice, 12,* 351.

Mass. Gen. Laws Ann. Ch. 71, § 94 (LexisNexis 2013).

Massachusetts Virtual Academy at Greenfield. (2015). *Massachusetts Virtual Academy Frequently Asked Questions.* Retrieved from http://mava.k12.com/faqs/enrollment-attendance-faqs

Mawdsley, R. D. (1999). Parental rights and home schooling: Current home school litigation. *West Education Reporter, 135*, 313.

McMullen, J. G. (2002). Behind closed doors: Should states regulate homeschooling? *South Carolina Law Review, 54*, 75.

Mead, J. F. (2003). Devilish details: Exploring features of charter school statutes that blur the public/private distinction. *Harvard Journal on Legislation, 40*, 349.

Medlin, R. G. (2000). Home schooling and the question of socialization. *Peabody Journal of Education, 75*(1–2), 107–123. doi:10.1080/0161956X.2000.9681937

Medlin, R. G. (2013). Homeschooling and the question of socialization revisited. *Peabody Journal of Education, 88*(3), 284–297. doi:10.1080/0161956X.2013.796825

Milliken v. Bradley, 418 U.S. 717 (1974).

Miron, G., & Urschel, J. L. (2012). *Understanding and improving full-time virtual schools.* Boulder, CO: National Education Policy Center.

Miron, G., Urschel, J. L., Aguilar, Y., Mayra, A., & Dailey, B. (2012). *Profiles of for-profit and nonprofit education management organizations: Thirteenth annual report, 2010–2011.* Boulder, CO: National Education Policy Center.

Molnar, A., Huerta, L., Barbour, M. K., Miron, G., Shafer, S. R., & Gulosino, C. (2015). *Virtual schools in the U.S. 2015: Politics, performance, policy, and research evidence.* Boulder, CO: National Education Policy Center.

Murphy, R., Snow, E., Mislevy, J., Gallagher, L., Krumm, A., & Wei, X. (2014a). *Blended learning report.* Michael & Susan Dell Foundation.

Murphy, R., Gallagher, L., Krumm, A ., Mislevy, J., & Hafter, A. (2014b). *Research on the use of Khan Academy in schools.* Menlo Park, CA: SRI Education.

Parker v. Hurley, 514 F.3d 87 (CA1) (2008).

Pelikan, J. (2005). The public schools as an institution of American constitutional democracy. In S. Fuhrman & M. Lazerson (Eds.), *The public schools.* New York, NY: Oxford University Press.

Picciano, A. G., & Seaman, J. (2009). *K-12 online learning: A 2008 follow-up of the survey of US school district administrators.* Newburyport, MA: Sloan Consortium.

Pierce v. Society of the Sisters of the Holy Names of Jesus and Mary. 268 U.S. 510 (1925).

Project Tomorrow. (2015). *Digital learning 24/7: Understanding technology—Enhanced learning in the lives of today's students.* Retrieved from http://www.tomorrow.org/speakup/pdfs/SU14StudentReport.pdf

Queen, B., Lewis, L., & Coopersmith, J. (2011). *Distance education courses for public elementary and secondary school students: 2009–10: First look.* Washington, DC: National Center for Education Statistics 2012-008.

Reese, W. J. (2007). *History, education, and the schools.* New York, NY: Palgrave Macmillan.

Rendell-Baker v. Kohn. 457 U.S. 830 (1982).

Reuben, J. A. (2005). Patriotic purposes: Public schools and the education of citizens. In S. Fuhrman & M. Lazerson (Eds.), *The public schools* (pp. 1–23). New York, NY: Oxford University Press.

Saiger, A. (1999). Disestablishing local school districts as a remedy for educational inadequacy. *Columbia Law Review, 99*, 1830. doi:10.2307/1123625

Saiger, A. J. (2013). Charter schools, the establishment clause, and the neoliberal turn in public education. *Cardozo Law Review, 34*, 1163.

Selwyn, N. (2011). *Schools and schooling in the digital age: A critical analysis.* Oxon, UK: Routledge.

Sengupta, S. (2011, December 5). Online learning, personalized. *The New York Times*, B1.

Setzer, J. C., Lewis, L., & Greene, B. (2005). *Distance education courses for public elementary and secondary school students: 2002–03*. Washington, DC: National Center for Education Statistics.

Sikora, A. C., & Carroll, C. D. (2002). *A profile of participation in distance education*. Washington, DC: National Center for Education Statistics.

Singer, N. (2014, November 17). Clicks, not gold stars. *The New York Times*, B1.

Staker, H., & Horn, M. B. (2012). *Classifying K–12 blended learning*. Innosight Institute. Retrieved from http://www.christenseninstitute.org/wp-content/uploads/2013/04/Classifying-K-12-blended-learning.pdf

Sugarman, S. D. (1991). Using private schools to promote public values. *University of Chicago Legal Forum, 1991*, 171–210.

Sugarman, S. D., & Kuboyama, E. M. (2001). Approving charter schools: The gate-keeper function. *Administrative Law Review, 53*, 869–942.

Tyack, D. B. (1974). *The one best system: A history of American urban education*. Cambridge, MA: Harvard University Press.

U.S. Department of Education, National Center for Education Statistics. (2015). *The condition of education 2015* (Report No. NCES 2015–144; supporting tables). Retrieved from https://nces.ed.gov/programs/digest/d14/tables/dt14_216.20.asp.

Va. Code Ann. § 22.1–212.24 (2011 & Supp. 2015).

Vergari, S. (2003). Charter schools: A significant precedent in public education. *NYU Annual Survey of American Law, 59*, 495.

Waddell, T. B. (2010). Bringing it all back home: Establishing a coherent constitutional framework for the re-regulation of homeschooling. *Vanderbilt Law Review, 63*, 541.

Waters, L. H., Barbour, M. K., & Menchaca, M. P. (2014). The nature of online charter schools: Evolution and emerging concerns. *Educational Technology & Society, 17*, 379.

Watson, J., Pape, L., Murin, A., Gemin, B., & Vashaw, L. (2014). *Keeping pace with K–12 digital learning: An annual review of policy and practice*. Mountain View, CA: Evergreen Education Group.

Wong, K. K. (2007). *The education mayor: Improving America's schools*. Washington, DC: Georgetown University Press.

Yudof, M., Levin, B., Moran, R. F., Ryan, J. E., & Bowman, K. L. (2012). *Educational policy and the law* (5th ed.). Belmont, CA: Wadsworth/Cengage.

Yuracko, K. A. (2008). Education off the grid: Constitutional constraints on homeschooling. *California Law Review, 96*, 123–184.

Zandberg, I., Lewis, L., & Greene, B. (2008). *Technology-based distance education courses for public elementary and secondary schools: 2002–03 and 2004–05*. Washington, DC: National Center for Education Statistics.

Zelman v. Simmons-Harris. 536 U.S. 639 (2002).

Types of Homeschool Environments and Need Support for Children's Achievement Motivation

Debra A. Bell, Avi Kaplan, and S. Kenneth Thurman

ABSTRACT

Working within a self-determination theory (SDT) framework, this study used cluster analysis to examine the naturally occurring types of homeschool-learning environments parents (N = 457) have created. Measures of support for student autonomy, mastery goal structure, and use of conditional regard were adapted for a homeschool context and used as constituting variables. Follow-up measures of parental need satisfaction, efficacy, student academic engagement, teaching practices, and demographics were used to identify significant differences among homeschooling motivational profiles. A five-cluster solution best fit the data: a *high need support* profile, *low need support* profile and three profiles of *mixed need support*. In general, the *high need* and *mixed need* support profiles were associated with higher student engagement, need satisfaction, efficacy for homeschooling, and frequent use of teaching strategies that promote autonomous motivation and support for student competence. The *low need support* profile was significantly associated with lower need satisfaction and teaching strategies associated with control. Higher levels of academic engagement were reported for those students homeschooled longer and at higher grade levels. Male teaching parents (N = 29) reported significantly less need satisfaction and were significantly more represented in the *low need support* profile. These findings point to the utility of self-determination theory for characterizing the motivational environments of homeschools.

Along many dimensions, homeschooling is increasing, diversifying, and spreading globally (Gaither, 2009; Home School Legal Defense Association, 2001). Few government regulations restrict the range of practices homeschooling parents may adopt. Arguably the largest natural experiment in the history of American education, this freedom allows for unimpeded innovation and experimentation not feasible in traditional settings. The question remains open as to how homeschooling parents configure appropriate learning environments for their children, given the meaningful differences among homeschools. Identifying these may provide a clearer picture of the characteristics of homeschool environments that support or hinder student learning and achievement. To date, no empirical study has sought to identify such differences, nor to examine the approaches to instruction that distinguish them. Our aim is to examine distinctions among homeschooling environments along axes of support for student autonomy, competence, and relatedness—the three inherent needs self-determination theory posits for the optimal development of achievement motivation.

Homeschools as learning environments

Many scholars have noted the opportunity for optimal learning a homeschool (in contrast to a conventional school) may provide (Knowles, 1991; Ray, 2002; Van Galen, 1988). Yet, few studies have investigated the opportunities, contingences, and constraints parents may face in reality. In a review of his research, Ray (2005) reported on practices of homeschooling parents that included "flexible and highly individualized [programs], involving both homemade and purchased curriculum materials" (pp. 16–17). However, Ray also reported other practices that might contradict the autonomy and individualized opportunity for students learning, such as limiting television and outside influences, required church attendance, and punishment and reward systems (Cai, Reeve, & Robinson, 2002; Kunzman, 2009). These reports were corroborated by one of the few empirical studies to examine homeschools as learning environments, which found that religiously motivated home educators ($n = 71$) endorsed a more controlling motivational style than did public school educators ($n = 76$) (Cai et al., 2002).

Several factors may explain differences in the motivational climate of homeschooling environments. Research has found that family demographics, including higher levels of income, parental education, parental occupations, and smaller family size are positively correlated with students' academic achievement. Research has also suggested that factors such as single-parent status, large family size, limited resources, or psychological stress may reduce the time and energy parents have to provide the opportunities that promote achievement motivation (e.g., Marjoribanks, 2002; Schneider & Coleman, 1993).

Researchers have also considered how parenting style may influence children's achievement motivation. Research has pointed to the positive relations of child's motivation with parents' consistent emotional warmth, involvement, and regard (e.g., Assor, Roth, & Deci, 2004; Grolnick, Kurowski, & Gurland, 1999; Gutman, Sameroff, & Eccles, 2002); involvement in academic work (Eccles, 1993; Fan & Chen, 2001); developmentally-appropriate structure and challenge (Grolnick et al., 1999; Grolnick & Ryan, 1989); valuing and modeling achievement (Eccles, 1993); and an autonomy-supportive motivational style in which choice, problem solving, and shared decision making is encouraged (Grolnick & Ryan, 1989).

Adoption of different teaching practices and beliefs may also be associated with differences in homeschooled students' achievement motivation. Research on teachers suggests that expectations for the individual student is paramount (Brophy, 1985; Eccles-Parsons et al., 1983; Weinstein, 1989), and that teacher's efficacy for promoting student learning (e.g., Midgley, Feldlaufer, & Eccles, 1989); and the teacher's provision of socioemotional support (Eccles & Midgley, 1989; Patrick, Ryan, & Kaplan, 2007) are also highly important. Teaching practices that promote student autonomy (Deci & Ryan, 1985; Grolnick & Ryan, 1987) in combination with appropriate structure (Grolnick, Gurland, Jacob, & Decourcey, 2002; Skinner & Belmont, 1993) and challenge (Brophy, 1999; Pintrich & Schunk, 2002) also correlate with students' achievement motivation and academic engagement. Conversely, teachers who emphasize peer competition and comparisons on ability and success undermine intrinsic motivation, especially in children who do not believe they possess the competence necessary for success (Kaplan & Maehr, 2007).

Homeschooling provides a unique opportunity for the development of achievement motivation—not only might students develop adaptive strategies, but parents are ostensibly unconstrained in their freedom to design adaptive learning environments for their children. At the same time, such factors as larger family size, limited financial resources, or overarching parenting beliefs and behavior may undermine this support.

Self-determination theory

One approach to conceptualize and better understand homeschool learning environments is with theories that characterize motivating learning environments. One motivational perspective that has demonstrated its utility across diverse contexts is self-determination theory (SDT; Deci & Ryan, 2000). SDT is a comprehensive perspective on human motivation and development that contends that all humans are motivated by three fundamental psychological needs—autonomy, competence, and relatedness. Autonomy refers to the need to perceive oneself as the locus of one's own behavior (Ryan & Deci, 2002) and to endorse actions that are valued by significant others. Competence refers to the need to feel capable in one's interactions with the social environment, increase these abilities, and have the opportunity to express one's capacities. Relatedness refers to the need to feel socially connected, accepted, and valued by others; to experience a sense of belongingness to other individuals and to one's community (Ryan & Deci, 2002). The satisfaction of these needs provides for the development of autonomous motivation—the optimal form of motivation that is associated with growth and social and psychological well-being (Deci & Ryan, 2000).

Parents and teachers can facilitate the development and maintenance of autonomous motivation in children by adopting an autonomy-supportive motivating style and instructional practices that manifest through the quality of their feedback, the design of activities that build on children's interests and preferences, provision of opportunities for optimal challenge, meaningful choice and opportunities for self-direction, and acknowledgement of negative feelings (Reeve, 2009; Ryan & Deci, 2000). In contrast, parents and teachers undermine autonomous motivation and psychological well-being when they adopt a controlling motivating style and practices that rely heavily on external regulation and evaluative pressure (Niemiec & Ryan, 2009). As such, SDT provides a theoretical framework to investigate meaningful sociocontextual differences among types of homeschool environments.

The current study

We applied self-determination theory to conceptualize and characterize the motivational profiles of homeschools, and to investigate the relations of these motivational profiles with parent- and student-desired motivational processes seeking to answer these questions:

(1) What profiles of homeschool environments do parents create along the dimensions of support for autonomy, competence, and relatedness?
(2) What teaching strategies characterize different motivational profiles of homeschool environments?
(3) What family, parent, and student characteristics are associated with different motivational profiles of homeschool environments?

Methods

Participants

Participants for the study were homeschooling parents recruited from a nonsectarian homeschool organization which offers online classes, several affinity groups associated with a particular homeschool demographic of interest (e.g., African-American, unschoolers, gifted and talented, urban regions), and readers of a popular blog related to homeschooling. A $5 Amazon gift card was offered to participants. Two hundred and fifteen (51% response rate) responded from the nonsectarian group. One hundred and fifty-three responded from the affinity groups. Estimates suggest that the respondents included between 25%–30% of the members. The blog owner estimated 5,000 U.S.-based homeschoolers subscribed to her blog. Two-hundred and ninety-six participants came from the blog readers. Together, 664 parents responded to the survey. Respondents were excluded from the analysis if they did not complete at least the first demographic measure, did not meet the operationalized definition of homeschooling, or entered non-sensical answers deemed as suspicious. The final sample included 457 participants.

Participant characteristics

Participants were characteristically married (N = 430; 94%), female (n = 407; 89%), White (n = 394; 86%) and between 35–54 years of age (n = 346, 76%). This sample was significantly better educated and wealthier than national means and previously reported homeschool samples (Planty et al., 2007; Princiotta & Bielick, 2006).

In contrast with a reportedly high quit rate among homeschoolers (Isenberg, 2007), this sample represented the highly committed: 74% of the participants (n = 341) stated they were "certain to homeschool next year." In addition, the sample represented a very experienced group of parent-teachers. Sixty-six percent (n = 309) reported having homeschooled 5 years or more.

A contentious issue between some American homeschoolers and authorities has been appropriate levels of oversight. The degree of monitoring was measured as a continuous variable on a 5-point Likert-response scale (5 = *closely monitored*, 3 = *some monitoring*, 1 = *no monitoring*). Generally speaking, the sample reported some to little monitoring of their program by authorities; 36% (n = 164) of the respondents selected "no monitoring" which positively skewed the distribution (M = 2.25; SD = 1.2).

Measures

Measures assessed demographic characteristics; parental support for student autonomy, competence, and relatedness; efficacy for homeschooling; parents' own basic need satisfaction; teaching practices; underlying motivations for homeschooling; and parental perception of the target student's academic engagement. Most measures came from prior research but were not previously established as reliable and valid for homeschool populations; thus all were adapted for a homeschool context. The teaching practices survey, motivations for homeschooling, and academic engagement measures were specifically designed for this study. To establish a unit of analysis, parents were asked to consider the child they had homeschooled the longest when answering the pedagogical questions. Those children equally divided by gender (213 girls, 48%; 238 boys, 52%), primarily from 11th–12th grade (167, 36%), and otherwise distributed relatively equally across grade levels (range 57–89, 12%–19%) except for Pre-K (10, 2%).

Motivation for homeschooling

Parents were asked to provide a short response to the questions, "Please list your initial reasons for deciding to homeschool. Was there a particular event or experience that contributed to your decision to homeschool?"

Three measures assessed the constructs used to typify the homeschooling environments:

Support for autonomy

Support for autonomy was assessed with *The Problems in School Questionnaire* (PIS), developed by Deci, Schwartz, Sheinman, and Ryan (1981). The measure poses eight vignettes which focus on a student's school-related problem followed by four strategies a teacher or parent might adopt to address this situation. This creates a 32-item measure consisting of four subscales which represent points along a continuum from a highly controlling motivational style to a highly autonomy supporting motivational style. Respondents must indicate on a 7-point Likert-like scale how appropriate (1 = *very inappropriate*, 4 = *moderately appropriate*, 7 = *very appropriate*) they believe each response would be in the situation. Cai and colleagues (2002) found all eight vignettes (unaltered) produced consistent scores with a religiously motivated homeschool sample ($N = 71$).

Our initial pilot of the PIS with 50 homeschool parents did not reach desirable levels of internal consistency. The measure was revised, and a new pilot with 49 homeschool parents suggested acceptable levels or reliability measured with Cronbach's alpha (High Autonomy = .72, Slight Control = .74, Moderate Control = .72, High Control = .79).

Support for competence

Support for competence was assessed with a 10-item scale from The Patterns of Adaptive Learning Survey (PALS) (Midgley et al., 2000) that assesses a teacher's mastery goal structure. Mastery goal structure refers to messages, emphases, and supports in the environment about the value of development of competence (Kaplan, Middleton, Urdan, & Midgley, 2002). These messages include emphasizing that mistakes are part of learning, that deep understanding is more important than memorization, and that effort is a virtue. Hence, a mastery goal structure constitutes support for students' need for competence. Minor adjustments were made to adapt the scale to a homeschool setting (e.g., *in this school the importance of trying hard is stressed* was changed to *in this homeschool the importance of trying hard is stressed with this child*). Respondents report the extent of their agreement with statements on a 5-point Likert scale (1 = *strongly disagree*, 3 = *somewhat agree*, 5 = *strongly agree*). The reliability of the scale in the pilot study was acceptable ($a = .72$).

Support for relatedness

Support for relatedness was assessed by the parent survey of the Positive and Negative Conditional Regard Scale (Assor, Roth, & Deci, 2004). Conditional regard constitutes a central psychological mechanism that undermines the need for relatedness, as it signifies the conditional nature of the relationship and of the acceptance of the child (Ryan, 1995). The researchers identified parental use of conditional negative regard (PCNR; i.e., emotional with-drawal and rejection as punishment for behaviors the parent dislikes) and conditional positive regard (PCPR; i.e., emotional warmth, praise, and accep-tance as a reward only for behaviors the parent desires) as two distinct constructs which *both* frustrate the child's need for relatedness (Assor, Roth, & Deci, 2004). The scale produces two scores; one for PCNR and one for PCPR, with scores falling between 1 and 5, respectively. Acceptable Cronbach's alphas were established with the first pilot study group (PCPR $a = .82$; PCNR $a = .76$). In the study, PCNR and PCPR were highly correlated ($r = .67$) and a confirmatory factor analysis indicated that all items loaded on a single factor. In order to avoid issues concern with multicollinearity, we used a composite score for Parental Conditional Regard.

Four measures were used to assess desirable and undesirable outcomes of different homeschooling environments:

Academic engagement

As a proxy for student outcomes, we designed an academic engagement scale based upon Reeve's (2002) list of observable clues for autonomous motiva-tion among children. The 8-item scale measured the parent's perception of the quality of the child's engagement along the dimensions of interest, effort, preference for challenge, initiative, enjoyment, persistence, expression of negative emotions, and independence (i.e., How interested is this student in his or her school studies? 1 = *never interested*, 3 = *sometimes interested*, 5 = *always interested*). Higher scores represent a higher degree of perceived academic engagement. This scale had a Cronbach's alpha of .88 in the first pilot study group.

Efficacy for homeschooling

A 4-item scale designed by Deci and Ryan to tap the motivators' (e.g., parents, coaches, teachers, managers) own sense of competence in a specific domain was adapted to fit the domain of homeschooling for this study (i.e., I feel confident in my ability to homeschool my children, 1 = *not at all true*, 4 = *somewhat true*, 7 = *very true*). Scores are summed and averaged, with higher scores indicating higher efficacy for homeschooling. The results of the pilot study yielded a Cronbach's alpha of .88 for this scale.

Need satisfaction

As a measure of parent outcomes, we included a 21-item scale also designed by Deci and Ryan and adapted for the domain of homeschooling. The scale has three subscales (i.e., autonomy, competence, and relatedness). Higher scores on each of the subscales are associated with higher need satisfaction. The initial pilot study yielded an overall Cronbach's alpha of .85 with alphas for subscales: need for autonomy $a = .45$, need for relatedness $a = .87$, and need for competence $a = .75$. An additional item was added to the need for autonomy scale to improve overall reliability in the main study.

Teaching practices

For the question concerning the instructional strategies that parents use, we developed a 42-item scale that asked about frequency of use of particular teaching practices from the beginning of this school year (i.e., 1 = *never*, 2 = *once or twice*, 3 = *once or twice a month*, 4 = *weekly*, 5 = *several times a week*, 6 = *daily*, 7 = *several times a day*). Items were drawn from the self-determination theory literature on teaching practices associated with student need-support (e.g., Reeve, 2002; Reeve & Jang, 2006) and from a content analysis of homeschooling practices in the literature on homeschooling.

Procedure

Responses for the pilot and the main study were collected online in one wave over the course of several weeks using Survey Monkey Pro. Owners of the lists and blog provided their contacts with a short description of the study and the incentive of the Amazon gift card via e-mail or a post. They also endorsed the study and noted the lead author's long affiliation with the homeschool community. Unique links to the study were provided for each source. Follow up e-mails were sent twice to the e-mail lists. The blog post generated so many responses that the link was removed after three days.

Data analysis

In order to characterize the sample of parents, we conducted a directed qualitative content analysis on their responses to the open-ended question about their motivation for homeschooling using the categories that have emerged from the NCES's regular data collection on homeschooling in the United States.

To investigate the naturally occurring motivational profiles of homeschools, we conducted a cluster analysis on the data set using z-scores of the variables assessing support for autonomy, competence, and relatedness: PIS, Mastery Goal Structure, and Conditional Parental Regard. Cluster analysis is a method that seeks and groups cases that are similar to each other. We first used Ward's method with a squared Euclidean distance as a measure of similarity, which is a method designed to minimize variance within clusters and maximize variance between clusters (Ward, 1963). The analysis is exploratory in nature. It begins with all the cases, and begins grouping the two most similar cases iteratively, until it ends with one group that includes all participants in the sample. Selecting the useful number of clusters in the data follows parsimony, theoretical signifi- cance, and magnitude of change in an agglomerative coefficient that indicates how much information is lost when two cases are combined. This analysis points to a number of clusters and provides the mean of the clustering variables for each cluster. We used these means with a confirmatory K-means clustering method (Gore, 2000; Hair, Anderson, Tatham, & Black, 1998; Tan, Steinbach, & Kumar, 2006). Following the identification of the clusters, we conducted a multivariate analysis of variance (MANOVA) with post hoc univariate tests with the clusters as the independent variable to determine the goodness of fit and the degree of variance the model explained in the variables that constituted the clusters (i.e., support for autonomy, competence, and relatedness). We then performed separate analysis of variance (MANOVAs) on the three external variables which served as proxy for parent and student outcomes, and which are theore- tically linked to self-determination theory: parent's basic needs satisfaction, efficacy for homeschooling, and parents' report on student academic engagement.

To investigate the teaching strategies associated with the different motivational profiles of homeschools, we first submitted the 42-item teaching practices survey to an exploratory factor analysis (EFA). After listwise deletion, 356 cases were available for analysis. After examining the correlation matrix, we removed 10 items from further analysis because they had a small number of correlations above .3 with other items (Tabachnick & Fidell, 2007). An examination of the scree plot suggested a six-factor solution based on the eigenvalue greater than 1 criterion. However, factor 6 only contained two items and explained a small amount of the variance. An EFA forcing a five-factor solution suggested underlying latent factors related to parents' pedagogue intended to (a) monitor the student's progress, (b) promote autonomous motivation, (c) support the need for competence, and (d) exert external control. The fifth factor was labeled "Independent" and suggested the target student was self-monitoring and self-motivating. The remaining items were retained as singular variables. We calculated composite scores for these five variables and conducted multivariate and univariate analysis of variance with these variables and the remaining single-item variables as outcomes and clusters as independent variables (see Appendix).

We then compared the different homeschool profiles on categorical and continuous demographic variables. Chi-square tests were used to examine the categorical variables and ANOVAs were performed on the continuous ones. Finally, we collapsed the clusters to look at the continuous and categorical variables across the sample.

Results

Ten main themes emerged from a content analysis of the open-ended question designed to tap parents underlying motivation for homeschooling. Overall, "a desire to provide a child-centered education" emerged as the predominant motivation (n = 169, 35%). Only 21% identified "a desire to provide a religious or moral instruction" as a primary trigger (see Table 1).

The psychometric characteristics of the variables are reported in Table 2. Most variables demonstrated satisfactory psychometric properties. However, high autonomy orientation, efficacy for homeschooling, and need for autonomy were significantly negatively skewed, indicating that this sample of homeschool parents endorsed a highly autonomous motivational profile on the PIS, and also reported high levels of efficacy for homeschooling, and autonomous need satisfaction.[1]

Descriptive characteristics of the teaching practices variables suggest that this sample of homeschool parents used the following teaching practices most frequently: (a) resources other than textbooks, (b) student manages his or her own time, (c) talk with the student about what he or she is learning, (d) encourage questions about what the student is learning, (e) praise student for his or her progress, and (f) ask student to explain something he or she is learning. Conversely this sample of homeschool parents reported using the following teaching practices most infrequently: (a) classes at a local private or public school, (b) college classes locally, (c) rewards as an incentive for doing work, (d) loss of privileges as an incentive for doing work, (e) take a field trip related to academic work, and (f) give a test (see Appendix).

Correlations among variables

Zero-order correlations among the substantive variables are presented in Table 3. The variables used for the cluster analysis (PIS, mastery goal

Table 1. Motivation for homeschooling.

Category	n	Percentage of sample
Initial reasons		
Concerns about the school environment	128	28
To provide religious or moral instruction	95	21
Concerns about academic instruction at other schools	105	23
Child has physical/mental health issues	23	5
Child has special needs	21	5
Pragmatic reasons	53	12
To promote family closeness	82	18
Influence of other homeschoolers	52	11
Desired a child-centered approach	160	35
Other	19	4

Table 2. Descriptives for variables.

Variable	N	M (SD)	Skewness	Kurtosis	Alpha
Problems in school (PIS)	457	.564 (3.2)	−.102	.646	—
High autonomy	457	5.93 (.80)	−1.65	5.87	.82
Slight control	457	4.13 (.77)	.105	.242	.67
Moderate control	457	4.27 (.85)	.064	.155	.70
High control	457	3.51 (1.0)	.157	.118	.80
Mastery goal orientation	457	4.06 (.52)	−.435	−.102	.71
Conditional regard	457	2.06 (.87)	.801	.205	.88
Positive	456	2.04 (1.0)	.818	−.033	.84
Negative	456	2.08 (.91)	.807	.033	.80
Efficacy for homeschooling	457	6.11 (.92)	−1.10	.661	.89
Parental need satisfaction	429	5.90 (.68)	−.869	.738	.84
Autonomy	451	6.08 (.75)	−1.17	1.11	.66
Relatedness	449	5.81 (.95)	−.784	.134	.80
Competence	440	5.80 (.91)	−.833	.499	.71
Academic engagement	448	3.97 (.57)	−.359	−.149	.88

structure, and conditional regard) were significantly correlated in the expected direction. The PIS and mastery goal structure were positively and moderately correlated ($r = .37$, $p < .01$), and both were negatively correlated with conditional regard ($r = −.501, −.223$, $p < .01$), with effect sizes large and small to medium, respectively.[2] The PIS subscales also were correlated in the expected direction. The parent's perception of student academic engagement variable was significantly correlated with all variables in the expected direction as well.

The factors extracted from the teaching practices survey correlated in expected ways with all variables except for monitoring and external control, which presented a less clear picture. Both variables correlated positively and most strongly with high control orientation on the PIS, conditional regard, and each other; but also had medium, positive correlations with the support for autonomous motivation and competence-supporting teaching practices. Of all variables, the use of external control was most strongly and negatively correlated with student academic engagement ($r = −.53$, $p < .01$).

Cluster analysis

The final-cluster solution was based upon parsimony of the cluster solution, explanatory power (50% of the variance for each of the constituting variables; Milligan & Cooper, 1985) and interpretability. A five-cluster solution explained 56% of the variance for the PIS, 70% of the variance in conditional regard, and 64% of mastery. The five-cluster solution also produced a clear High Need Support cluster (i.e., support for student autonomy, competence, and relatedness), Low Need Support cluster and three Mixed Need Support clusters which were interpretable. Based upon this analysis, we retained the

Table 3. Correlation among variables.

	1	2	3	4	5	6	7	8	9	10	11	12	13	14	15
1. HghAut	—														
2. SlghtCntr	.148**	—													
3. ModCntrl	.069	.682**	—												
4. HghCntrl	-.157**	.527**	.640**	—											
5. PIS	.580**	-.435**	-.628**	-.872**	—										
6. Mstry	.365**	-.002.	-.024**	-.198**	.312**	—									
7. CndRgd	-.186**	.343**	.386**	.490**	-.501**	-.223**	—								
8. Effcy	.228**	-.002	.028	-.134**	.191**	.370**	-.241**	—							
9. Engmnt	.170**	-.068	-.048**	-.222**	.236**	.260**	-.310**	.403**	—						
10. NdStftn	.304**	-.144**	-.146**	-.304**	.382**	.362**	-.423**	.488**	.371**	—					
11. Autmov	.182**	.010	-.076	-.096*	.169**	.382**	-.012	.158**	-.005	-.004	—				
12. Comp	.154**	.016	.002	-.026	.093	.370**	-.115	.289**	-.011	.172**	.517**	—			
13. Mntr	-.050	.194**	.265**	.317**	-.290**	.032	.205**	.080*	-.268**	-.109*	.242**	.569**	—		
14. Cntrl	-.014	.209**	.214**	.359**	-.285**	.007	.344**	-.114**	-.530**	-.215**	.340**	.453**	.587**	—	
15. Indp	.035	.056	.130**	.014	-.025	.056	.129**	.146**	.431**	.054	-.091	-.212**	-.197**	-.306**	—

Note. HghAut = High Autonomy Orientation; SlghtCntr = Slightly Controlling; ModCntrl = Moderately Controlling; HghCntrl = Highly Controlling; PIS = Problems in School Composite Score; Mstry = Mastery Goal Orientation; CndRgd = Use of Conditional Regard; Effcy = Efficacy for Homeschooling; Engmnt = Parent Perception of Academic Engagement; NdStftn = Need Satisfaction; TEACHING STRATEGIES SCALE: Aut_Mot = Support for Autonomous Motivation; Comp = Support for Competence; Mntr = Monitoring; Cntrl = Use of Control; Indp = Student Independence.

*p < .05. **p < .01.

five-cluster solution. A double-split cross validation indicated the five-cluster solution was stable (Breckenridge, 2000).

Figure 1 presents the final-cluster solution. The *y*-axis in the figure represents *z* scores on the support for autonomy, competence, and relatedness proxies. The distance between the cluster means and the total sample standardized means, in standard deviation units, can be interpreted as effect sizes (Scholte, van Lieshout, de Wit, & van Aken, 2005) similar to Cohen's *d*, *.2 SD* is a small effect, 0.5 *SD* is a medium to moderate effect, and 0.8 *SD* is a large effect (Vansteenkiste et al., 2009). Profile 1 represents the High Need Support motivational profile (*n* = 131, 29%) and is characterized by high autonomy support (large effect), high mastery support (large effect), and low use of conditional regard (large effect). Profile 5 (*n* = 49, 11%) represents the Low Need Support motivational profile, with large effect sizes for control orientation, use of conditional regard, and low mastery orientation.

The three Mixed Need Support groups were characterized by the following differences: Profile 2 represents a Low Competence Support motivational profile (*n* = 86, 19%), characterized by a moderate autonomy orientation (small effect), modest use of conditional regard (small effect), and low mastery goal orientation (large effect). Profile 3 represents a Moderate Competency Support motivational profile (*n* = 103, 23%), characterized by a slight control orientation, moderate use of conditional regard (moderate effect) and moderate mastery goal orientation (moderate

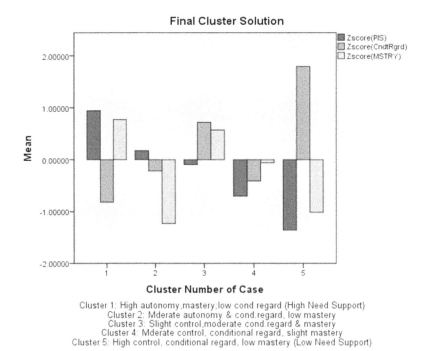

Figure 1. Final cluster solution.

effect). Profile 4 represents a Low Autonomy Support motivational profile (n = 88, 19%), characterized by moderate control orientation (moderate effect), moderate conditional regard (small to medium effect) and slight mastery orientation.

Before proceeding with further analyses, we evaluated whether the gender and grade-level categories for the child of interest were evenly distributed among the groups. Both chi-square tests were nonsignificant. Descriptive statistics for the clusters and results of follow up analyses are presented in Table 4.

Need satisfaction, efficacy, and academic engagement

ANOVAs for parent need satisfaction, efficacy for homeschooling, and perception of student academic engagement suggested meaningful differences between the profiles. Parents in the High Need Support profile differed significantly from all other profiles on need satisfaction

Table 4. Z Scores of the cluster dimensions and means of external variables and teaching practices factors and variables together with F values and effect sizes.

Variable	Group 1 n = 131 (29%)	Group 2 n = 86 (19%)	Group 3 n = 103 (23%)	Group 4 n = 88 (19%)	Group 5 n = 49 (11%)	F	η^2
Cluster dimensions						$F_{(4, 452)}$	
PIS	0.94_a	0.18_b	-0.10_b	-0.70_c	-1.36_d	141.48***	.56
Mastery	0.77_a	-1.23_c	$.57_a$	-0.06_b	-1.01_c	261.85***	.70
Conditional regard	-0.82_a	-0.22_b	$.72_c$	-0.41_b	1.80_d	202.83***	.64
External variables						$F_{(4, 424, 452, 442)}$	
Need satisfaction	6.26_a	5.77_b	5.93_b	5.97_b	5.03_c	37.05***	.26
Efficacy	6.42_a	5.84_b	$6.17_{a,b}$	6.27_a	5.40_c	13.93***	.12
Academic engagement	4.21_a	$3.95_{a,b}$	3.90_b	$3.99_{a,b}$	3.58_c	13.74***	.11
Teaching practices						$F_{(4, 369)}$	
Autonomous motivation	4.63_a	3.75_b	$4.30_{a,c}$	$4.00_{b,c}$	$4.12_{b,c}$	9.17***	.10
Control	3.10_a	$3.41_{a,b}$	$3.99_{b,c}$	$3.59_{a,b}$	4.26_c	10.09***	.10
Competence	5.76_a	5.29_b	5.75_a	$5.57_{a,b}$	4.83_c	9.77***	.10
Monitoring	3.80_a	$4.12_{a,b}$	4.39_b	4.48_b	$4.35_{a,b}$	4.48**	.05
Independence	$4.69_{a,b}$	4.34_a	$4.65_{a,b}$	4.35_a	5.16_b	3.39**	.04
Conventional materials	3.08_a	$3.70_{a,b}$	$3.58_{a,b}$	$3.85_{a,b}$	4.49_b	4.40**	.04
Takes college classes	1.75_a	1.24_a	1.77_a	1.33_a	3.34_b	16.34***	.14
Private/public school classes	1.59_a	1.28_a	1.39_a	1.54_a	2.83_b	10.43***	.10
You set deadlines	3.50_a	4.06_a	4.70_b	4.72_b	4.60_b	10.59***	.10
Student takes a test	3.34_a	$3.89_{a,b}$	$3.58_{a,b}$	$3.97_{b,c}$	4.51_c	7.60***	.07
Praise student for progress	$5.49_{a,b}$	5.05_b	$5.68_{a,b}$	$5.67_{a,b}$	4.90_b	4.81***	.05

Note. Cluster means are significantly different if they have different subscripts. PIS = Problems in School Composite Score.

**p < .01. ***p < .001.

(M = 6.26) and reported the highest academic engagement (M = 4.21) and efficacy for homeschooling (M = 6.42), reaching significance with some but not all groups. Parents in the Low Need Support profile reported significantly lower need satisfaction (M = 5.03), student academic engagement (M = 3.58), and efficacy for homeschooling (M = 5.40) than all other motivational profiles. Among the Mixed Need Support profiles, the Profile 2 (Low Competence Support) reported significantly lower efficacy for homeschooling than Profile 4 (Low Autonomy Support).

Teaching practices among the motivational rofiles

Wilk's lambda for the MANOVA with cluster membership as the independent variable and the five factors extracted from the teaching practices measure (Autonomous Motivation, Control, Competence, Monitoring, and Independence) as dependent variables was significant, $F(4, 369)$ = 10.82, $p < .001$, η^2 = .13. Follow-up univariate F values showed groups differed significantly on all five factors: support for autonomous motivation, $F(4, 369)$ = 9.17, $p < .001$, η^2 = .09; support for competence, $F(4, 369)$ = 9.77, $p < .001$, η^2 = .10; use of external control, $F(4, 369)$ = 10.09, $p < .001$, η^2 = .10; monitoring, $F(4, 369)$ = 4.48, $p < .01$, η^2 = .05; and student independence, $F(4, 369)$ = 3.38, $p < .01$, η^2 = .04. Tukey's post hoc comparisons showed the High Need Support parents reported the highest mean scores for support for autonomous motivation (M = 4.64), reaching significance with Profiles 2, 4, and 5; and support for competence (M = 5.76), reaching significance with Profiles 2 and 5. These parents also reported the lowest use of external control (M = 3.10) and practices intended to monitor student progress (M = 3.80), reaching significance with Profiles 3 and 5 and 3 and 4, respectively. The Low Need Support parents reported significantly lower support for competence than all other groups (M = 4.84), along with the highest use of external control (M = 4.26), differing statistically from all profiles except Profile 3. These parents were also most likely to report a student functioning independently (M = 5.16).

Demographic characteristics of the motivational profiles

A comparison of the continuous demographic variables is reported in Table 5. No significant differences were reported among the profiles except for religious activity, $F(4, 428)$ = 4.49, $p < .01$, η^2 = .04, political leanings, $F(4, 428)$ = 6.03, $p < .05$, η^2 = .05 and work concurrent with homeschooling, $F(4, 428)$ = 7.28, $p < .01$, η^2 = .06. The High Need Support parents reported less religious activity and were more left-leaning politically than all groups, reaching significance with Profiles 2 and 4. The Low Need Support parents reported significantly higher hours of work per week than all other groups. And while it did not reach significance, the

Table 5. Significant and nonsignificant continuous variables among groups.

Variable	Group 1 n = 110 (29%)	Group 2 n = 77 (19%)	Group 3 n = 92 (23%)	Group 4 n = 79 (19%)	Group 5 n = 44 (11%)	$F(4, 428)$	η^2
Religious activity	3.86_a	4.49_b	$4.26_{a,b}$	4.63_b	$4.28_{a,b}$	4.49**	.04
Political leanings	3.23_a	3.74_b	$3.59_{a,b}$	3.84_b	$3.58_{a,b}$	6.03**	.05
Work concurrent with homeschooling	2.15_a	2.16_a	2.16_a	1.65_a	3.20_b	7.28***	.06
Degree of monitoring	2.19	2.29	2.03	2.42	2.61	2.23	.02
Years homeschooling	4.02	4.17	3.97	4.15	4.02	.415	.00
Household income	3.68	4.01	3.70	3.53	3.96	2.14	.02
Level of education	5.32	5.38	5.47	5.22	5.50	.630	.00
Number of children	2.62	3.02	2.72	2.88	2.52	3.17	.03

Note. Means are significantly different if they have different subscripts.
**$p < .01$. ***$p < .001$.

Low Need Support parents also reported the highest degree of external monitoring.

The remaining categorical variables were entered into crosstabs for chi-square testing. These included gender of the parent teacher, homeschooling a special needs child, and holding a teaching certificate. Only the chi-square test for the gender of the teaching parent had a significant group effect, χ^2 (4, 434) = 72.32, $p < .001$, Cramer's $V = .41$. Close inspection of the percentages revealed that males were overrepresented in the Low Need Support profile ($n = 17$, 58% of males in this study). However, this finding must be interpreted with caution, as less than five males were reported in each of the other four groups.

We also conducted an independent sample t-test for need satisfaction and efficacy for homeschooling on the basis of gender of teaching parent. The Levene's test for homogeneity of variance was significant, $p < .05$. Need satisfaction for females ($M = 5.96$, $SE = .032$) was significantly higher than males ($M = 4.9$, $SE = .154$), t (28.34) = 6.47, $p < .001$, which represented a large effect $r = .77$. Females ($M = 6.16$, $SE = .043$) also had significantly higher efficacy for homeschooling than males ($M = 5.46$, $SE = .207$); t (30.55) = 3.35, $p < .001$, $r = .52$, also considered a large effect.

The correlations between student engagement and the grade of the student of interest and the number of years the student had been homeschooled were both positive with relatively moderate effect ($r = .351, .286$; $p < .01$). Finally, we conducted an independent sample t-test for school engagement on the basis of gender of the child of interest. Overall, parents reported significantly higher student engagement scores, t (438) = 3.24, $p < .001$, for female students ($M = 4.07$, $SE = .036$) than male students ($M = 3.9$, $SE = .038$). This represented a small effect, $r = .16$.

Discussion

In the last 25 years homeschooling has become a fixture of the U.S educational landscape. State legislation that legalized this option did little to dictate parental curricular choices or teaching practices. Concurrently, classroom teachers have been subjected to ever-increasing external control, high stakes testing, and adherence to core standards—conditions self-determination theorists have cautioned can undermine the development of students' autonomous motivation for learning. Further concerning are studies that show students' academic engagement declines overtime in conventional settings (Eccles & Roeser, 2010; Meece & Schaeffer, 2010; Planty et al., 2008). This dichotomy gave rise to our interest in investigating support for achievement motivation in a homeschool context.

The parents in our sample reported little to no monitoring of their program by outside authorities. Thus, they were ostensibly free from the external sources of surveillance, pressure, and constraints SDT research postulates may contribute to the controlling practices that undermine autonomous motivation in conventionally educated students. Inferentially then the practices that characterized this sample may be assumed to emanate from underlying psychological processes such as, the beliefs, values, and needs of the primary teaching parent.

In this context, it is significant that overall, this sample of highly experienced, highly efficacious, and highly committed homeschool parents endorsed a highly autonomous motivational orientation on the PIS, high mastery goal orientation, and low use of conditional regard. Further this correlated with high parental need satisfaction on all subscales: autonomy, relatedness, and competence. As theory would predict, these in turn were moderately and positively correlated with student academic engagement. Perhaps more significant, the child of interest held in mind for the academic engagement measure—in contrast with the reverse findings among conventionally educated students—indicated higher academic engagement the longer a child was homeschooled and the higher his or her reported grade level.

Our study may also add further insight to the findings in Cai and colleagues (2002). That study showed religiously motivated homeschool parents endorsed a more controlling motivational style on the PIS ($M = 2.44$; $SD = 2.81$) than public school teachers ($M = 4.67$; $SD = 2.82$). Using the same scoring procedure reported in Cai and colleagues (2002), our sample of parents endorse a more autonomy supporting motivational style ($M = 4.7$; $SD = 2.97$). A comparison of descriptive statistics in Cai and colleagues suggests that our larger sample of homeschool parents had homeschooled longer (65% of our sample reported homeschooling five or more years; Cai and colleagues reported a mean of 3.7 years), taught at higher grade levels (50% of parents in our study reported homeschooling at high school grades in comparison with 14% in Cai and colleagues), were more highly educated (70% of parents in our study held a bachelor degree or higher, parents in Cai and colleagues reported less formal education than the public school teachers), and reported less religious motivation for homeschooling (see Table 1). We revised the PIS twice in order to achieve acceptable internal reliability scores. In particular, several vignettes were rewritten to be more meaningful to a homeschool setting. This also may explain some of the differences in scores.

Further insight is gleaned from examining the teaching practices that characterized the homeschools represented in this study. In general, parents reported frequent use of the strategies self-determination theorists have recommended classroom teachers adopt to promote autonomous motivation: They use age-appropriate materials other than textbooks, allow the student the freedom to manage his or her own time, talk with the student about things he or she is learning, encourage questions, take the student's preferences into consideration, encourage the pursuit of the student's own interests, and frequently praise the student for his or her progress. Conversely, they are less likely to use strategies associated with control, and which undermine autonomous motivation: They do not use rewards or loss of privileges as an incentive for doing work, they are less likely to give tests or set deadlines, they infrequently point out areas that need to improve or address unacceptable behavior, and they are not likely to set a schedule for the student to follow.

The antecedents of these outcomes nor the interactions that are suggested by these central tendencies cannot be untangled from this study. But these correlations give a rare picture of a context where teachers were free to adapt their motivational approach and teaching practices in response to the needs and preferences of the child. It appears many parents in this study are doing just that, and they perceive their children as being highly academically engaged along the dimensions associated with autonomous motivation. That this dynamic has been found in a natural learning environment where at least parents, if not students, are unconstrained, lends credence to self-determination theory's humanistic claim that the human organism actively seeks integration and optimal functioning through the satisfaction of the need for autonomy, competence, and relatedness (Deci & Ryan, 2002).

There were fewer differences that emerged among the groups at the family-, parent-, and child-levels than anticipated. This is likely due to the overall similarities this sample shared in common; that is, highly educated, well-off, large families. The most surprising and significant differences were based on the gender of the teaching parent. Male teaching parents were significantly outnumbered in this study because, as documented elsewhere, females are far more likely to be the teaching parent. However, the high use of control associated with the group overrepresented by men, the hours worked concurrent with homeschooling, and the low need satisfaction reported by all men across the groups suggests these sources of psychological stress may reduce the time and energy male teaching parents have to promote autonomous motivation (Marjoribanks, 2002; Schneider & Coleman, 1993). Further, because of their minority status within this population, they may feel marginalized and may encounter obstacles to integration and support within the homeschool community.

It is also interesting to note the distribution of the types of homeschools found; for example, the High Need Support as the largest single cluster (29%), the three Mixed Need Support groups taken as a whole representing the most common condition (61%), and the Low Need Support cluster representing only slightly more than 10% of this sample. One likely explanation is homeschool parents who experience high need satisfaction and desired outcomes in their children, persist in homeschooling; those who don't, quit (and are therefore underrepresented here.) The option to opt out is not readily available to teachers, parents, or students in conventional settings so the prevalence of extrinsically motivated students in that context and less desirable outcomes is not surprising. Therefore, these results cannot be construed to mean homeschooling is a more efficacious context for learning. Rather, it may explain *why* homeschooling is efficacious when it is so. This interaction between parental need satisfaction and student academic engagement is a dynamic that warrants further investigation and may have more explanatory power than consideration of parental motivations for homeschooling as to why homeschooling is surging.

The final goal of this study was to extend self-determination theory to this important emerging learning context; one, ostensibly suited for examining some of the assumptions SDT researchers may not be able to test in more conventional settings. The SDT measures adapted for use with this sample had sound psychometric properties and findings are consistent with SDT results elsewhere, extending the universality and robustness of this particular theoretical paradigm.

Further, it is noteworthy that many participants reported in unsolicited follow-up e-mails, they enjoyed completing this study and found the survey questions thought provoking. Some even stated they recognized patterns in their teaching practices they planned to change. Participants frequently thanked us for giving them this opportunity to talk about their teaching practices and experiences; and no small number ask to know more about how they might promote achievement motivation in their homes. These comments contribute to the practical significance of these results and also the utility of self-determination theory as a lens for examining homeschools and distinguishing meaningful differences among them.

Notes

1. The slight control subscale of the PIS had a less than satisfactory reliability (a = .67). However, following Reeve's recommended scoring procedure (Reeve, Bolt, & Cai, 1999), this subscale on the PIS is effectively canceled out.
2. These correlations among the variables used for the cluster analysis also met the recommended relationship among variables for performing a MANOVA (e.g., high, negative correlations or moderate correlations in either direction; Tabachnick & Fidell, 2007).

References

Assor, A., Roth, G., & Deci, E. L. (2004). The emotional costs of parents' conditional regard: A Self–Determination Theory analysis. *Journal of Personality, 72*(1), 47–88.

Breckenridge, J. N. (2000). Validating cluster analysis: Consistent replication and symmetry. *Multivariate Behavioral Research, 35*(2), 261–285.

Brophy, J. (1999). Toward a model of the value aspects of motivation in education: Developing appreciation for. *Educational Psychologist, 34*(2), 75–85.

Brophy, J. E. (1985). Teacher-student interaction. In J. B. Dusek (Ed.), *Teacher expectations* (pp. 303–328). Hillsdale, NJ: Erlbaum.

Cai, Y., Reeve, J., & Robinson, D. (2002). Home schooling and teaching style: Comparing the motivating styles of home school and public school teachers. *Journal of Educational Psychology, 94*(2), 372–380.

Deci, E., Schwartz, A., Sheinman, L., & Ryan, R. (1981). An instrument to assess adults' orientations toward control versus autonomy with children: Reflections on intrinsic motivation and perceived competence. *Journal of Educational Psychology, 73*(5), 642–650.

Deci, E. L., & Ryan, R. M. (1985). *Intrinsic motivation and self-determination in human behavior.* New York, NY: Plenum.

Deci, E. L., & Ryan, R. M. (2000). The "what" and "why" of goal pursuits: Human needs and the self-determination of behavior. *Psychological Inquiry, 11*(4), 227–268.

Deci, E. L., & Ryan, R. M. (2002). Self-determination research: Reflections and future directions. In E. L. Deci & R. M. Ryan (Eds.), *Handbook of self-determination theory research* (pp. 431–441). Rochester, NY: University of Rochester Press.

Eccles, J. (1993). School and family effects on the ontogeny of children's interests, self-perceptions, and activity choice. In J. Jacobs (Ed.), *Nebraska symposium on motivation: Developmental perspectives on motivation* (Vol. 40, pp. 145–208). Lincoln, NE: University of Nebraska Press.

Eccles, J. S., & Midgley, C. (1989). Stage-environment fit: Developmentally appropriate classrooms for young adolescents. *Research on Motivation in Education, 3*, 139–186.

Eccles, J., & Roeser, R. (2010). An ecological view of schools and development. In Meece, J., & Eccles, J. (Eds.), *Handbook of research on schools, schooling and human development.* New York, NY: Routledge.

Eccles, J. S., Adler, T. F., Futterman, R., Goff, S. B., Kaczala, C. M., Meece, J. L., & Midgley, C. 1983. Achievement and achievement motivation. In J. T. Spence (Ed.), *Expectancies, values and academic behaviors* (pp. 75–146). San Francisco, CA: Freeman.

Fan, X., & Chen, M. (2001). Parental involvement and students' academic achievement: A meta-analysis. *Educational Psychology Review, 13*(1), 1–22.

Gaither, M. (2009). Homeschooling in the USA: Past, present and future. *Theory and Research in Education*, 7(3), 331–346.

Gore, P. A., Jr. (2000). Cluster analysis. In H. E. A. Tinsley & S. D. Brown (Eds.), *Handbook of applied multivariate statistics and mathematical modeling* (pp. 297–321). San Diego, CA: Academic Press.

Grolnick, W. S., Gurland, S. T., Jacob, K. F., & Decourcey, W. (2002). The development of self-determination in middle childhood and adolescence. In A. Wigfield & J. S. Eccles (Eds.), *Development of achievement motivation* (pp. 147–171). San Diego, CA: Academic Press.

Grolnick, W. S., Kurowski, C. O., & Gurland, S. T. (1999). Family processes and the development of children's self-regulation. *Educational Psychologist*, 34, 3–14.

Grolnick, W. S., & Ryan, R. M. (1987). Autonomy in children's learning: An experimental and individual difference investigation. *Journal of Personality and Social Psychology*, 52, 890–898.

Grolnick, W. S., & Ryan, R. M. (1989). Parent styles associated with children's self-regulation and competence in schools. *Journal of Educational Psychology*, 8, 143–154.

Gutman, L., Sameroff, A., & Eccles, J. (2002). The academic achievement of African American students during early adolescence: An examination of multiple risk, promotive, and protective factors. *American Journal of Community Psychology*, 30, 367–399.

Hair, J. R., Anderson, R. E., Tatham, R. L., & Black, W. C. (1998). *Multivariate data analysis*. New York, NY: Macmillan.

Home School Legal Defense Association. (2001, October 2). Homeschooling expands around the globe. *HSLDA News*. Retrieved from http://www.hslda.org/hs/international/200110020.asp.

Isenberg, E. (2007). What have we learned about homeschooling? *Peabody Journal of Education*, 82(2–3), 387–409.

Kaplan, A., & Maehr, M. (2007). The contributions and prospects of goal orientation theory. *Educational Psychological Review*, 19, 141–184.

Kaplan, A., Middleton, M. J., Urdan, T., & Midgley, C. (2002). Achievement goals and goal structures. In C. Midgley (Ed.), *Goals, goal structures and patterns of adaptive learning* (pp. 21–53). Mahwah, NJ: Lawrence Erlbaum.

Knowles, J. G. (1991, April 3–7). Now we are adults: Attitudes, beliefs, and status of adults who were home-educated as children. Paper presented at the Annual Meeting of the American Educational Research Association, Chicago, IL.

Kunzman, R. (2009). *Write these laws on your children: Inside the world of conservative Christian homeschooling*. Boston, MA: Beacon Press.

Marjoribanks, K. (2002). *Family and school capital: Towards a context theory of students' school outcomes*. Dordrecht, The Netherlands: Kluwer Academic.

Meece, J. & Schaefer, V. (2010). Schools as a context of human development. In Meece, J., & Eccles, J. (Eds.), *Handbook of research on schools, schooling and human development*, (pp. 3–5). New York, NY: Routledge.

Midgley, C., Feldlaufer, H., & Eccles, J. (1989). Change in teacher efficacy and student self- and task-related beliefs in mathematics during the transition to junior high school. *Journal of Educational Psychology*, 81(2), 247–258.

Midgley, C., Maehr, M. L., Hruda, L. Z., Anderman, E., Anderman, L., Freeman, K. E., & Urdan, T. (2000). *Manual for the patterns of adaptive learning scales*. Ann Arbor, MI: University of Michigan.

Milligan, G. W., & Cooper, M. C. (1985). An examination of procedures for determining the number of clusters in a data set. *Psychometrika*, 50, 159–179.

Niemiec, C. P., & Ryan, R. M. (2009). Autonomy, competence, and relatedness in the classroom: Applying self-determination theory to educational practice. *Theory and Research in Education, 7*(2), 133–144.

Patrick, H., Ryan, A. M., & Kaplan, A. (2007). Early adolescents' perceptions of the classroom social environment, motivational beliefs, and engagement. *Journal of Educational Psychology, 99*(1), 83.

Pintrich, P. R., & Schunk, D. H. (2002). *Motivation in education: Theory, research, and application* (2nd ed.). Englewood Cliffs, NJ: Merrill-Prentice-Hall.

Planty, M., Provasnik, S., Hussar, W., Snyder, T., Kena, G., Hampden-Thompson, G., ... & Choy, S. (2007). The Condition of Education, 2007. NCES 2007-064. National Center for Education Statistics.

Planty, M., Hassar, W., Snyder, T., Kena, G., Dinkes, R., Kewal Ramani, A., et al. (2008). The conditions of education 2008 (NCES 2008-31). Washington, D.C.: National Center for Educational Statistics, Institute of Education Sciences, U.S. Department of Education. Retrieved from http://nces.ed.gov

Princiotta, D., & Bielick, S. (2006). *Homeschooling in the United States: 2003* (p. 2005). Washington, DC: (NCES 2006-042) U.S. Department of Education. National Center for Education Statistics.

Ray, B. (2002). Customization through homeschooling. *Educational Leadership, 59*(7), 50–54.

Ray, B. (2005). A homeschool research story. In B. S. Cooper (Ed.), *Home schooling in full view: A reader* (pp. 1–19). Greenwich, CT: Information Age.

Reeve, J. (2002). Self-determination theory applied to educational settings. In E. L. Deci, & R. M. Ryan (Eds.), *Handbook of self-determination theory research* (pp. 183–203). Rochester, NY: University of Rochester Press.

Reeve, J. (2009). Why teachers adopt a controlling motivating style toward students and how they can become more autonomy supportive. *Educational Psychologist, 44*(3), 159–175.

Reeve, J., Bolt, E., & Cai, Y. (1999). Autonomy-supportive teachers: How they teach and motivate students. *Journal of Educational Psychology, 91*(3), 537–548.

Reeve, J., & Jang, H. (2006). What teachers say and do to support students' autonomy during a learning activity. *Journal of Educational Psychology, 98*, 209–218.

Ryan, R. M. (1995). Psychological needs and the facilitation of integrative processes. *Journal of Personality, 63*(3), 397–427.

Ryan, R. M., & Deci, E. L. (2000). Self-determination theory and the facilitation of intrinsic motivation, social development and well-being. *American Psychologist, 55*, 68–78.

Ryan, R. M., & Deci, E. L. (2002). Overview of self-determination theory: An organismic dialectic perspective. In E. L. Deci & R. M. Ryan (Eds.), *Handbook of self determination research*. Rochester, NY: University of Rochester Press.

Schneider, B., & Coleman, J. S. (1993). *Parents, their children, and schools*. Boulder, CO: Westview Press.

Scholte, R. J., van Lieshout, C. M., de Wit, C. M., & van Aken, M.G. (2005). Adolescent personality types and subtypes and their psychosocial development. *Merrill-Palmer Quarterly, 51*, 258–286.

Skinner, E., & Belmont, M. (1993). Motivation in the classroom: Reciprocal effects of teacher behavior and student engagement across the school year. *Journal of Educational Psychology, 85*, 571–581.

Tabachnick, B. G., & Fidell, L. (2007). *Using multivariate statistics* (5th ed.). Boston, MA: Allyn & Bacon.

Tan, P. N., Steinbach, M., & Kumar, V. (2006). *Introduction to data mining*. Boston, MA: Addison-Wesley.

Van Galen, J. A. (1988). Ideology, curriculum, and pedagogy in home education. *Education and Urban Society, 21*, 52–68.

Vansteenkiste, M., Sierens, E., Soenens, B., Luyckx, K., & Lens, W. (2009). Motivational profiles from a self-determination perspective: The quality of motivation matters. *Journal of Educational Psychology, 101*(3), 671–688.

Ward, J. (1963). Hierarchical grouping to optimize an objective function. *Journal of the American Statistical Association, 58*, 236–244.

Weinstein, R. S. (1989). Perception of classroom processes and student motivation: Children's views of self-fulfilling prophecies. In R. E. Ames & C. Ames (Eds.), *Research on motivation in education* (Vol. 3, pp. 187–221). New York, NY: Academic Press.

Appendix

Table A1. Descriptives for Teaching Practices Survey.
Frequency of use since beginning of the school year with child of interest: 1 = *never*, 2 = *once or twice*, 3 = *once or twice per month*, 4 = *once a week*, 5 = *several times per week*, 6 = *once a day*, 7 = *several times a day*.

Item	N	M (SD)	Skewness	Kurtosis	Alpha
This student:					
uses resources designed for a conventional school	444	3.6 (2.1)	.117	−1.42	
uses resources designed primarily for a home school	446	5.6 (1.8)	−1.297	.758	
takes college classes locally (e.g., not online)	448	1.8 (1.6)	1.874	1.964	
takes classes at a local private or public school	448	1.6 (1.5)	2.111	2.971	
participates in co-op classes or other group learning	448	3.6 (1.7)	−.351	−.904	
uses age-appropriate literature and nonfiction (i.e., other than textbooks)	445	6.1 (1.3)	−1.449	2.127	
takes a test	448	3.8 (1.4)	−.237	−.235	
You:					
set deadlines	448	4.2 (1.7)	−.209	−.738	
praise student for his or her progress	443	5.4 (1.4)	−.519	−.181	
provide student with the opportunity to work with others	442	4.5 (1.4)	−.318	.086	
work collaboratively with the student on a task	446	4.5 (1.7)	−.205	−.821	
show student how to complete an academic task	444	4.4 (1.8)	−.162	−.993	
This student (INDEPENDENCE SCALE):					
participates in classes conducted online	445	3.4 (2.3)	.284	−1.55	.74
self-checks his or her work	447	4.7 (2.1)	−.611	−.896	
uses materials or activities found online	447	5.3 (1.6)	−.830	.031	
uses a tutor or teacher other than you	447	3.7 (2.0)	−.243	−1.23	
is responsible for managing his or her time	447	6.1 (1.7)	−1.97	2.80	
You (MONITORING SCALE):					
show student how to answer problems in the text	444	4.3 (1.8)	−.158	−.883	.85
assign academic work for the student to complete	444	4.8 (1.8)	−.563	−.565	
enforce deadlines	443	4.2 (1.8)	−.277	−.772	
grade the student's work	445	4.0 (2.0)	−.139	−1.171	
give tests	448	3.3 (1.5)	−.031	−.770	
evaluate the student's work	445	4.8 (1.6)	−.321	−.507	
set a schedule for the student to follow	446	3.8 (1.8)	.016	−1.04	
You (AUTONOMOUS MOTIVATION SCALE):					
let student choose his or her books or activities	447	4.7 (1.9)	−.383	−.877	.78
encourage student to pursue his or her interests	445	5.3 (1.5)	−.594	−.393	
use projects to promote learning	445	3.7 (1.7)	.387	−584	
take a field trip related to academic work	448	2.7 (1.1)	1.247	2.826	
ask student what he or she would like to study or do	441	4.0 (1.7)	.410	−.886	
take student's preferences into consideration	440	4.8 (1.7)	−.211	−1.123	
explain the reason for learning the material	443	4.2 (1.7)	.102	−.906	
You (SUPPORT FOR COMPETENCE SCALE):					
encourage the student to persist in his or her efforts	447	5.3 (1.4)	−.469	−.314	.83
encourage questions about what the student is learning	446	5.9 (1.2)	−1.05	.925	
give the student feedback on the quality of his or her work	448	5.1 (1.5)	−.449	−.253	
talk with the student about things he or she is learning	444	6.1 (1.2)	−1.067	.760	
ask the student to explain something he or she is learning	443	5.4 (1.3)	−.594	.032	

(Continued)

Table A1. (Continued).

Item	N	M (SD)	Skewness	Kurtosis	Alpha
You (EXTERNAL CONTROL SCALE):					
redirect student's attention back to his or her schoolwork	447	4.9 (2.0)	−.602	−.813	.86
use rewards as an incentive for doing work	447	2.6 (1.6)	1.003	.187	
use loss of privileges as an incentive for doing work	448	2.6 (1.6)	.975	.124	
address unacceptable student behavior	441	3.7 (1.9)	.342	−.986	
point out areas of academic work that need to improve	445	3.5 (1.5)	.312	−.390	
address negative attitudes	445	4.0 (1.7)	.199	−.962	

A Descriptive Survey of Why Parents Choose Hybrid Homeschools

Eric Wearne

ABSTRACT

"Hybrid home schools" are schools in which students attend school with other students for 2 or 3 days per week in traditional classroom settings, and are homeschooled the balance of the week. This exploratory study presents self-reported reasons parents choose these schools, using an electronic survey of parents from four such schools ($n = 136$; 19% return rate). Findings indicate that families in these schools are relatively wealthier and more suburban than parents using tax credit programs, that they value school structures more than particular student achievement outcomes, and that they seek information on accreditation, curriculum, and the religious nature of schools in making their choices.

Introduction

Several factors in American education policy have been converging to cause parents to seek new options for schooling. A consensus among elite policy-makers has emerged, focusing on "college and career readiness," along with a push for more centralized, standardized practices such as the Common Core State Standards. At the same time more choice options are becoming available to parents, including online options, more charter schools, various private choice programs within states, and a growing acceptance of home-schooling. One option growing alongside full-time homeschooling is *hybrid homeschools*. Hybrid homeschools for the purposes of this study are schools in which students attend school with other students for 2 or 3 days per week in traditional classroom settings, and are homeschooled the balance of the week. A school need not necessarily be private to be a hybrid homeschool, though nearly all are. In this study, all of the schools are private. These are not online schools, but a combination of homeschooling and brick-and-mortar schooling, giving students the experiences of being homeschooled as well as that of a traditional classroom setting with teachers and other students. Often these schools are called *university model schools* (UMS). Some of the schools in this study use that term. "University Model

Schools," however, is also a brand name; one school in this study is a formal University Model School, another uses the term informally, and the others do not use it at all. The term hybrid homeschool will be used hereafter to include all such schools which follow the organizational structure of holding school 2–3 days per week in a physical, traditional-looking classroom setting, and homeschooling the rest of the week. While work has been done on reasons parents choose private schools, or homeschooling, very little has been done to explore hybrid homeschools and their particular appeals. This study is a descriptive survey exploring the reasons parents in the metropolitan area of a city in the state of Georgia in the southeastern United States say they choose to send their children to hybrid homeschools.

To learn parents' stated preferences, an electronic survey was sent to four schools' respective lists of parents. We address three questions:

(1) What are the characteristics of families who choose to send their children to hybrid homeschools?
(2) What do these parents say they value as part of a hybrid homeschool education?
(3) What sources of information do these parents say they seek to decide on this school option?

Literature review

Very little work has studied hybrid homeschools. These schools have grown from the homeschooling movement, from the traditional private school sector, and more recently from the public sector, due to improvements in technology. Some work has addressed university model hybrid homeschool; those and particular public school analogs are the closest comparisons in the literature. Finally, work on the reasons parents choose homeschooling or private schools can help indirectly address the central question here: why do parents choose hybrid schools for their children?

Homeschooling

The homeschooling population in the United States has been larger than other segments of the school choice movement, such as the charter school population, for some time (Bauman, 2002; Murphy, 2012). Ray (2011) estimated the homeschooling population at over 2 million students. Recent estimates suggest approximately 3% of school-aged children in America are homeschooled; in Georgia estimates range from 50,000 to 73,000 students (Coalition for Responsible Homeschooling, 2011). A fraction of these students would be attending hybrid homeschools and registered as homeschoolers with the state, depending on the structure of their particular school.

Murphy (2012) has written the most comprehensive account of the various forms of homeschooling in the United States. Murphy describes four frameworks for parents' reasons for choosing homeschooling:

- religion,
- academic deficiencies in the assigned public school,
- social/environmental problems in the assigned public school, and
- other family-based motivations (such as a desire to be with one's children, or for special needs or other special circumstances).

All of these frameworks appear in some form in the parent responses to this survey, and will be discussed as follows.

Hybrid schools

The vast majority of hybrid homeschools are private entities, incorporated as nonprofits, with their own independent boards of directors, though some programs in public school settings are beginning to adopt hybrid characteristics, as will be described as follows. Hybrid homeschools might be considered more formal, structured versions of homeschool cooperatives ("co-ops"). Muldowney (2011, p. 35) has written about these co-ops, reporting that the existing research on them is minimal. She writes that:

> According to Topp, one benefit of joining a co-op is the opportunity to work with people with similar values since co-ops are formed by parents with likeminded goals. Co-ops also allow homeschooled children to socialize with similar-aged children and to get a "taste" of group learning without being overwhelming. (as cited in Topp, 2008, p. 6)

Co-ops tend to be more ad hoc arrangements than the hybrid schools considered in this study. In co-op arrangements, students often take a select number of classes largely for social interaction; hybrid schools are generally full-day schools on the days they are in session. The hybrid schools choose curriculum, hire teachers, set day-long schedules, and generally take a more dominant role in academic instruction than co-ops. Still, hybrid homeschools resemble co-ops in many ways, as noted as follows.

A common form of hybrid homeschool is the UMS. *University Model* is a brand name many of these schools formally adopt or informally employ. UMS schools follow a collegiate schedule with students taking some classes as a group, and working at home on other days. The schools emphasize character development, parental involvement, and a college-preparatory curriculum. The limited research on these schools suggests that graduates resemble homeschoolers in their reasons for choosing and their academic success—a desire for parents to have more influence over their children's academic development and slightly better than average academic scores on standardized tests (Brobst, 2013).

Recently, hybrid schools have appeared as public schools, often driven by the improved quality and accessibility of technology. State-sponsored online schools such as the Florida Virtual School (Gaither, 2009) are examples of schooling hybridization (though this school, fully online, does not typically include physical classrooms, unlike the hybrid schools considered here). Another example, closer to the hybrid homeschools surveyed here, is that of a public school system experimenting with a very structured form of hybrid schooling. Forsyth County, Georgia schools recently experimented with a small, select group of high school juniors, allowing them to study in a synchronous online environment at home twice per week, and attend school as traditional students the rest of the week (Wearne, 2013). In addition, some public schools are beginning to use technology to eliminate snow days by having students work from home, a temporary hybrid homeschool approach (Farner, 2015).

Finally, *micro-schools* have appeared in technology centers such as Austin and the San Francisco Bay Area. These are mostly private schools with different areas of curricular emphasis, but with structures resembling university-model/hybrid homeschools (Horn, 2009). Ultimately, parents, school systems, and other organizations are experimenting with various methods of personalizing instruction, with a variety of motivations and formats.

What parents value

A recent nationwide survey measured parental criteria of school options: most valued some version of academic success or "college and career readiness" (Zeehandelaar & Winkler, 2013). Indeed, that study classifies approximately 71% of parents ("pragmatists," "test-score hawks," and "strivers") as mainly favoring some form of "college and career readiness." Ray (2015a) and Murphy (2012) have reported on reasons parents choose homeschooling, which often differ from those reported by Zeehandelaar and Winkler. For example, the latter reported greater emphasis on academic success or "college and career readiness" rather than religious, family, or other social values suggested by Murphy.

Schneider and colleagues (2000), as well as Stewart and Wolf (2014) discuss the demand side of school choice, finding that parents mostly prioritize criteria other than academic metrics when choosing schools. Similarly, Greene, Hitt, Kraybill, and Bogulski (2015), and Greene, Kisida, and Bowen (2014) discuss schooling aspects that parents value other than typical academics or school structures (and which seem to have a positive academic impact as well)—museum and live theater visits. Hybrid homeschools are neither homeschools nor traditional schools, and the motivations of parents to choose them have not been explored.

In a particular local context relevant to this study, Kelly and Scafidi (2013) surveyed low-income parents receiving tax credit scholarships in Georgia to attend private schools regarding their criteria for choosing and the information valued in making their choices. Georgia's Private School Tax Credit program allows individuals to receive state tax credits for donations to approved Student Scholarship Organizations (SSOs). SSOs then pay out scholarships to (typically) low-income students to pay the cost of private schools. These authors found that the parents in their survey typically valued issues such as school climate, discipline, safety, and smaller classes ahead of academic reasons such as test scores. Parents choosing schools in New Orleans after Hurricane Katrina, similarly, chose factors other than academics, including school location and extracurricular activities, ahead of academic performance (Harris & Larsen, 2015). Trivitt and Wolf (2011) and Cheng and colleagues (2016) examine the effects of branding on parents' private school choices, among families participating in private choice programs. The choices made by hybrid homeschool families have not yet been examined.

Funding

As private institutions, these schools do not receive state funding, instead relying on tuition, grants, and other fundraising. Some schools generally (and in this study) charge annual tuition, while others provide *a la carte* services, charging by the credit hour. The mean annual tuition at these schools (including a "full load" as defined by the schools charging by the credit hour) was just over $3,000 at the K–8 level, just over $3,500 at the high school level. These are substantially below tuition at full-time private schools in the area. The major costs hybrid homeschools save are personnel and benefits—most of the teachers at the schools in this study are part-time employees and/or contractors.

Methods

The respondents to this survey were drawn from a convenience sample of parents of students in hybrid homeschools in the metropolitan area of a large southeastern city. Eight formal hybrid homeschools were identified. All were invited to participate in this survey; four agreed. The participating schools served a mean of 183 families, with a high of 353 and a low of 45. Two of the schools declining to participate had enrollments larger than this mean, two smaller. Three of the participating schools are nondeno-minational Christian schools; the fourth is Catholic (though not affiliated with the Archdiocese). Three of the nonparticipating schools are nonde-nominational Christian as well, and the fourth is Catholic (also not affiliated with the Archdiocese).

A link to a survey within an invitation to participate was sent to the school leaders at the four schools, who then sent the invitation and link on to their parents. Approximately 700 families were contacted, and 136 surveys were completed, for a 19% response rate. School leaders were asked to send a reminder approximately 1 week after the original survey link. Response rates for external online surveys are generally low: this rate falls within Nulty's (2008) guidelines for adequacy. While existing research on hybrid home-schools is very thin and these results may not warrant wide generalization, the participating schools generally mirror the nonparticipating schools in size and religious affiliation.

The survey included 18 questions modeled after Kelly and Scafidi's (2013) survey, which asked parents of students receiving state tax credit scholarships in Georgia why they chose their private schools. The two surveys were likely given to very different sets of parents, as described as follows. Parents in these hybrid homeschools likely considered the questions in very persona-lized contexts—their children entered hybrid homeschools from full home-school environments and from traditional public and private schools, though some have always attended hybrid schools. When asked to compare their hybrid schools to other options, then, respondents likely had varying alter-natives in mind. Both this survey and the Kelly and Scafidi survey asked questions concerning income range, educational attainment, and other demographics. They also asked parents to choose and rank reasons regarding their choice of schooling options (or to add their own reasons), and what information parents sought in making their choices.

Results

Demographic characteristics

Table 1 reports summary demographic data for respondents.

A plurality of respondents reported family income in the $100,000–$124,999 range; 84.4% have at least an undergraduate degree. Respondents tended to be White (92.6%), married (96.7%), and live in a suburb (91.8%). Kelly and Scafidi's respondents, by comparison, had lower incomes (57.3% earned $60,000 or less), 68.4% had at least an undergraduate degree, 72.8% were "White or Asian" (racial/ethnic categories were slightly different between the two surveys), 73.1% were married, and 61.0% lived in a suburban area.

Table 1. Summary data for respondents.

	Percent
Income	
$0–$24,999	0.0
$25,000–$49,999	2.6
$50,000–$74,999	9.5
$75,000–$99,999	19.8
$100,000–$124,999	29.3
$125,000–$149,999	9.5
$150,000–$174,999	9.5
$175,000–$199,999	5.2
$200,000 and up	14.7
Educational attainment	
Did not graduate high school	0.0
Graduated from high school	1.6
Some college	13.9
Undergraduate degree	50.8
Graduate or professional degree	33.6
Marital status	
Married	96.7
Not married	3.3
Race/Ethnicity	
American Indian or Alaskan Native	0.8
Asian/Pacific Islander	0.0
Black or African American	3.3
Hispanic American	2.5
White/Caucasian	92.6
Multiple ethnicity/Other (please specify)	0.8
Urbanicity	
Urban	0.0
Suburban	91.8
Rural	8.2

Reasons for choosing a hybrid homeschool

Why do parents choose hybrid homeschools? To address this, respondents were first asked: "There are many possible reasons why families send their children to a hybrid school, rather than to some other kind of school. Please select each of the following reasons you had for sending your child to a hybrid school (you may mark as many or as few reasons as applied to your situation)." Table 2 reports parents' responses.

"Religious education" was listed by the largest percentage, perhaps to be expected as all four schools are religious. This resembles results from Ray's (2015a) survey of African-American homeschooling families. "Better learning environment" and "smaller class sizes," the second- and third-most common choices for these respondents, were the also among the three most-common choices for respondents to Kelly and Scafidi. Respondents' higher-ranked answers resemble those given by homeschooling parents in general (Ray, 2015b). It should be noted, however, that while nearly all of the respondents to Kelly and Scafidi have had some experience with traditional public schools (a requirement of the state tax credit scholarship program), students

Table 2. All reasons parents reported for choosing a hybrid homeschool.

Answer options	Response percent
Religious education	81.7
Better learning environment	79.4
Smaller class sizes	79.4
Less time wasted during the school day	76.2
More individual attention for my child	64.3
Better education	59.5
Better preparation for college	54.8
More meaningful opportunities for parental involvement	54.8
More responsive teachers and administrators	53.2
Greater respect for my rights as a parent	53.2
Other students would be a better influence on my child	51.6
Better student discipline	46.8
Greater sense of community	46.8
More attention to the unique needs of my child	42.9
Improved student safety	38.9
Other parents would be more concerned about their children's education	38.1
Less gang activity	23.0
Other (please specify)	23.0
Higher standardized test scores	19.0
Would prefer full-time private school, but the hybrid is more affordable	14.3
More extracurricular opportunities	13.5
More tutorial and other supplemental learning services than at a five-day school	9.5

attending these hybrid schools come from various environments: public schools, private schools, and full-time homeschools. For the purposes of these surveys, "Better learning environment," for example, means better, in the responder's opinion, than their other available school options or experiences.

The least-common reasons for choosing a hybrid school were "More tutorial and other supplemental learning services than at a five-day school" (9.5%) and "More extracurricular opportunities" (13.5%). Additionally, 14.3% of respondents reported that they "Would prefer full-time private school, but the hybrid is more affordable." While Kelly and Scafidi found more than a third of parents prioritizing test scores, here only 19.0% did so.

"Other" reasons respondents provided involved items such as increased time with family, or influence by family (e.g., "Family as primary sphere of influence," and "We chose a hybrid school so that we would remain the main influence in our children's' lives, they would have more time with siblings learning together, we would be able to partner with teachers in their education and have time to developed specific interests.")—"family" reasons were the most common "other" response. Additional "Other" reasons included religion more specifically (e.g., "Biblical world view," as stated by two respondents); specifics about homeschooling (e.g., "homeschooling support," and "No after school homework, as all is completed in school day"); and finally, general flexibility for nonacademic pursuits (e.g., "Flexibility for travel and lifestyle," and "schedule, my daughter is an elite gymnast").

Table 3. "Most important reason" parents reported for choosing a hybrid homeschool.

Answer options	Response percent
Other (please specify)	16.7
Better learning environment	13.0
Better education	13.0
Religious education	13.0
More individual attention for my child	8.7
More meaningful opportunities for parental involvement	5.8
Better preparation for college	5.1
Greater respect for my rights as a parent	5.1
Smaller class sizes	4.3
More attention to the unique needs of my child	3.6
Other students would be a better influence on my child	2.9
Less time wasted during the school day	2.9
Better student discipline	1.4
Would prefer full-time private school, but the hybrid is more affordable	1.4
Improved student safety	0.7
Greater sense of community	0.7
Other parents would be more concerned about their children's education	0.7
More tutorial and other supplemental learning services than at a five-day school	0.7
More responsive teachers and administrators	0.0
Better teachers	0.0
Higher standardized test scores	0.0
Less gang activity	0.0
More extracurricular opportunities	0.0

The following tables reflect additional questions about what parents valued in their hybrid homeschools. Table 3 reports responses to: "What is the MOST important reason for choosing a hybrid school for your child(ren)?"

Here, the highest response was for "Other" reasons. As above, the most common "other" reasons were "family" related (e.g., "Spend more time with my children," or "More time to build relationship with my child"), followed by homeschooling support or other education-specific reasons (e.g., "Balance of school and homeschool," and "Looking for education model that promotes joy in learning vs. learning to pass a test"), and finally, general flexibility (e.g., "More opportunities for real life learning, for example, via field trips"). Several respondents also named specific religious or political reasons. A sample of "Other" responses are categorized in Table 4. Versions of some responses (particularly the religious and political answers) were given by multiple respondents.

Of the given response options, parents also said they valued a "better learning environment," "better education," and "religious education" as their next-most common choices. Those three answers ("better learning environment," "better education," and "religious education") account for 39.0% of the most important reasons these respondents choose hybrid homeschools. No respondent chose "More responsive teachers and administrators," "Better teachers," "Higher standardized test scores," "Less gang activity," or "More extracurricular opportunities" as their Most Important reason.

Respondents were also asked to name their top five reasons for choosing a hybrid homeschool. Those results are reported in Table 5.

Table 4. "Other" responses.

Type of reason	Respondents' stated reasons
Family	• Spend more time with my children • More family time • More time to build relationship with my child • More time at home with family • Retaining parental influence is our primary reason • Being the primary influence on our child during formative years • Family as primary sphere of influence
Homeschool support/ Education-specific	• Nontraditional environment classical, Catholic—creative, outside the box thinking • Homeschooling support • Balance of school and homeschool • Avoiding peer pressure at traditional school • The children as well as mom benefit from the rhythm of 2 days at school, 3 days at home. By being with other students those 2 days and being accountable to an outside teacher in addition to mom, my children get a better grasp of what personal responsibility is and apply it • Looking for education model that promotes joy in learning vs. learning to pass a test • Next best thing to homeschooling
Flexibility	• Schedule flexibility • More flexible schedule • More opportunities for real life learning, for example, via field trips • Flexibility for travel and lifestyle • Schedule, my daughter is an elite gymnast
Religious/Political	• Biblical world view (multiple respondents) • No Common Core (multiple respondents)

"Better learning environment" (60.0%), "Religious education" (55.2%), "Smaller class sizes" (48.8%), "Better education" (44.8%), and "Better preparation for college" (31.2%) were the next five reasons listed by respondents. The fewest respondents listed "Better teachers" (6.4%), "More extracurricular opportunities" (4.8%), "Less gang activity" (1.6%), "More tutorial and other supplemental learning services than at a five-day school (1.6%), or "Higher standardized test scores" (0.8%) as one of the top five reasons for choosing a hybrid homeschool.

Information and decision making

The survey asked respondents about the information they would value and seek out in deciding to choose a hybrid homeschool, much as did Kelly and Scafidi (2013). Table 6 reported responses to "What information about hybrid schools is most important in helping select the best private school for your child? (you may mark as many or as few reasons as applied to your situation)."

Table 5. "Top 5 reasons" parents reported for choosing a hybrid homeschool.

Answer options	Response percent
Better learning environment	60.0
Religious education	55.2
Smaller class sizes	48.8
Better education	44.8
Better preparation for college	31.2
More individual attention for my child	29.6
Greater respect for my rights as a parent	29.6
More meaningful opportunities for parental involvement	29.6
Less time wasted during the school day	24.0
Other (please specify)	24.0
More attention to the unique needs of my child	20.8
Other students would be a better influence on my child	19.2
More responsive teachers and administrators	16.0
Better student discipline	14.4
Greater sense of community	11.2
Improved student safety	8.0
Other parents would be more concerned about their children's education	8.0
Would prefer full-time private school, but the hybrid is more affordable	8.0
Better teachers	6.4
More extracurricular opportunities	4.8
Less gang activity	1.6
More tutorial and other supplemental learning services than at a five-day school	1.6
Higher standardized test scores	0.8

Table 6. Types of information sought by parents.

Answer options	Response percent
The curriculum (i.e., content of instructional areas) and course descriptions	80.8
The ratio of students per teacher and the average class size	72.8
Evidence that the school is accredited by a recognized school accrediting agency	71.2
Whether the private school teaches your religion or any religion with which you are comfortable	67.2
The percentage of students who are accepted and attend college	53.6
The duration of the school year and the hours spent by the students in class	44.0
Evidence that the private school teaches character education	43.2
Whether parents have access to the head of school to express any concerns	35.2
The years of teaching experience and credentials of the teachers at the school	33.6
The disciplinary policy of the school	31.2
The financial condition of the school	25.6
The graduation rate for students attending the school	24.8
The quality and availability of extracurricular activities	24.8
The average performance on standardized tests by students in different grades	24.0
The colleges attended by graduates of the school	24.0
The percent of teachers and administrators who leave from year to year	24.0
The frequency and nature of disciplinary actions	16.8
The governance of the school, including the members of the board of trustees	16.0
Whether computers are used effectively in classroom instruction	8.0
Whether students have access to tablet, laptop, and classroom computers	7.2
Other (please specify)	7.2
The racial, ethnic, and socioeconomic makeup of the student population	4.8

Most respondents desired information about a hybrid homeschool's curriculum, class size, and accreditation status, and its religious nature and success in sending graduates on to college. The five most-named responses

Table 7. "Most important" type of information sought by parents.

Answer options	Response percent
Evidence that the school is accredited by a recognized school accrediting agency	26.1
The curriculum (i.e., content of instructional areas) and course descriptions	25.2
Whether the private school teaches your religion or any religion with which you are comfortable	25.2
The ratio of students per teacher and the average class size	13.0
The percentage of students who are accepted and attend college	5.2
Other (please specify)	5.2
The graduation rate for students attending the school	1.7
The average performance on standardized tests by students in different grades	0.9
The years of teaching experience and credentials of the teachers at the school	0.9
Whether parents have access to the head of school to express any concerns	0.9
The frequency and nature of disciplinary actions	0.9
The disciplinary policy of the school	0.0
Evidence that the private school teaches character education	0.0
The quality and availability of extracurricular activities	0.0
The colleges attended by graduates of the school	0.0
The financial condition of the school	0.0
Whether students have access to tablet, laptop, and classroom computers	0.0
The percent of teachers and administrators who leave from year to year	0.0
Whether computers are used effectively in classroom instruction	0.0
The racial, ethnic, and socioeconomic makeup of the student population	0.0
The governance of the school, including the members of the board of trustees	0.0
The duration of the school year and the hours spent by the students in class	0.0

Table 8. Steps to gain information about hybrid homeschools.

Answer options	Response percent
Attend an information meeting for potential families sponsored by the school	95.1
Ask to tour the school	94.3
Review the school Web site in detail	94.3
Ask neighbors, friends, relatives, or other parents for their views	81.3
Review information available on the internet	74.0
Determine how convenient the private school is to where I live	67.5
Ask to observe a class being taught	45.5
Ask to meet privately with the head of school	42.3
Other (please specify)	4.9

Table 9. Parental confidence about obtaining information.

Answer options	Response percent
I believe I could typically get enough information to make an informed decision	91.9
Unless the hybrid school provided me additional information, I would be unable to make an informed decision	8.1

in this survey are the same as the top five in Kelly and Scafidi's survey (though in a different order). Six respondents found value in every type of information suggested, and nine added others, most often a desire to have a strong parental influence within the context of the school and classroom environments (i.e., "The systems in place to make the partnership between parent and teacher work well," and "The ability to have a say/influence in education. To be true partners with teachers at school"). One respondent also gave a more extensive answer to this question:

> While the checkboxes above are important, many other factors are equally important: non-traditional/living books/original source documents, creativity in teaching (sometimes best teachers not those with teaching degrees/less lecture, more student initiative), fewer worksheets, less time on assessments, more "real" learning, Socratic discussion, teaching students to think critically, not check boxes or just learn material for tests, opportunities for students to take courses of interest/use to them personally.

Respondents were then asked: "What information about hybrid schools is MOST important in helping select the best hybrid school for your child?" (Table 7).

When asked to name the most important information, only three answers were given by a quarter or more of respondents: accreditation, the content of the curriculum, and religious instruction. Eleven of the given responses were chosen by no respondents as the most important piece of information; in Kelly and Scafidi, all but two response options were selected at least once. Additional "other" responses focused on curriculum or the school environment, such as, "School's philosophy on education," "the feeling of family—all the teachers care about my children," "Their ability to support our Biblical world view," or "the authentic teaching of the Catholic faith."

Respondents were then asked about how they would obtain information about hybrid homeschools, how confident they felt about their ability to obtain it, and how a lack of information might affect their school choice: "What steps would you take to get desired information about hybrid schools? (you may select as many or as few steps as you choose)." (Table 8).

Over 90% of respondents said they would attend an information meeting, ask to tour the school, and/or review the hybrid school's Web site in detail. In Kelly and Scafidi, only asking to tour the school drew over 90% of respondents. Six respondents to this survey also said they would, for example, "review curriculum that is taught," "talk to existing families that attend the school," or "pray about it."

Finally, respondents were asked whether they felt they could obtain the information needed for an informed decision: "In your experience, how confident are you that you could obtain the desired information about possible hybrid schools to which you might send your children?" (Table 9).

Nearly all respondents (91.9%) believed they could get enough information for an informed decision, comparable to the 83.3% reported by Kelly and Scafidi.

Discussion

Family characteristics

Regarding characteristics of hybrid homeschool families, respondents are wealthier and more educated than those in Kelly and Scafidi, and the metropolitan area. They are typically married, White, and suburban, college educated, and earn over $100,000. Perhaps this is because hybrid school parents bear the financial burdens of both homeschool parents and private school parents: they must be available to homeschool their children and so have the means to support one homemaker (or have workplace flexibility), *and* pay tuition to the hybrid school.

These factors and school locations suggest that most of these students come from public school zones considered academically successful. In fact, financial factors may explain school locations in affluent settings. Many of the families in this survey come from full-time homeschooling environments. Although these parents are wealthier on average than the Kelly and Scafidi respondents, many lack the discretionary income for full-time private schools, especially if they have multiple children (as some parents noted). One school explicitly considers these middle-income families its target market, suggesting a growth area for such schools. Homeschool enrollment is rising, as is charter school enrollment, though charter school enrollment is not growing rapidly in suburban areas. Hybrid homeschools may be emerging to fill this demand for reasonably priced school choice in the suburbs.

The value of hybrid homeschool

Regarding what parents say they value in hybrid homeschooling, all four of Murphy's (2012) motivational frameworks seemingly appear. Parents of hybrid homeschool students tend to value overall school structure ("Better learning environment," "Better education," etc.) over specific school outcomes ("Higher standardized test scores," or "More extracurricular opportunities," for example). Relatively few respondents listed aspects such as "Better student discipline," "Improved student safety," or "Less gang activity," compared to respondents to Kelly and Scafidi. No respondent listed higher standardized test scores as one of their top three reasons for choosing a hybrid homeschool, and only one listed it in their top five. (This contrasts Zeehandelaar and Winkler, who classified 23% of parents "test score hawks.") In addition, while 29.6% of respondents to this survey listed "More meaningful opportunities for parental involvement" as a top five reason in this survey, only 4.6% did so for Kelly and Scafidi's less affluent subjects. Differential parental motivations accord with prior findings on the demand side of school choice, such as Harris and Larsen (2015) and Stewart and Wolf (2014) who find limited motivation from test scores as such; rather they prioritize their decision making along Maslow s hierarchy of needs. Parents of students coming from lower-performing schools focus on the more pressing needs of safety and basic skills, while the parents in the market for hybrid homeschools, having had those needs satisfied at home or through other schooling options, seek other things.

Finally, it is worth noting again that all of the schools in this study are explicitly religious. Eighty one point seven percent of respondents listed religion as a reason they chose their hybrid homeschool, but only 55.2% listed "Religious education" as a top five reason, and fewer than 20% of responding parents included religion as the most important reason for choosing one of these schools, suggesting that religious education, while important to these parents, may not be as important as other academic priorities. (In comparison, 29.7% of respondents listed "Religious education" as a top five reason for Kelly and Scafidi.)

Sources of information

Respondents reported that they would seek out and value information regarding a hybrid homeschool's curriculum, class size, accreditation status, religious nature, and success in sending graduates on to college. This accords with reported valued criteria by the private school parents surveyed by Kelly and Scafidi. However, the parents in this survey seem more definite in judging the "most important" evidence. They rated accreditation, curriculum, and religion as their top priorities more consistently than did the Kelly and Scafidi respondents. This may reflect the sample: unlike Kelly and Scafidi, all these schools are explicitly religious, and Georgia's HOPE Scholarship program provides college tuition and book funding for students graduating from accredited programs, perhaps sensitizing parents to accreditation (Kelly and Scafidi's respondents all come from public schools, per the regulations of Georgia's K–12 tuition tax credit program, and may have assumed their new schools were accredited). Both sets of parents seem confident that they could acquire sufficient information for informed decisions about their school options.

Conclusion

More work would be useful in drilling down into hybrid homeschool parents' responses to gain a fuller picture of their values and motivations. Interviewing hybrid homeschool parents (especially a group of parents who arrived from a variety of other schooling options) would be a fruitful next step. Other research paths would likely yield additional insight. For example, because of the explicitly religious nature of the schools here, one might expect a higher percentage of respondents to list that as a choice motivator.

It would be useful to know more about this aspect of parental choice (and if, for example, there is a gap between school founders/leaders, and the rest of the parent population at such schools). Second, several families indicated that they would prefer a full-time private education, but could not afford it. Given the large commitment even part-time homeschooling entails in terms of work and forgone income, these families likely differ qualitatively from those who would choose full-time homeschooling absent their hybrid schools. This suggests a third avenue: looking at the differences among the families who choose hybrid homeschools. Hybrid homeschools seem to attract families from a wide range of schooling experiences; parental motivations may vary depending on whether a family is choosing between a hybrid school versus full-time homeschooling, or a hybrid school versus a full-time private or public school. Finally, issues such as curriculum, finances, and the push/pull of the motivations suggested by Murphy (2012) would add to the discussion.

References

Bauman, K. J. (2002). Home schooling in the United States. *Education Policy Analysis Archives EPAA*, *10*(0), 26. doi:10.14507/epaa.v10n26.2002

Brobst. (2013). *Academic college readiness indicators of seniors enrolled in university-model schools and traditional, comprehensive Christian schools*. Retrieved from http://digitalcom mons.liberty.edu/cgi/viewcontent.cgi?article=1739&context=doctoral.

Cheng, A., Trivitt, J. R., & Wolf, P. J. (2016). School Choice and the Branding of Milwaukee Private Schools*. *Social Science Quarterly*, *97*, 362–375. doi: 10.1111/ssqu.12222

Coalition for Responsible Homeschooling. (2011). *Homeschooling numbers*. Retrieved from http://www.responsiblehomeschooling.org/homeschooling-101/homeschooling-numbers/

Farner, K. (2015, September 21). *GCPS considering cyber school for inclement weather periods*. Lawrenceville, GA: *Gwinnett Daily Post*.

Gaither, M. (2009). Home schooling goes mainstream. *Education Next*, *9*(1), 11–18.

Greene, J., Hitt, C., Kraybill, A., & Bogulski, C. (2015). Learning from live theater. *Education Next*, *15*(1), 54–61.

Greene, J., Kisida, B., & Bowen, D. (2014). The educational value of field trips. *Education Next*, *14*(1), 78–86.

Harris, D. N., & Larsen, M. (2015). *What schools do families want (and why)?* New Orleans, LA: Education Research Alliance for New Orleans and Tulane University.

Horn, M. (2009). The rise of altschool and other micro-schools. *Education Next*, *15*(3), 77–78.

Kelly, J. P., & Scafidi, B. (2013, November 13). *More than scores: An analysis of why and how parents choose private schools*. Indianapolis, IN: Friedman Foundation for Educational Choice.

Muldowney, H. M. (2011). *The operation of cooperative education for homeschooled children: The quality homeschool cooperative as a case study*. Retrieved from http://search.proquest. com/docview/909575665?accountid=11244

Murphy, J. (2012). *Homeschooling in America: Capturing and assessing the movement*. Thousand Oaks, CA: Corwin Press.

Nulty, D. D. (2008). The adequacy of response rates to online and paper surveys: What can be done? *Assessment & Evaluation in Higher Education, 33*(3), 301–314. doi:10.1080/02602930701293231

Ray, B. (2011). *2.04 million homeschool students in the United States in 2010*. Salem, OR: National Home Education Research Institute.

Ray, B. (2015a). African American homeschool parents' motivations for homeschooling and their Black children's academic achievement. *Journal of School Choice, 9*(1), 71–96. doi:10.1080/15582159.2015.998966

Ray, B. (2015b). *Research facts on homeschooling*. Salem, OR: National Home Education Research Institute.

Schneider, M., Teske, P., & Marshall, M. (2000). *Choosing schools: Consumer choice and the quality of American schools*. Princeton, NJ: Princeton University Press.

Stewart, T., & Wolf, P. J. (2014). *The school choice journey: School vouchers and the empowerment of urban families*. New York, NY: Palgrave Macmillan.

Trivitt, J. R., & Wolf, P. J. (2011). School choice and the branding of Catholic schools. *Education Finance and Policy, 6*(2), 202–245. doi:10.1162/edfp_a_00032

Wearne, E. (2013). *South Forsyth war eagles look to incubate hybrid learning*. Atlanta, GA: Georgia Public Policy Foundation.

Zeehandelaar, D., & Winkler, A. (2013). *What parents want: Education preferences and trade-offs*. Washington, DC: Thomas B. Fordham Institute.

African American Homeschool Parents' Motivations for Homeschooling and Their Black Children's Academic Achievement

BRIAN RAY

This study explores the motivations of African American parents for choosing homeschooling for their children and the academic achievement of their Black homeschool students. Their reasons for homeschooling are similar to those of homeschool parents in general, although some use homeschooling to help their children understand Black culture and history. The average reading, language, and math test scores of these Black homeschool students are significantly higher than those of Black public school students (with effect sizes of .60 to 1.13) and equal to or higher than all public school students as a group in this exploratory, cross-sectional, and explanatory nonexperimental study.

Federal researchers (Noel, Stark, & Redford, 2013; United States Department of Education, 2010) found that the rate of Black families homeschooling their children in the United States nearly doubled from 1999 to 2012. Very few studies, however, have focused on this population. The purpose of this study is to examine the motivations of African American parents for homeschooling and the academic achievement of their Black children.

REVIEW OF LITERATURE AND CONCEPTUAL FRAMEWORK

Commentators are noting a substantial rise in the percentage of Black parents who are intentionally seeking alternatives to conventional institutional public schools for a better education for their children (Hess, 2010; Lomotey, 2012). African Americans have been some of the most vociferous supporters over the past 10 to 15 years of public charter schools and vouchers as ways to improve their children's educational lot (Cooper, 2005; Williams, 2002). Some have even tried establishing schools for Black students only (Jesse, 2010). This comes 60 years after of the U.S. Supreme Court case *Brown v. Board of Education* (1954) that many hoped would be the key to equalizing academic opportunity or performance between Black and White children. Nevertheless, many researchers still find great disparities between White children and those of Color, specifically African Americans[1] (Ladson-Billings, 2006; Vanneman, Hamilton, Anderson, & Rahman, 2009), despite the fact that institutional racism might have notably subsided (Ogbu, 2004; Williams, 2011). Either way, many Black parents have become "active school choice-makers and educational advocates" (Cooper, 2007, p. 508).

One educational alternative to which African Americans are gravitating is parent-led home-based education, that most call homeschooling. "Homeschooling is a form of private education that is parent led and home based" and "homeschooling does not rely on either state-run public schooling or institutional private schooling for a child's education" (Ray, 2013, p. 324). Although homeschooling was quite common from colonial times until about 1920 (Ray, 2012), by the 1960s homeschooling was nearly extinct (Lines, 1991). Beginning in the late 1970s homeschooling began to grow again. It is estimated that by early 2014 there were about 2.2 million K–12 homeschool students in the United States (Noel et al., 2013; North Carolina, Department of Administration, 2013; Ray, 2011).

Entrance of Blacks to the Modern Homeschool Movement

Few studies have addressed the ethnic/racial makeup of the homeschool population despite the fact that homeschooling has spread well beyond White non-Hispanic families. African American children comprised about 8% (Noel et al., 2013, p. 17) of the roughly 2.04 million K–12 students homeschool students in the spring of 2010 (Ray, 2011). In 1999, only 1.0% of Black children were homeschooled but by 2010 it had grown to 1.9% (Noel et al., 2013; United States Department of Education, 2010). This suggests a 90% increase in the rate of Blacks home educating their children over the course of 11 years. This prominent increase is consistent with what I have been told by grassroots homeschool organizations across the nation. This trend raises important questions. Why are these parents choosing homeschooling when so many African Americans and others fought hard for so long to have access to and be mainstreamed into the nation's public schools? What impact might homeschooling have on their children's academic achievement? I now offer a synopsis of homeschool research, while the reader may find more extensive reviews by Murphy (2012) and Ray (2013).

Reasons for Home Educating

Most parents and youth decide to homeschool for more than one reason, and their reasons often change over time (Resetar, 1990). The most common reasons given by parents or youth for homeschooling are to (a) customize or individualize the child's education, (b) accomplish more academically, (c) use pedagogical approaches other than those typical in institutional schools, (d) enhance family relationships, (e) provide guided and reasoned social interactions with peers and adults, (f) provide a safer learning environment, (g) avoid negative experiences parents had in institutional schools, and (h) fulfill the parents' job to teach and impart a particular set of values, beliefs, and worldview to their children and not delegate such to schools (Murphy, 2012; Noel, Stark, & Redford, 2013; Stevens, 2001). Only a few studies to date have focused on African Americans and their motivations for homeschooling.

Taylor's (2005) view is that improved academic achievement and increasing expectations of every child are perhaps the key reasons for Blacks homeschooling. She wrote the following:

> The legacy of the *Brown* decision is not only about access but is also about options. We African Americans owe it to our children to exercise all available opportunities to ensure their current and future success. We are not obligated to wait for schools to improve to better meet our needs; we are obligated to provide our children the best education available. (pp. 131–132)

In addition, some scholars have found that race/ethnicity plays a part in motivations for Black homeschool parents (Fields-Smith & Williams, 2009). They studied 24 Black parents via surveys, interviews, and focus groups. Their report focused on two motivators for homeschooling. One was "the role of ethnicity" (p. 376). "Black families' perceived that institutional norms and structures within schools created destructive, rather than supportive, learning environments for children of African descent" (p. 376). The other motivator was the "role of religion" (p. 379). A majority of the parents reported that religious beliefs influenced their decisions to homeschool. Some "directly shared a belief that God had actually led them to home schooling" while others "described home schooling as a complement and support to their religious beliefs" (p. 379).

Fields-Smith and Kisura (2013) presented a synthesis of two independently conducted studies of Black homeschool families; one was situated in Metro-DC and the other in Metro-Atlanta. Their findings, based on interviews and focus groups, represent the voices of 54 Black home educators. The researchers focused on five "key motivations" (p. 272) in their article. These were the negative experiences in schools of a "culture of low expectations" (p. 272), the "plight of Black boys" (p. 274), the "psychology of safety" (p. 276), and the "positive opportunities in home education" (p. 276) of "imparting Black/African American culture" (p. 277) and "seeking a global perspective" (p. 277). Fields-Smith and Kisura (2013) theorized as follows:

> Thus, contrary to the negative depictions of black families as disengaged from the educational pursuits of their children, we evoke hooks' (1990) notion of *homeplace* to argue that black home education represents a vehicle of resistance to institutionalized racism and ideological mismatches between black families and their children's educational needs. (p. 266)

Mazama and Lundy (2013b) interviewed 74 Black parents, and surveys, focus groups, and participant observations of Black homeschooling parents were also done. Regarding reasons for homeschooling, they found that:

> most parents gave two to three reasons for homeschooling and rarely were they motivated by a single cause. Among the many reasons given was a concern with the quality of education provided in brick and mortar schools, which was most often mentioned (23.2%). . . . The second most cited factor was the desire to strengthen family bonds (13.7%), which respondents felt schools systematically undermined. (pp. 131–132)

The third most-mentioned reason (by 12.6 % of the subjects) was "the desire on the part of parents to teach their children using a curriculum that positively reflects African American culture" (p. 132) and the fourth most frequently cited motive (by 10% of the parents) was racism. Mazama and Lundy concluded that "many African American homeschoolers believe that a Eurocentric curriculum is bound to gravely interfere with their children's self-esteem and sense of purpose" (p. 123). Motivations for Blacks homeschooling have many similarities to others' motivations and some research suggests that other catalysts are also at play.

Learning and Academic Achievement

Numerous studies by various researchers have examined the academic achievement of home-educated students, and state departments of education have provided relevant data that show homeschool students score, on average, at the 65th to 80th percentile on standardized tests (Martin-Chang, Gould, & Meuse, 2011; Murphy, 2012; Oregon Department of Education,

1999; Ray, 1990a, 1994, 1997, 2000b, 2005, 2010, 2013; Rudner, 1999; Van Pelt, 2004; Wartes, 1990; Washington State Superintendent of Public Instruction, 1985). Some scholars have carefully posited that the elements of pedagogical practice, lifestyle, and philosophy of education that are generally systemic to home-based education might be causally related to higher academic achievement (Murphy, 2012; Ray, 1990b, 1997, 2000b, 2013). Several academics (e.g., Murphy, 2012; Ray, 2013) have cautioned, however, about the methodological limitations of many studies on homeschooling so that readers do not conclude that homeschooling necessarily causes high (or low) academic achievement. Most of the studies involve serious sampling challenges and have been descriptive and cross-sectional, and not causal-comparative, in design (Johnson, 2001; Murphy, 2012). Researchers have had considerable difficulty in getting guaranteed representative samples.

Social, Emotional, and Psychological Development

Many ask, related to homeschooling, "What about socialization?" "This question arises mainly in societies in which the institutionalization of children has been the norm for several generations of children between the ages of 6 to 18" (Ray, 2013, p. 327). Medlin's (2013) review of research found that homeschooled children are acquiring the "skills, behavior patterns, values, and motivations" they need to function competently as members of society:

> In fact, some indicators—quality of friendships during childhood, infrequency of behavior problems during adolescence, openness to new experiences in college, civic involvement in adulthood—suggest that the kind of socialization experiences homeschooled children receive may be more advantageous than those of children who attend conventional schools. (p. 293)

Medlin found there is no empirical evidence that adults who were home educated are somehow less able than those who attended institutional schools to civically interact with individuals and their communities. These research findings might make homeschooling more attractive to Black parents than if such discoveries were not available.

Adults Who Were Home Educated

Many also ask, "How will the home-educated person do once in the 'real world' of adulthood?" Research generally shows that the home educated are faring well, compared to those who attend public and private schools, in their adulthood (Belfield, 2005; Cheng, 2014; Cogan, 2010; Galloway & Sutton, 1995; Gloeckner & Jones, 2013; Jones & Gloeckner, 2004; Knowles & Muchmore, 1995; Montgomery, 1989; Murphy, 2012, p. 148; Oliveira, Watson,

& Sutton, 1994; Ray, 2004; Sheffer, 1995; Sutton & Galloway, 2000; White, Moore, & Squires, 2009; White et al., 2007). Some have wondered, for example, whether the homeschooled will learn to be tolerant or willing "to extend civil liberties to people who hold views with which one disagrees" (Cheng, 2014, p. 49). Surprisingly to many critics of homeschooling, Cheng found that "greater exposure to homeschooling is associated with more political tolerance" (p. 49). There is no research showing a negative long-term effect of homeschooling. These research findings might also make home education more attractive to African Americans than if they were not available.

Society in General and Black Community and Culture

Some posit that if millions of children and youth are individually benefitted by home-based education then the overall society will be benefitted (e.g., Howell, 2005; Ray, 2000a, 2013). Others argue that the common good is advanced if more parents put their children into state institutional schools rather than seek their children's good via home-based education (e.g., Apple, 2000, 2006; Evans, 2003; Lubienski, 2000). Apple (2000) and Lubienski (2000), for example, associate the choice to homeschool with self-ishness on the part of parents. Scholars have found, however, that Black homeschool parents are highly motivated to proactively seek out and construct the best education possible for their children, for their children's sake (Fields-Smith & Kisura, 2013; Fields-Smith & Williams, 2009; Mazama & Lundy, 2012, 2013a, 2013b; Taylor, 2005). There is still relatively little known about homeschooling by Black families. A few researchers have examined African Americans' motivations for homeschooling and apparently no findings on the academic achievement of Black homeschool students had been published when this study commenced.

Purpose and Hypotheses

The purpose of this study is to explore the academic achievement of Black homeschool students in Grades 4 to 8 as it relates to various demographic features of the students and their families and to better understand these parents' motivations for homeschooling. I expected to find that the academic achievement of Black homeschool students is, on average, higher than that of Black public school students (see reviews, e.g., Murphy, 2012; Ray, 2000b, 2005, 2013). I also hypothesized that Black homeschool students might not perform as well on these tests as do White homeschool students. Many studies and national data on the performance of Black students in public schools on standardized achievement tests show they score lower than Whites, regardless of the reasons for such disparity in public schools, than do Whites (Ladson-Billings, 2006; Vanneman et al., 2009). Also, the Black homeschooling community is relatively new and has not had as much time to develop support infrastructure. Finally, I hypothesized that Black parents' reasons for homeschooling are similar to those of homeschool parents in general, except that they might mention shielding their children from race-based or racist behaviors in public schools (Fields-Smith & Kisura, 2013; Fields-Smith & Williams, 2009; Mazama & Lundy, 2012, 2013a, 2013b).

METHODOLOGY

Design

This is a cross-sectional, explanatory nonexperimental study (Johnson, 2001), or causal-comparative study (Borg & Gall, 1989, p. 537). The design controlled for limited background independent variables for the homeschool and public-school students in a way that very few studies to date have accomplished. Data were collected from homeschool parents and students at only a single point in time. One objective of this study was to identify potential causal factors that produce differences in academic achievement, if any, between homeschool and public-school Black students.

Definitions

The following definitions are used in this study:

1. "Academic achievement" is the amount learned in terms of knowledge, skills, and understanding as measured by a well-recognized, nationally normed, standardized academic achievement test (e.g., *Iowa Tests of Basic Skills [ITBS]*).
2. A "homeschool student" is a person who is in Grades 4 to 8 during the collection of data (roughly ages 9 to 14) and engaged or enrolled in private home-based education and not enrolled in public or private institutional (or classroom) schooling for 50% or more of his or her Kindergarten through current grade-level years.
3. A "public school student" is a person in Grades 4 to 8 enrolled in public schooling/education when he or she took the academic achievement test and used by the publisher of the ITBS to establish norms.
4. "Black," when referring to the homeschool students in this study, is defined as the parent having identified the child as "Black (or African American)" and both of the child's parents were identified as "Black (or African American)" regarding race/ethnicity. Black and African American will be used interchangeably in the general narrative of this article.
5. "Parent was teacher certified" means the student's mother or father is/was (ever) certified to teach in any state.
6. "Degree of structure" in the practice of home education varies greatly. It ranges from a very unstructured learning approach, (e.g., centered upon

the child's interests or the eclectic nature of the teaching parent) to the use of a preplanned, structured, and highly prescribed curriculum. To the statement, "The main method used for this child during his/her school-age homeschool years has been," the parent made a choice from a 7-point list from *very unstructured* to *very structured*.

7. "Structured learning" is time during which the child is engaged in learning activities planned by the parent; it is a time during which the child is not free to do whatever he or she chooses. The parent was asked, "On average, how many hours per day has this child been engaged in structured learning?"

8. "Formal instruction" is considered to be planned or intentional instruction in areas such as reading, writing, spelling, or mathematics; it is done to meet a learning objective. The parent was asked at what age formal instruction began for this child.

9. Whether the child was eligible for "free or reduced lunch" (per United States Department of Agriculture, 2011) served as a proxy for the family's socioeconomic status.

10. "Cost per child" is the amount of money that was spent on the student's education during the conventional school year for textbooks, lesson materials, tutoring and enrichment services, testing, counseling, evaluation, and so forth.

The dependent variable of concern is academic achievement as measured by a nationally normed standardized academic achievement test (i.e., ITBS). The independent variables are type of education/schooling (i.e., public schooling, homeschooling), gender of student, and socioeconomic status.

Population and Sample

The homeschool target population was primarily middle-class Black homeschool families with students in grade levels 4 to 8 (roughly ages 9 to 14) who had been home educated at least half of their K–12 grade-level school years. I accessed these families via several sources. The main effort to gain participants was through a nationwide support organization that serves mainly African American homeschoolers, National Black Homeschoolers (NBH; only pseudonyms are used in this paragraph). NBH is the oldest and best-known support group of its kind. NBH promoted the study to their approximately 140 member families, and to a larger list that included anyone who wanted to be on it (e.g., of any race/ethnicity, pedagogical preference, or religious affiliation, and homeschooling or not). Any child in a member household or on the list who the parents might consider Black would qualify for this study only if the child fit the definition given previously (i.e., number 2). The study was also promoted to all Black homeschool support groups that could be identified as such. An announcement about the study also went out to statewide homeschool support organizations (e.g., those listed by The Teaching Home, 2014) and a well-known nationwide organization (Homeschool Protection Group) with a history of decades of support to the homeschooling community with respect to many topics; all of these lists, however, included a small minority of Black families. The study was also promoted to African American families via word of mouth. I contacted various support organizations and they assisted me in contacting Black homeschool families who might be willing to participate in the study. These organizations and I firmly encouraged any and all Black families to participate, regardless of their reasons for homeschooling, socioeconomic status, or prediction of how their children might score on a standardized academic achievement test.

It was very challenging to obtain the sample of the families and their 81 students who fit the criteria for this study. There were several reasons for this. First, it was not easy to find active support groups that included or focused on serving African American homeschool families. Second, homeschool families are difficult to study (e.g., resistance to engage with researchers) and wary of researchers (Murphy, 2012). They like privacy for their families and many of them have experienced criticism and harsh treatment from government agencies, academics, and others. From doing this study, my experience is that Black homeschool parents are extra cautious about participating. Third, I found out that restricting my study to only children for whom both of the child's parents identified as "Black" notably reduced the pool of who might participate in the study. Fourth, organizing and managing (from 50 to 3,000 miles away and on a very limited budget) volunteer local test managers in several cities to find and/or organize several homeschool families on a mutually agreeable testing date is a very demanding logistical challenge. As many studies by various academics have shown, homeschool parents and their children are not a group of people who are constrained by a regular daily schedule and a location that easily fit the needs of a researcher who wants to work with a group all at one time, rather than a single family or one student at a time. The resource-intensive nature of this kind of research likely explains why few have undertaken it.

Data from 1,299 Black public school students are used in this study as a comparison group. These data were provided by the publisher, Riverside Publishing, of the ITBS (i.e., the same test administered to the Black homeschool students). The publisher provided fully anonymized data for these public school students. The only variables included in the dataset that were usable for this study were test scores, grade level of test, sex, race/ethnicity, and whether the student's family qualified for free or reduced lunch. Table 1 provides some comparative demographic statistics for the homeschool and public school students.

TABLE 1 Some Comparative Information for the Black Public School and Black Homeschool Participants

Variable	Public school (total sample *n*)	Homeschool (total sample *n*)
Students gender, male/female	51.3%/48.7% (1287)	39.5%/60.5% (81)
Free or reduced lunch qualified	2.2% (1299)	40% (75)
Both parents Black?	Not available	100% (81)
Number children in family	Not available	mean, 4.15; median, 4.00
Household income	Not available	median = $70,000 (76)
		$0 to $29,999 less, 11.8%
		$30,000 - $89,999, 52.7%
		$90,000 or more, 35.5%
Family structure	Not available	Married couple, 98.8%
		Divorced parent, 1.2%

Instruments, Data, and Data Analysis

I administered a 39-item, paper-and-pencil survey to homeschool parents that was comprised of items on topics such as parent and family demographics, student's demographics and schooling history, approach to homeschooling, and parents' motivations or reasons for homeschooling their children. Most items were identical or similar to those used in previous studies (e.g., Noel et al., 2013; Ray, 2004). Family eligibility for free or reduced lunch (United States Department of Agriculture, 2011) served as a proxy for the socioeconomic status of the student's family. Data gathered by the survey were used to categorize homeschool students' families as "free lunch" or not and data provided by the test publisher (on students' "free lunch" status) were used for comparison with public school students.

The standardized academic achievement tests used in this study were the ITBS (Form A, levels 10–14, Grades 4 to 8). The ITBS is published by Riverside Publishing Company. The tests were designed and developed by University of Iowa professors to measure skills and standards important to growth across the curriculum in the nation's public and private schools. The ITBS reflects many years of test development experience and research on measuring achievement and critical thinking skills in reading, language arts, mathematics, science, social studies, and information sources. These tests are considered to have strong and well-established validity and reliability (e.g., Iowa Testing Programs, 2005). The tests were administered during the Spring of 2012 by publisher-qualified test administrators; all tests administered for the study were used in the data analysis (i.e., none were rejected).

The statistical software *IBM SPSS Statistics* (IBM SPSS, 2013) was used for data analysis. Students' scores on tests were handled in the following manner. Percentile equivalents were converted to z-scores (Hopkins, Glass, & Hopkins, 1987). Means were calculated and statistical tests were performed using z-scores (Loveless, 2002; Pattison, Grodsky, & Muller, 2013; Tallmadge & Wood, 1978; Yin, Schmidt, & Besag, 2006). Missing data were handled listwise. In many cases, simple descriptive statistics and frequencies were appropriate and reported. Stepwise regressions were used (with p-level-in set at .05 and p-level-out set at .10). Indicator (dummy) variables (Cohen & Cohen, 1983) were used for categorical variables such as free/reduced lunch, gender, and study group. Hopkins' (2000) qualitative terms regarding the amounts of variance explained in correlations or regressions were used; his terms that range from least to most significant are trivial, small, moderate, large, very large, nearly perfect, and perfect.

Assumptions, Limitations, and Delimitations

I assumed that parents accurately answered the survey items and that they were honest, that the publisher-qualified test administrators properly administered the academic achievement tests to the students, and that the data I received from the test publisher regarding public-school students were dependable. I was not studying whether these parents and their children were successful at meeting various objectives related to their reasons for homeschooling. This study is not designed to compare Black homeschool students' achievement to all homeschool students' achievement in preceding studies. It is not known whether this sample is representative of all U.S. Black homeschool families, and therefore one should be cautious regarding generalizations. There is no comprehensive list of Black homeschool families from which to sample. This should be considered as part of groundwork in studies of its type, focusing on African American families who homeschool.

This is a cross-sectional, explanatory nonexperimental study (Johnson, 2001) and controlled for limited background independent variables for the homeschool and public-school students in a way that very few studies (if any) have accomplished using the limited data available to any researcher with the fairly limited resources available. It is not an experimental study that is designed, in and of itself, to establish causation. This is meant to be a simple, efficient, and hardy study of Black homeschool parents and children. This study is designed to uncover findings that might develop perceptions and increase understanding of fitting policies or outlooks on homeschooling in general, and homeschooling by African Americans in particular.

A study such as this of Black homeschool students' academic achievement might raise the issues of stereotype threat (American Psychological Association, 2005) or the Hawthorne effect (McCarney et al., 2007). Regarding the stereotype threat, I have no reason to believe that either parents or test administrators said anything about the students' race or ethnicity in connection with the testing and I did not instruct them to do so. Further, if the effects of stereotype threat were involved in this study, it would mean that the Black homeschool students performed worse on the tests than their actual abilities would predict, and their scores would have been higher had there been no stereotype effect. Regarding the Hawthorne effect, it is possible that these homeschool students tried harder than normal because they were being tested or perhaps knew that they were part of a study. I have no evidence that the parents or test administrators promoted to the students that they were being watched, so to speak. I think, however, that it is also possible that public school students in the norming groups for standardizing the tests might have tried just as hard during their testing as did these homeschool students. It would be difficult to confidently argue one way or another on this point.

FINDINGS

Characteristics of Students and Families

The Black homeschool students in the study lived in 15 states and the District of Columbia. The 81 students were from all four regions of the United States, as follows: Northeast (8), Midwest (14), South (52), and West (7). Regarding gender, 39.5% of the students were male. Their mean age was 11.62 ($SD = 1.617$) and the mean grade level was 5.96 ($SD = 1.495$). The mean number of children, ages 21 and under, in the home was 4.15 ($SD = 2.122$). There were 5 or more children in 39.5% of the families. Eighty students were tested by a qualified test administrator other than the student's parent; one was tested by his/her parent who was a qualified test administrator. The mother was the main home-education teacher for 79 of the students. Some 11.1% of the mothers had ever been certified to teach in any state. Of the fathers, 12.7% had ever been certified to teach in any state. Table 1 provides some comparative demographic statistics for the homeschool and public school families and students.

Most studies find close to a one-to-one gender ratio among homeschool students (e.g., Ray, 2010; Noel, Stark, & Redford, 2013). Some have found homeschooled students to be somewhat disproportionately female (e.g., United States Department of Education, National Center for Education Statistics, 2010: 58% female), and this was consistent with the present study (60% female). Aud, Fox, and Ramani (2010) found that that 74% of Black public school 4th graders were eligible for free or reduced-price lunches in 2009. Perhaps, then, the present study included Black public school students who were, on average, from wealthier Black families than the general population of Black families with school-aged children.

Reasons for Homeschooling

Parents were asked to mark all the reasons or motivations why they homeschool their child. They chose from a list of 21 reasons, including other/another. Their responses are noted in Table 2. The six reasons most commonly selected for homeschooling by these Black parents were (a) the parents "prefer to teach the child at home so that you [parent] can provide religious or moral instruction" (chosen by 96.3% of parents), (b) "for the parents to transmit values, beliefs, and worldview to the child" (95.1%), (c) "develop stronger family relationships between children and parents and among brothers and sisters" (87.7%), (d) "to customize or individualize the education of each child" (80.2%), (e) "accomplish more academically than in conventional schools" (76.5%), and (f) "want to provide religious or moral instruction different from that taught in public schools" (76.5%).

Parents were also asked to list "the three main reasons, from [the] pevious [list], for homeschooling this child." Their responses are tabulated in

TABLE 2 Reasons Parents Gave for Homeschooling Their Children

Reason[a]	Frequency	Percent
1. Prefer to teach the child at home so that you can provide religious or moral instruction.	78	96.3
2. For the parents to transmit values, beliefs, and worldview to the child.	77	95.1
3. Develop stronger family relationships between children and parents and among brothers and sisters.	71	87.7
4. To customize or individualize the education of each child.	65	80.2
5. Accomplish more academically than in conventional schools.	62	76.5
6. Want to provide religious or moral instruction different from that taught in public schools.	62	76.5
7. Concerned about the school environment, such as safety, drugs, or negative peer pressure.	59	72.8
8. Provide guided and reasoned social interactions with youthful peers and adults.	56	69.1
9. Dissatisfied with the academic instruction at other schools.	43	53.1
10. Use pedagogical (teaching) approaches other than those typical in institutional schools.	43	53.1
11. Provide safety from teasing, ostracizing, bullying, and pressures toward premarital sex.	42	51.9
12. The child's parents should be his/her main teachers.	37	45.7
13. Give the child a more international perspective or worldview.	32	39.5
14. Give the child more instruction on African American/Black culture and history.	32	39.5
15. You are interested in a nontraditional approach to children's education.	32	39.5
16. You have another reason for homeschooling your child.	19	23.5
17. Desire to avoid racism in public schools.	16	19.8
18. Would prefer private school but cannot afford the tuition.	4	4.9
19. Child has other special needs that you feel the school can't or won't meet.	3	3.7
20. Child has a physical or mental health problem that has lasted 6 months or more.	0	0.0
21. Child has a temporary illness that prevents (him/her) from going to school.	0	0.0

[a]Parents were told: "Please mark all the reasons that apply for this child."

TABLE 3 Parents' Main Reasons for Homeschooling This Child

Reason[a]	Frequency	Percent
Prefer to teach the child at home so that you can provide religious or moral instruction.	38	46.9
Accomplish more academically than in conventional schools.	31	38.3
For the parents to transmit values, beliefs, and worldview to the child.	28	34.6
To customize or individualize the education of each child.	23	28.4
Want to provide religious or moral instruction different from that taught in public schools.	22	27.2
Develop stronger family relationships between children and parents and among brothers and sisters.	19	23.4
Concerned about the school environment, such as safety, drugs, or negative peer pressure.	18	22.2
The child's parents should be his/her main teachers.	15	18.5
You have another reason for homeschooling your child.	14	17.3
Provide safety from teasing, ostracizing, bullying, and pressures toward premarital sex.	8	9.9
Dissatisfied with the academic instruction at other schools.	7	8.6
Provide guided and reasoned social interactions with youthful peers and adults.	5	6.2
Give the child a more international perspective or worldview.	3	3.7
Use pedagogical (teaching) approaches other than those typical in institutional schools.	3	3.7
Desire to avoid racism in public schools.	2	2.5
Give the child more instruction on African American/Black culture and history.	2	2.5
Child has a physical or mental health problem that has lasted 6 months or more.	1	1.2
Would prefer private school but cannot afford the tuition.	1	1.2
You are interested in a nontraditional approach to children's education.	1	1.2
Child has a temporary illness that prevents (him/her) from going to school.	0	0.0
Child has other special needs that you feel the school can't or won't meet.	0	0.0

[a]Parents were asked to list the "three main reasons" for homeschooling this child. Responses are arranged in descending order according to reasons most frequently given by parents.

Table 3. The five reasons most often chosen were (a) "prefer to teach the child at home so that you can provide religious or moral instruction" (selected as one of the "three main reasons" by 46.9% of parents); (b) "accomplish more academically than in conventional schools" (38.3%); (c) "for the parents to transmit values, beliefs, and worldview to the child" (34.6%); (d) "to customize or individualize the education of each child" (28.4%); and (e) "want to provide religious or moral instruction different from that taught in public schools" (27.2%).

The five most frequently cited important reasons for homeschooling in a nationwide study (that included fewer options for reasons from which parents could choose but included all the reasons used in the present study,

Noel et al., 2013) were "a concern about environment of other schools" (91% of parents chose this), "a desire to provide moral instruction" (77%), "a dissatisfaction with academic instruction at other schools" (74%), "a desire to provide religious instruction" (64%), and "a desire to provide a nontraditional approach to child's education" (44%). In the same study, the four most important reasons chosen most often were "a concern about environment of other schools" (25%), "other reasons" (21%), "a dissatisfaction with academic instruction at other schools" (19%), and "a desire to provide religious instruction" (16%).

Academic Achievement

Following are descriptive statistics about and relationships between the homeschool and public school students' academic achievement.

HOMESCHOOL STUDENTS

Table 4 shows the mean z-scores for Black home-educated students on the reading total, language total, and mathematics total, and core subtest scores and according to the family's free/reduced lunch status. These Black homeschool students scored at or above the 50th percentile in reading, language, math, and core (i.e., a combination of reading, language, and math) subtests. By definition, the 50th percentile is the mean for all students nationwide. The effect sizes were .47 for reading ($SD = .81$), .15 for language

TABLE 4 Black Homeschool Students' Mean z-Scores and Corresponding National Percentile by Subject Area and Free/Reduced Lunch Status

Subject area	N	Mean z-score[a]	Standard deviation, z-score	Percentile, Black homeschool[b]	Percentile, national mean, all races/ethnicities
Reading total	81	.4694	.8071	68	50
Language total	81	.1473	.7731	56	50
Math total	81	.0096	.8533	50	50
Core[c]	81	.2080	.7742	58	50

	Free/Reduced Lunch?[d]	
	Yes	No
Reading total	66 (.4210, .7016, 30)	71 (.5400, .8563, 45)
Language total	46 (−.1037, .6527, 30)	63 (.3447, .7511, 45)
Math total	44 (−.1440, .8564, 30)	57 (.1678, .8254, 45)

[a]Following are a few z-score/percentile equivalents: $-0.67 = $ 25th percentile, $0.00 = $ 50th percentile, $0.20 = $ 58th percentile, $0.67 = $ 75th percentile, $1.00 = $ 84th percentile for comparative purposes.
[b]Percentiles in this study were converted from z-scores using http://www.measuringusability.com/pcalcz.php and confirmed with Hopkins, Glass, and Hopkins (1987). The corresponding percentiles shown in the table are the within-grade percentile scores for the nation that correspond to the given z-scores.
[c]Core is comprised of combination of a student's reading, language, and mathematics scores.
[d]Percentile (z-score, z-score standard deviation, sample size).

TABLE 5 Black Public School Students' Mean z-Scores and Corresponding National Percentile by Subject Area and Free/Reduced Lunch Status

Subject area	N	Mean z-score[a]	Standard deviation, z-score	Percentile, Black public school	National percentile mean, all races/ethnicities
Reading total	1240	−.6830	.8840	25	50
Language total	1238	−.5105	.9356	30	50
Math total	1219	−.5831	.9220	28	50
		Free/Reduced Lunch?[b]			
	Yes			No	
Reading total	24 (−.7207, .7074, 28)			25 (−.6821, .8879, 1212)	
Language total	18 (−.9107, .7032, 27)			31 (−.5016, .9384, 1211)	
Math total	17 (−.9657, .7295, 28)			28 (−.5741, .9244, 1191)	

[a]Following are a few z-score/percentile equivalents: −0.67 = 25th percentile, 0.00 = 50th percentile, 0.20 = 58th percentile, 0.67 = 75th percentile, 1.00 = 84th percentile for comparative purposes.
[b]Percentile (z-score, z-score standard deviation, sample size).

(s.d. = .77), .01 for math (s.d. = .85), and .21 for core (s.d. = .77), compared to the norm group of all races/ethnicities nationwide in public schools.

PUBLIC SCHOOL STUDENTS

Table 5 shows the achievement test scores of Black public school students in this study by subtest subject and whether or not the student's family qualified for free/reduced lunch. They scored at or below the 30th percentile in reading, language, and math. The simple effect sizes of Black homeschool students compared to Black public school students were, therefore, roughly 1.15 for reading, .66 for language, and .59 for math in the present study.

Explaining Variance in Achievement Scores

I examined which independent variables, if any, explain these Black students' achievement scores. First only the home educated were considered, and then both the homeschooled and public schooled were considered.

WITHIN HOMESCHOOLING SAMPLE

A regression analysis of the independent variables of (a) gender of the student, (b) certification status of the mother, (c) certification status of the father, (d) household income, (e) cost per child, (f) degree of structure, (g) amount of structured time, and (h) age at which formal instruction began on the dependent variables of the homeschool students' reading, language, and math scores revealed no significant relationships. That is, the eight independent variables were not statistically significantly helpful in explaining variance in homeschool students' achievement scores.

A regression analysis of the independent variables of (a) gender of the student, (b) socioeconomic status of the student's family (i.e., free/reduced lunch), and (c) type of schooling (i.e., public school or homeschool) on the dependent variables of reading, language, and math scores revealed some significant relationships. Regarding reading scores, only the type of schooling was a significant independent variable ($F = 118.84$; $df = 1,1211$; $p = .000$); gender and socioeconomic status were not significant. While controlling for gender and socioeconomic status, type of education explained 8.9% of the variance in the reading score, a moderate amount of variance. While controlling for the other variables, being homeschooled had an effect size of about 42 percentile points higher ($B = 1.13$; i.e., an effect size or change in z-score of 1.13; e.g., $-.68$ to .45).

All three independent variables explained significant amounts of variance in language scores. Type of education explained the most variance in language scores and the first regression model included only that variable ($F = 35.20$; $df = 1,1211$; $p = .000$). Model 2 included type of schooling and socioeconomic status ($F = 10.36$; $df = 1,1210$; $p = .001$). Finally, the third model, with type of schooling, socioeconomic status, and gender all included, was also significant ($F = 6.58$; $df = 1,1209$; $p = .010$). While controlling for gender and socioeconomic status, type of schooling accounted for a small amount of variance (2.7%) in scores, while socioeconomic status and gender explained even smaller amounts of additional variance (0.8% and 0.5%). That is, the homeschooled scored significantly higher than the public schooled while controlling for the other variables. While controlling for the other variables (i.e., regression Model 1), being homeschooled had an effect size of about 26 percentile points higher than if public schooled ($B = .65$; i.e., a change in z-score or effect size of .65; e.g., $-.51$ to .14).

Two of the three independent variables (type of schooling, socioeconomic status, and gender) explained significant amounts of variance in math scores. Regression analysis revealed that type of schooling explained the most variance in the math scores without other controls included in the model ($F = 30.74$; $df = 1,1211$; $p = .000$). Model 2 included type of schooling and socioeconomic status ($F = 8.16$; $df = 1,1210$; $p = .004$). While controlling for socioeconomic status, type of schooling accounted for a small amount of variance (2.4%) in scores, while socioeconomic status explained an even smaller amount of additional variance (0.7%). That is, the homeschooled scored significantly higher than the public schooled while controlling for the other variables. With the other variables controlled, being homeschooled had an effect size of about 23 percentile points higher than if public schooled ($B = .60$; i.e., a change in z-score or effect size of .60; e.g., $-.58$ to .02).

TABLE 6 Summary of Significance of Independent Variables in Explaining Test Scores

Subject area	Independent variable		
	Type of schooling	Socioeconomic status (SES)	Gender
Reading	Yes, Homeschooling[a]	No	No
Language	Yes, Homeschooling	Yes, Higher SES	Yes, Female
Math	Yes, Homeschooling	Yes, Higher SES	No

[a]"Yes" or "no" indicates whether the variable explained significant amounts of variance; if "yes," then the variable category associated with a positive effect is given.

Table 6 summarizes the regression analyses of the three independent variables of type of schooling, socioeconomic status, and gender of student on reading, language, and math test scores. Schooling type emerged as the only variable that explained variance in all three subject areas and type of schooling explained the most variance in these scores.

CONCLUSIONS AND CONSIDERATIONS

This project explores the academic achievement of Black homeschool students in Grades 4 to 8 as it relates to various demographic and educational features of the students and their families and to better understand these parents' motivations for homeschooling.

Motives for Homeschooling

These parents' reasons for homeschooling are similar to those of homeschool parents at large in the United States. In addition, some of them mentioned race/ethnicity-related issues as part of their many reasons for homeschooling. Findings in this study offer no solid evidence that this group of Black homeschoolers chose home-based education primarily to promote anything like Afrocentrism or its thinking to their children, even though Mazama and Lundy (2013b) found in their study that "many African American homeschoolers believe that a Eurocentric curriculum is bound to gravely interfere with their children's self-esteem and sense of purpose" (p. 123). Evidence from the current study, however, indicates that these parents are not promoting Afrocentric essentialism. It may be that they are generally satisfied with the American identity, and the "Euro-American cultural influence" in their children's lives (Adeleke, 2009, p. 177). At the same time, data from this study show that a notable portion of homeschool Black parents want their children to understand and appreciate the history and value of culture related to Africa and Black Diaspora, but there is no evidence that they are Afrocentric essentialists (Adeleke, 2009, pp. 179–180).

Academic Achievement

The Black homeschool students' relatively high achievement, compared to Black public school students, is consistent with decades of research on homeschooling in general (Murphy, 2012; Ray, 2013). Some will not be surprised since home-based education, by nature, generally involves pedagogical practices and an educational ecology that are conducive to improving achievement (Murphy, 2012; Ray, 1997, 2000b, 2005, 2013). For example, Murphy posited a theory of action—to understand and explain the generally high academic achievement by home-educated students—that includes what he called the three planks of parental involvement (i.e., much), instructional program (e.g., considerable flexibility, extensive two-way dialogue between adults and children), and learning environment (e.g., safe and orderly, less negative peer culture) that are advantageous compared to public and private institutional school settings.

The Black homeschool students in this study performed as well or better than the national average of public school students of all races/ethnicities, while Black students in public schools score, in general, far below average (Ladson-Billings, 2006; Vanneman et al., 2009). The scores of these Black homeschool students were far above the scores of the Black public school norm students in this study. Analysis revealed that having been home educated was a consistent, significant predictor of higher achievement while controlling for gender of student and the socioeconomic status of the student's family. Being homeschooled was associated with a positive effect size of roughly 42 percentile points in reading, 26 percentile points in language, and 23 percentile points in math.

Some studies on homeschooling have reported significant portions of the students out of grade level, on average, compared to institutional school students and their chronological ages. For example, Rudner (1999) found that "25% of home school students are enrolled one or more grades above their age-level public and private school peers" Assuming that the majority of fourth graders in institutional schools in the United States are 9 or 10 years old, and that for each additional grade level students are a year older than this range, only one student (1.2%) in the present study was tested at a grade level one year higher than his or her age and four (4.9%) were tested at a grade level one year lower than their age. No others were out of grade level, on average, compared to public and private school students. That is, these students' chronological ages largely matched their public and private school peers' ages for any given grade level and this finding might make this study more methodologically sound than some other studies.

Within the Black homeschool student group, the independent variables of (a) gender of the student, (b) certification status of the mother, (c) certification status of the father, (d) household income, (e) cost per child, (f) degree of structure, (g) amount of structured time, and (h) age at which formal instruction began had no significant effect on achievement scores. In addition, and especially considering the especially low academic performance of Black males in public schools, it is noteworthy to consider that gender was not a significant predictor of these homeschool students' achievement. Murphy (2012) and Ray (1997, 2000b, pp. 91–99) have considered whether there might be some traits of home-based education that ameliorate the effect of background factors that are consistently associated with lower academic achievement in public schools (e.g., household income). Factors that are typically systemic to homeschooling and related to improved achievement in institutional schools that were mentioned by one or both of these writers include plenty of one-on-one instruction, low student-to-teacher ratios, holding high and reasonable expectations of students, individualizing or customizing curriculum for each student, increased feedback from teacher to the student, extensive dialogue between adults and children, increased academic learning time (and/or academic engaged time), a safe and orderly learning environment, high parental involvement, and greater amounts of social capital among students and teacher.

Final Comments

I must revisit some important limitations of this study. It is a cross-sectional, explanatory nonexperimental study (Johnson, 2001), or causal-comparative study (Borg & Gall, 1989, p. 537). It controls for limited background independent variables for the homeschool and public school students in a way that very few studies (if any) have accomplished using the limited data available to any researcher with the fairly limited resources available. It is not possible to know whether the Black families and students in this study are representative of all Black homeschool families and students in the United States, thus one should be circumspect regarding generalizations. Data were collected from homeschool parents and students and public school students at a point in time and one of the objectives of this study, in which variables were not manipulated, was to identify potential causal factors that produce differences in academic achievement, if any, between groups of Black students.

This is a simple, parsimonious, and robust study of Black homeschool parents and children and there is good reason to believe that these families are demographically like other homeschool families, both Black and otherwise, in general in the United States. There is much overlap between these parents' reasons for homeschooling and those of homeschool parents in general. The Black homeschool students in this study are performing academically above the national average in general and well above Black public school students in particular. Advocates of Black children's education should consider whether homeschooling might have any useful or significant predictive power (Phillips, 2014; Wieman, 2014) regarding improving Black children's achievement. Although we still have little direct evidence on the academic achievement of Black homeschool students, this study's findings and past research on homeschoolers in general might help us develop insights and increase our understanding of effective policies or attitudes regarding homeschooling.

Quantitative researchers of homeschooling must know that they will face many confounding variables. They might also consider philosopher of education, Phillips' (2014), words here: "In the hard physical sciences, confounding variables can eventually be controlled, but in research in educational settings, these factors are not nuisances but are of great human and educational significance—control here removes all semblance of ecological validity" (p. 10). Erickson (1993) addressed the ecological invalidity he perceived in many attempts to control the variables in private schooling to compare it to public schooling, and Ray (1995, p. 23) used Erickson's analysis to address research on homeschooling. For example, it might be pointless to try to "control for" the amount of parental involvement (i.e., differences between classroom public schooling and homeschooling) in order to determine whether this variable has an effect on achievement because very high parental involvement is near the essence of homeschooling.

In reflecting on the value of predictive power in research, Wieman (2014, p. 13) put forward the following: "In cutting-edge research in the hard sciences, there are always things that one wants to know or measure or control that one cannot, just as there are in education research." I have tried to control some of the most significant variables in this study and I have tried to heed Wieman's warning that "it is possible to be too careful" (p. 13). I think it is likely that this study provides findings "that are reproducible and have adequate predictive power to advance the field" (Wieman, 2014, p. 14). More sound studies of Black families will provide even more predictive power about homeschooling and African Americans. Future research on Black homeschooling and achievement should consider tightly controlled designs that focus on high participation by some local homeschool groups. A matched-pair design could be very useful (c.f., Martin-Chang et al., 2011). Researchers must be prepared to develop personal and trusting relationships to gain participants and execute such studies.

Although some (e.g., Fineman, 2009) argue that the government should control all Black children's education and outlaw homeschooling, or that "individualized atomistic decisions to school one's [Black] child at home" are bad for "for the large scale transformations that are necessary" (Apple, 2006), two African American scholars have posited that "homeschooling may be the most provocative and courageous act of self-determination and resistance undertaken by blacks since the decolonization and civil rights movements of the 1950s, 1960s, and 1970s" (Fields-Smith & Kisura, 2013, pp. 279–280; see also, Ray, 2007).

NOTE

1. I use the terms Black and African American as synonyms in this article.

REFERENCES

Adeleke, T. (2009). *The case against Afrocentrism*. Jackson, MS: The University Press of Mississippi.

American Psychological Association. (2005, July 15). *Stereotype threat widens achievement gap: Reminders of stereotyped inferiority hurt test scores*. Retrieved from http://www.apa.org/research/action/stereotype.aspx

Apple, M. W. (2000). The cultural politics of home schooling. *Peabody Journal of Education, 75*(1 & 2), 256–271.

Apple, M. W. (2006, December 21). The complexities of Black home schooling. *Teachers College Record*, www.TCRecord.org. Retrieved from http://cockingasnook.wordpress.com/2007/03/07/michael-apple-expert-on-black-homeschooling-now/

Aud, S., Fox, M. A., & Ramani, A. K. (2010). *Status and trends in the education of racial and ethnic groups* (NCES 2010-015). Washington, DC: United States Department of Education. Retrieved from http://nces.ed.gov/pubs2010/2010015.pdf

Belfield, C. R. (2005). Home-schoolers: How well do they perform on the SAT for college admission? In B. S. Cooper (Ed.), *Home schooling in full view: A reader* (chapter 11, pp. 167–177). Greenwich, CT: Information Age Publishing.

Borg, W. R., & Gall, M. D. (1989). *Educational research: An introduction* (5th ed.). New York, NY: Longman.

Brown v. Board of Education, 347 U.S. 483 (1954).

Cheng, A. (2014). Does homeschooling or private schooling promote political intolerance? Evidence from a Christian university. *Journal of School Choice: International Research and Reform, 8*(1), 49–68.

Cogan, M. F. (2010, Summer). Exploring academic outcomes of homeschooled students. *Journal of College Admission*, Summer 2010, 18–25.

Cohen, J., & Cohen, P. (1983). *Applied multiple regression/correlation analysis for the behavioral sciences* (2nd ed.). Hillsdale, NJ: Lawrence Erlbaum Associates, Publishers.

Cooper, C. W. (2005). School choice and the standpoint of African American mothers: Considering the power of positionality. *The Journal of Negro Education, 74*(2), 174–189.

Cooper, C. W. (2007). School choice as 'motherwork': Valuing African-American women's educational advocacy and resistance. *International Journal of Qualitative Studies in Education, 20*(5), 491–512.

Erickson, D. A. (1993). Research that lies. *Private School Monitor, 14*(3 & 4), 1–19.

Evans, D. L. (2003, September 2). *Home is no place for school*. Retrieved from http://www.usatoday.com/news/opinion/editorials/2003-09-02-oppose_x.htm

Fields-Smith, C., & Kisura, M. W. (2013) Resisting the status quo: The narratives of Black homeschoolers in Metro-Atlanta and Metro-DC. *Peabody Journal of Education, 88*(3), 265–283.

Fields-Smith, C. & Williams, M. R. (2009). Sacrifices, challenges and empowerment: Black parents' decisions to home school. *Urban Review, 41*, 369–389.

Fineman, M. A. (2009). Taking children's interests seriously. In M. A. Fineman & K. Worthington (Eds.), *What is right for children? The competing paradigms of religion and human rights* (pp. 229–237). Burlington, VT: Ashgate Publishing Company.

Galloway, R. A., & Sutton, J. P. (1995). Home schooled and conventionally schooled high school graduates: A comparison of aptitude for and achievement in college English. *Home School Researcher, 11*(1), 1–9.

Gloeckner, G. W., & Jones, P. (2013). Reflections on a decade of changes in homeschooling and homeschooled into higher education. *Peabody Journal of Education, 88*(3), 309–323.

Hess, F. M. (2010, Fall). Does school choice "work"? *National Affairs, 5*, 35–53.

Hopkins, K. D., Glass, G. V., & Hopkins, B. R. (1987). *Basic statistics for the behavioral sciences* (2nd ed.). Englewood Cliffs, NJ: Prentice-Hall, Inc.

Hopkins, W. G. (2000). *A new view of statistics*. Internet Society for Sport Science. Retrieved from http://www.sportsci.org/resource/stats/.

Howell, C. (2005). Parental duty and the shape of the future. *Home School Researcher, 16*(3), 1–14.

IBM SPSS. (2013). *IBM SPSS Statistics, version 22*. Armonk, NY: IBM.

Iowa Testing Programs. (2015). *ITBS Research Guide*. Iowa City, IA: University of Iowa, College of Education. Retrieved from https://itp.education.uiowa.edu/ia/documents/ITBS-Research-Guide.pdf

Jesse, D. (2010). Ann Arbor elementary school's Black-only program violated state law, district policy. *The Ann Arbor News*. Retrieved from http://www.annarbor.com/news/ann-arbor-elementary-schools-black-only-program-violated-state-law-district-policy/

Johnson, B. (2001). Toward a new classification of nonexperimental quantitative research. *Educational Researcher, 30*(2), 3–13.

Jones, P., & Gloeckner, G. (2004, Spring). A study of home school graduates and traditional school graduates. *The Journal of College Admission, 183*, 17–20.

Knowles, J. G., & Muchmore, J. A. (1995). Yep! We're grown-up home-school kids—And we're doing just fine, thank you. *Journal of Research on Christian Education, 4*(1), 35–56.

Ladson-Billings, G. (2006). From the achievement gap to the education debt: Understanding achievement in U.S. schools. *Educational Researcher, 35*(7), 3–12.

Lines, P. M. (1991, October). *Estimating the home schooled population* (working paper OR 91-537). Washington DC: Office of Educational Research and Improvement, U.S. Department of Education.

Lomotey, K. (2012). Black educational choice: Race (still) matters [book review]. *Educational Researcher, 41*(6), 233–235.

Loveless, T. (2002). *How well are American students learning?* Washington, DC: Brookings Institute. Retrieved from http://www.brookings.edu/~/media/Files/rc/reports/2002/09education/09education.pdf

Lubienski, C. (2000). Whither the common good?: A critique of home schooling. *Peabody Journal of Education, 75*(1 & 2), 207–232.

Martin-Chang, S., Gould, O. N., & Meuse, R. E. (2011, July). The impact of schooling on academic achievement: Evidence from homeschooled and traditionally schooled students. *Canadian Journal of Behavioural Science (Revue canadienne des sciences du comportement)*, 43(3),195–202.

Mazama, A., & Lundy, G. (2012). African American homeschooling as racial protectionism. *Journal of Black Studies*, 43(7), 723–748.

Mazama, A., & Lundy, G. (2013a). African American homeschooling and the quest for a quality education. *Education and Urban Society*, 20(10), 1–22.

Mazama, A., & Lundy, G. (2013b). African American homeschooling and the question of curricular cultural relevance. *The Journal of Negro Education*, 82(2), 123–138.

McCarney, R., Warner, J., Iliffe, S., van Haselen, R., Griffin, M., & Fisher, P. (2007). The Hawthorne effect: A randomised, controlled trial. *BMC Medical Research Methodology*, 7(30), 1–8.

Medlin, R. G. (2013). Homeschooling and the question of socialization revisited. *Peabody Journal of Education*, 88(3), 284–297.

Montgomery, L. R. (1989). The effect of home schooling on the leadership skills of home schooled students. *Home School Researcher*, 5(1), 1–10.

Murphy, J. (2012). *Homeschooling in America: Capturing and assessing the movement*. Thousand Oaks, CA: Corwin, a Sage Company.

Noel, A., Stark, P., & Redford, J. (2013). *Parent and family involvement in education, from the National Household Education Surveys Program of 2012* (NCES 2013-028). Washington, DC: National Center for Education Statistics, Institute of Education Sciences, U.S. Department of Education. Retrieved from http://nces.ed.gov/pubs2013/2013028.pdf

North Carolina, Department of Administration. (2013). *North Carolina home school statistical summary*. Raleigh NC: Author. Retrieved from http://www.ncdnpe.org/documents/hhh238.pdf

Ogbu, J. U. (2004). Collective identity and the burden of "acting White" in Black history, community, and education. *The Urban Review*, 36(1), 1–35.

Oliveira (de Oliveira), P. C. M., Watson, T. G., & Sutton, J. P. (1994). Differences in critical thinking skills among students educated in public schools, Christian schools, and home schools. *Home School Researcher*, 10(4), 1–8.

Oregon Department of Education. (1999). *Home school data collection 1998-99, test scores by percentiles*. Retrieved from http://www.ode.state.or.us/teachlearn/specialty/home/1999/percen99.pdf

Pattison, E., Grodsky, E., & Muller, C. (2013). Is the sky falling? Grade inflation and the signaling power of grades. *Educational Researcher*, 42(5), 259–265.

Phillips, D. C. (2014). Research in the hard sciences, and in very hard "softer" domains. *Educational Researcher*, 43(1), 9–11.

Ray, B. D. (1990a). *A nationwide study of home education: Family characteristics, legal matters, and student achievement*. Salem, OR: National Home Education Research Institute.

Ray, B. D. (1990b, April 16–20). *Social capital, value consistency, and the achievement outcomes of home education*. A paper presented at the Annual Meeting of the American Educational Research Association, Boston, MA.

Ray, B. D. (1994). *A nationwide study of home education in Canada: Family characteristics, student achievement, and other topics*. Salem, OR: National Home Education Research Institute.

Ray, B. D. (1995, April 18–22). *Home education science learning in the context of family, neighborhood, and society*. A paper presented at the Annual Meeting of the American Educational Research Association, San Francisco, CA.

Ray, B. D. (1997). *Strengths of their own—Home schoolers across America: Academic achievement, family characteristics, and longitudinal traits*. Salem, OR: National Home Education Research Institute.

Ray, B. D. (2000a). Home schooling for individuals' gain and society's common good. *Peabody Journal of Education, 75*(1 & 2), 272–293.

Ray, B. D. (2000b). Home schooling: The ameliorator of negative influences on learning? *Peabody Journal of Education, 75*(1 & 2), 71–106.

Ray, B. D. (2004). *Home educated and now adults: Their community and civic involvement, views about homeschooling, and other traits*. Salem, OR: National Home Education Research Institute.

Ray, B. D. (2005). A homeschool research story. In B. S. Cooper (Ed.), *Home schooling in full view: A reader* (pp. 1–19). Greenwich, CT: Information Age Publishing.

Ray, B. D. (2007). On Blacks choosing home-based education. *Home School Researcher, 17*(4), 9–12.

Ray, B. D. (2010). Academic achievement and demographic traits of homeschool students: A nationwide study. *Academic Leadership Journal, 8*(1). Retrieved from http://contentcat.fhsu.edu/cdm/compoundobject/collection/p15732coll4/id/456.

Ray, B. D. (2011). *2.04 million homeschool students in the United States in 2010*. Salem, OR: National Home Education Research Institute. Retrieved from http://www.nheri.org/research/nheri-news/homeschool-population-report-2010.html.

Ray, B. D. (2012). Evangelical Protestant and other faith-based homeschooling. In J. C. Carper & T. C. Hunt (Eds.), *Praeger handbook of faith-based schools in the United States, K-12* (chapter 12, pp. 123–135). Santa Barbara, CA: Praeger, ABC-CLIO.

Ray, B. D. (2013). Homeschooling associated with beneficial learner and societal outcomes but educators do not promote it. *Peabody Journal of Education, 88*(3), 324–341.

Resetar, M. A. (1990). An exploratory study of the rationales parents have for home schooling. *Home School Researcher, 6*(2), 1–7.

Rudner, L. M. (1999). Scholastic achievement and demographic characteristics of home school students in 1998. *Educational Policy Analysis Archives, 7*(8). Retrieved from http://epaa.asu.edu/ojs/article/viewFile/543/666

Sheffer, S. (1995). *A sense of self: Listening to homeschooled adolescent girls*. Portsmouth, NH: Boynton/Cook Publishers, Heinemann.

Stevens, M. L. (2001). *Kingdom of children: Culture and controversy in the homeschooling movement*. Princeton, NJ: Princeton University Press.

Sutton, J. P., & Galloway, R. (2000). College success of students from three high school settings. *Journal of Research and Development in Education, 33*(3), 137–146.

Tallmadge, G. K., & Wood, C. T. (1978, January). *ESEA Title I evaluation and reporting system: User's guide* (Rev. Ed.). Mountain View, CA: RMC Research Corporation.

Taylor, V. (2005). Behind the trend: Increases in homeschooling among African American families. In B. S. Cooper (Ed.), *Home schooling in full view: A reader* (pp. 121–133). Greenwich, CT: Information Age Publishing.

The Teaching Home. (2014). *Statewide homeschool organizations.* Retrieved from http://www.teachinghome.com/

United States Department of Agriculture. (2011). Food and nutrition service, child nutrition programs—income eligibility guidelines. *Federal Register, 76*(58), 16724. Retrieved from http://www.fns.usda.gov/cnd/Governance/notices/iegs/IEGs11-12.pdf

United States Department of Education, National Center for Education Statistics. (2010). Table 40. Number and percentage of homeschooled students ages 5 through 17 with a grade equivalent of kindergarten through 12th grade, by selected child, parent, and household characteristics: 1999, 2003, and 2007. Homeschooling in the United States: 2003; and Parent Survey (Parent:1999) and Parent and Family Involvement in Education Survey (PFI:2003 and PFI:2007) of the National Household Education Surveys Program. Retrieved from http://nces.ed.gov/programs/digest/d11/tables/dt11_040.asp.

Van Pelt, D. (2004, March). The choices families make: Home schooling in Canada comes of age. *Fraser Forum,* 15–17.

Vanneman, A., Hamilton, L., Anderson, J. B., & Rahman, T. (2009). *Achievement gaps: How Black and White students in public schools perform in mathematics and reading on the National Assessment of Educational Progress, statistical analysis report* (NCES 2009-455). Washington DC: U.S. Department of Education.

Wartes, J. (1990). Recent results from the Washington Homeschool Research Project. *Home School Researcher, 6*(4), 1–7.

Washington State Superintendent of Public Instruction. (1985). *Washington State's experimental programs using the parent as tutor under the supervision of a Washington State certificated teacher 1984-1985.* Olympia, WA: Author

White, S., Moore, M., & Squires, J. (2009). Examination of previously home-schooled college students with the Big Five model of Personality. *Home School Researcher, 25*(1), 1–7.

White, S., Williford, E., Brower, J., Collins, T., Merry, R., & Washington, M. (2007). Emotional, social and academic adjustment to college: A comparison between Christian home schooled and traditionally schooled college freshmen. *Home School Researcher, 17*(4), 1–7.

Wieman, C. E. (2014). The similarities between research in education and research in the hard sciences. *Educational Researcher, 43*(1), 12–14.

Williams, A. T. (2002). Black Alliance for Educational Options: Promoting school choice and empowering parents through No Child Left Behind. Retrieved from http://www.mackinac.org/4853

Williams, W. E. (2011). *Race and economics: How Much can be blamed on discrimination?* Stanford CA: Hoover Institution at Leland Stanford Junior University.

Yin, R. K., Schmidt, R. J., & Besag, F. (2006). Aggregating student achievement trends across states with different tests: Using standardized slopes as effect sizes. *Peabody Journal of Education, 81*(2), 47–61.

Homeschooling Is Not Just About Education: Focuses of Meaning

Ari Neuman and Oz Guterman

ABSTRACT
This article explores the meanings parents attribute to homeschooling. The literature reveals two main approaches to this subject: a view of homeschooling as a pedagogical practice and a holistic perspective. Employing qualitative methodologies, we administered in-depth interviews to 30 mothers who engaged in homeschooling in Israel, in order to gain a better understanding of what homeschooling meant to them. Analysis of the interviews indicated that the participants attributed diverse meanings to homeschooling. These represented many themes, which were gathered into four super-themes: control, lifestyle, family, and child. The first two themes were emphasized more often than the latter two.

Introduction

This article explores the meaning that parents attribute to homeschooling (also known as elective home education). The literature reveals two main approaches to research on this subject: that of homeschooling as a pedagogical practice and a holistic view of the practice. We begin with a brief description of homeschooling, followed by a review of research on what homeschooling means for parents who choose this form of education for their children. We conclude that in order to fully understand the spirit of homeschooling, it is necessary to consider not only the pedagogical characteristics but additional aspects as well.

Homeschooling is a practice in which parents do not send their children (of any age) to school but educate them at home instead. This is not a new practice; in fact, throughout most of human history, parents bore the responsibility for their children's education. Most children were taught in their parents' homes or, alternatively, learned a trade as apprentices. The few schools that existed served a very small percentage of the population of children, usually those expected to fulfill religious positions or children of the well-to-do. In most cases, these schools focused on teaching different aspects of religion and not general studies (Avner, 1989; Cai, Reeve, & Robinson, 2002; Hiatt, 1994; Tyack, 1980).

In response to the Industrial Revolution, governments established public schools, enacted mandatory education laws, and over time assumed the responsibility for the education of children (Evangelisti, 2013; Gaither, 2009; Hiatt, 1994; Wilhelm & Firmin, 2009).

Over the past few decades, parents have begun to share the responsibility for their children's education, and some have even chosen to refrain from giving an external organization charge, instead assuming full responsibility for the educational process by means of homeschooling.

The beginnings of this trend in the United States appeared in the 1970s; at that time reports indicated that about 13,000 children were being home-schooled. Nowadays, 40 years later, the estimated figure is 2 million, and in Britain the estimate is about 80,000 (Blok & Karsten, 2011; Davis, 2006; Ray, 2011). In Canada it is about 50,000, in Australia about 30,000, and in France about 2,800 (Authors, 2013).

This rise in the number of children being homeschooled may stem from increasing dissatisfaction among parents with the conventional school system, coupled with growing public legitimation of this practice. In many places in the world, and particularly in the United States and England, parents who educate their children at home and meet certain criteria are deemed to be fulfilling the mandatory education laws.

In Israel, homeschooling is a relatively recent development; it began only two decades ago. However, it is a growing practice. The number of home-schooling families in Israel is estimated to be about 400, whereas two decades ago it was only about 60 (Authors, 2013).

The state of Israel, which was established about 70 years ago, did not undergo a process of transferring the responsibility for education from parents to the state. From the time it was established, the state was responsible for the education of children. However, parents in Israel today are allowed to homeschool their children, provided they obtain permission and meet certain criteria. Thus, the processes currently under way in many Western countries have affected Israel as well.

In light of the recent development of homeschooling in Israel, the legal aspects of the practice were established over the past decade, most notably in a 2006 and later a 2009 directive from the Ministry of education's director general, which stated, among other things, that

homeschooling applications will be approved in cases where the parents present a very well-established worldview which rejects education in a school, or cases in which there are exceptional, special and extreme circumstances for which the Ministry of education allows an exemption from the Mandatory Education Law for parents who request that their child not study in a recognized educational institution, on the condition that the child is found to be receiving a systematic, satisfactory education in his home. (Ministry of Education, 2009, our translation and emphasis)

The Ministry of education also established a unit to supervise and assist parents who homeschool their children. These legal arrangements paved the way for families who wish to homeschool to do so legally, but because they were instituted only a few years ago, the number and percentage of home-schooled children are relatively small compared with other Western countries. However, as noted, the practice is growing rapidly. To date, there is no organized, updated database on the characteristics of families that home-school in Israel.

These developments represent a universal trend that is not specific to any one country: Parents are once again assuming more responsibility for their children's education. In particular, they are becoming more involved in the public school system, sending their children to special or private schools, or taking them out of the school system and educating them at home.

Parallel to the increase in the number of families that educate their children at home, many studies have been conducted to examine this practice. Some have compared the scholastic achievements of children of the same age who attend schools and those who are educated at home. Others have examined the reasons why parents choose homeschooling (Bates, 1991; Marchant & MacDonald, 1994; Neuman & Aviram, 2003; Ray & Warez, 1991; Rothermel, 2005; Snyder, 2013) and the processes that occur within the homeschooling context (see Kunzman & Gaither 2013, for a recent review of the literature on this subject).

Researchers have attempted to distinguish between different homeschool-ing groups, such as structured and unstructured homeschooling (the latter is also referred to as unschooling; Authors, 2016; Kunzman & Gaither, 2013; Ray, 2011; Rothermel, 2011). Homeschoolers who advocate structured schooling follow a defined curriculum, usually of their own design; propo-nents of unstructured homeschooling teach varying subjects, based on the wishes of the children, without any external dictates. These parents provide a supportive environment for learning and enable the children to choose the materials, methods of learning, and times for study (Aurini & Davies, 2005; Barratt-Peacock, 2003; Bertozzi, 2006; Kunzman & Gaither, 2013; Ray, 2011; Rothermel, 2005).

However, many researchers of homeschooling treat this practice as an educational and pedagogical option, a means by which parents can be involved in the schooling as well as the education of their children. It is one of several possible alternatives to the conventional education system, which also includes public and private schools. Studies based on such a pedagogical perspective examine the curriculum, the role of the child in the learning process, scholastic achievements, teaching methods, teaching materials, and other educational aspects of homeschooling (Bagwell, 2010; Coleman, 2010; Gaither, 2008, 2009; Kunzman & Gaither, 2013; Meighan, 1997; Ray & Warez, 1991; Rothermel, 2002, 2004).

Although this is the most popular approach today, it is also possible to extend the study of homeschooling beyond the purely pedagogical aspects. Neuman & Aviram (2003) described two approaches to the study of homeschooling, one purely pedagogical and the other holistic. The pedagogical study of homeschooling considers the educational aspects of this practice; in comparison, the holistic approach examines the ways in which homeschooling affects the lifestyle of those who choose this practice. Literature based on this approach has viewed homeschooling as life changing; accordingly, it has examined factors such as the influence of homeschooling on parents and children, family structure, marriage, career and employment, income and standard of living, attitudes and perceptions regarding life, the daily life routine, as well as other life-changing factors (on this, see also Ray, 2013).

The pedagogical and the holistic approaches to homeschooling examine different questions. In this article we further broaden the holistic approach by examining what homeschooling means, beyond a pedagogical option, to parents who practice it.

In the majority of cases, homeschooling is a choice that parents make for their children; therefore, it is important to understand the focuses of the meaning that parents attribute to this choice, or in other words what it is that they choose.

The pedagogical choice of homeschooling is well documented in the literature. However, it is also important to understand the other components involved in the decision to homeschool. Accordingly, the present research sought to answer the following question: "When you say *homeschooling*, what do you mean?"

Method

In this study, we used a qualitative participant-centered research methodology based on the hermeneutic phenomenological approach (Glense & Peshkin, 1992; Maykut & Morehouse, 1997; Shkedi, 2011).

Hermeneutics takes its name from the Greek god Hermes, who interpreted the messages of the gods for humans. Accordingly, this type of research involves giving meaning to texts, language, and behavior by means of interpretation; it is one of the most common qualitative approaches used in the social sciences (Bleicher & Bleicher 1980). This approach enables us to examine a phenomenon as it is experienced and perceived by the subject participating in it (the phenomenon). In order to understand the phenomenon, the researcher must first understand the significance that the subject ascribes to the phenomenon (Jorgensen, 1989; Willis, 1991). Consequently, a study such as this must collect descriptions of experiences and their significance.

In-depth interviews with the participants is one of the central tools in such a study (Creswell, 1995). The aim of the present research was to gain a better understanding of the meaning of the practice of homeschooling to parents who engage in it; therefore, the hermeneutic approach, which focuses on interpretations of reality, was appropriate.

Participants

The research population comprised 30 mothers who engaged in homeschooling in Israel. The research participants volunteered to participate in response to a notice distributed among homeschoolers by various means. Only two families refused to participate in the research; thus, it can be assumed that refusal to participate did not affect the research results.

The families that were interviewed lived in urban and rural communities in northern and central Israel. All of the participants were from the Jewish sector and led a nonreligious or traditional (not Orthodox) Jewish lifestyle. In all of the families, the fathers were the main breadwinners and the mothers spent most of their time at home with the children.

The number of children in each of the participating families ranged from one to five, with an average of 2.13 children ($SD = 1.03$). In each of the families there was at least one child who was between 6 and 12 years old. The average education of the mothers was 15.94 years ($SD = 2.80$). For the sake of comparison, in Jewish families in Israel, the average number of children is 2.3 and the average education of mothers is 14.6 years (Central Bureau of Statistics, 2016a, 2016b).

The choice to interview the mothers was based on the fact that usually the mother is the family member responsible for homeschooling. In addition, in our study, the mothers were the family members who spent the most hours every day with the children and were involved in the teaching and learning processes.

As noted in the Introduction, there is a lack of data on the people who homeschool in Israel. Therefore, it was not possible to establish the extent to which the interviewees were representative of all homeschoolers in the country. It is hoped that the development of research in this field will result in the creation of a larger base of reliable data about the characteristics of this group.

Procedure

In accordance with the gender of the interviewees, all of the interviewers in this research were also women. Some were students and others were not. The interviewers participated in a 1-day training seminar in which they learned how to carry out the interview. The training included general knowledge about homeschooling and knowledge about qualitative research methods in general. In addition, each of the interviewers practiced administering the specific interview chosen for this study, followed by reflection.

The interviewers arranged a convenient time for the mothers and went to their homes. The interviewees received an explanation about the study and signed an informed consent form required for their participation in the study. They were then interviewed for 60–75 min. The interviews were semistructured: The mothers were asked a series of structured questions, the purpose of which was to understand the significance of homeschooling for the interviewees ("Tell me about your family," "What is homeschooling for you, for your family, and for your children?" "Tell me about the way you conduct your homeschooling"). In addition, the interviewers conducted an open conversation on the subject of homeschooling in order to elicit indirect comments by the interviewees regarding the meaning of homeschooling for them. All of the participants responded to all of the questions asked during the interview. The interviews were recorded and then transcribed.

Analysis

We used ATLAS.ti software to analyze the transcripts. One researcher carried out the analysis. The results of this analysis were then reexamined critically by a second researcher, according to Lincoln and Guba's (1986) peer debriefing. Disagreements between the two researchers were resolved through discussion.

The first stage of analysis involved analysis of the relevant texts and their division into themes. Each segment of the text was linked to a theme whose name reflected the written content. Sometimes a number of segments of text were linked to the same theme. At the end of this stage, every relevant segment of text had been linked to a theme, which in effect generated a list of themes.

In the next stage, a mapping analysis was carried out that examined whether there were links between various themes and identified common denominators. During this stage of the analysis, some of the themes were divided into groups of super-themes with a common denominator.

We did not include the themes related to homeschooling as a pedagogical choice in the analysis, and they are not described in this article, as these were beyond the defined focus of the research question.

Results

In this section, we present our analysis of the interviews with the parents regarding the question of what homeschooling meant to them. The results are presented according to the super-themes that arose from the analysis.

Sense of family

Some of the respondents noted that the family setting was right for their children and homeschooling was natural for them and the rest of the family in terms of both the children's lifestyle and their style of learning. They referred to homeschooling, or to the child who stayed with the family and did not go to school, as a natural "default":

> Children should live in the community within their own family. Ideally, it's really a tribe, but that doesn't happen in our world. We live far from our family, but the default is that children live within the family, the family lives within the tribe or community, [so there] has to be a really good reason to [go to] school. (Participant 9)

Moreover, Participant 8 said, "In our family at any rate, the home is the center; the siblings are the center and the parents are in the center—not society."

These comments suggest that sending children to school is not the right thing to do; it contradicts the desired lifestyle within the family and the desirable learning style, which is also within the family.

> I try to recall how I used to feel about school. Now it's a lot about this being our family, how we live; we can't do it any other way. The thought that [name withheld] would go to school and we would start the day—every day—without him, that my daughters would be away from him all day and he would have all sorts of personal and social experiences without most of his time being at home seems very unusual to me and it doesn't fit at all with our life. (Participant 8)

The child in the center

For some of the research participants, homeschooling was a means of placing the child at the center of their activity. In order to enable children to express their full potential and grant them rights regarding decisions that affected their own lives, the parents chose to educate them at home and not send them to school. This enabled each child to discover and explore his or her interests at the pace and in the manner suited to the individual.

This theme of the child in the center might be considered a pedagogical characteristic of homeschooling (in this respect, see Dewey, 1986, 1997, who emphasized the importance of teaching according to the child in the center). However, in the present research, it emerged as part of the holistic aspect of homeschooling.

From this perspective, the theme of the child in the center referred to the parents' perceptions of the process that their children underwent within the family, that is, the experience of reconciling family-related collectivist values with individualist values that focus more on personal desires. Who knows better what is right for the children—the collective (in this case, represented by the parents as the family leaders) or the individuals themselves? For example, "Homeschooling is enabling and opens things up compared with conventional education, which closes things ... because homeschooling puts the child in the center" (Participant 7) and "These are not my goals; how can I decide? These are their goals, their life ... I can't decide that this is the right way for them just because it's good" (Participant 12).

Responsibility, choice, and control

The analysis of the interviews indicated that homeschooling enabled parents to take responsibility for their lives and those of their children. Furthermore, the choice of homeschooling gave the parents a great deal of responsibility— which parents who sent their children to school transferred to the education system. For example, "He is my child and I am responsible for him. I am with him and I take responsibility for everything good or bad that happens to him. I think this happens less among conventional parents" *(Participant 14) and* "The whole idea of giving someone else the responsibility for education is difficult for me" (Participant 21).

Some of the parents referred to this responsibility as a hardship, especially with respect to the responsibility to provide the child's learning needs.

> If something doesn't go right you have to figure out what the difficulty is yourself ... I think the parents of children who attend school also have responsibility, but here it is very great and sometimes it is heavy and stressful ... there's the calm, but on the other hand there are the questions when you don't go with the mainstream: What am I doing to my child and is it right and do I really understand him? (Participant 4)
>
> It's not freedom and ... I always said that it means taking responsibility ... There is no freedom here. I constantly have to be responsible for this and for that, for the transportation of that one, and for the studies of the other one, so there's no freedom here. (Participant 24)

Moreover, Participant 22 said, "I have a lot of responsibility. There's nobody else to blame. For better or for worse."

The findings also revealed that parents felt that homeschooling enabled them to exercise their right of choice regarding their and their children's lives.

> I don't want to just let life pass by, especially not as a person who chose this [i.e., homeschooling]. It's not something that someone dictated; I chose it. It gives me a great deal of strength when I talk with you; it reinforces what I wanted to say. I chose it every time. Even when it was very difficult, I said, "This is our choice." (Participant 2)

It is interesting that the parents also referred to the subject of choice and responsibility when they spoke about their children's education. They tried to give their children the same sense of responsibility for their actions and for exercising their right to choose. Participant 5 said, "It is also a responsibility to come to the pool with all your swimming gear. There's no way around it— this is your responsibility, not mine. I always say that."

Furthermore, some of the interviewees referred to homeschooling as a way for them to control different aspects of their and their children's lives, for example, by reducing the volume of stimuli the children and adults were exposed to in the contemporary world:

> I'm talking about this class of 40 children in a room. It's much more. I think that our world today is full of much more stimulation than we were meant to tolerate, and we succeed a bit in distancing ourselves from this and surviving with a slightly lower level of stimuli ... and this [overstimulation] attacks us every time from every direction. I can take only as much of this as I want and am capable of, and the children can, too. (Participant 9)
>
> I am really very happy not to be part of that consumer culture. I'm not interested in stores. I go to the mall once in a while and I don't find anything. It doesn't interest me and really isn't part of my world. (Participant 17)

The parents reported on their control over the study materials the children were exposed to:

> I control the study material. For instance, sometimes [name withheld] comes home with stories, first-grade reading material that shocks me. For instance, there was a story ... a boy whose hair was very long and everyone laughed at him and said he had girl's hair and he should get a haircut. So in the end he got a haircut. The moral of the story was that he should cut his hair, understand? (Participant 6)
>
> It's the films we choose with messages that we definitely accept even though every movie with acceptable messages always has small things. We are ultimately the main figures that they look up to, if you can say that. We have the right to express an opinion and it is our opinion, and not the film itself that determines things in the end. (Participant 7)

They also spoke about their control over the children's actions and their social encounters.

> There's more parental supervision over what the children do. We are around all the time so they have much less opportunity to behave inappropriately, you could say, without us or someone else knowing about it and dealing with it. (Participant 15)
>
> The kids at school, especially the older ones really frighten me. I also see some cases with children and I know what it leads to; they influence each other. I know I have a child who is very sociable and cares a lot about his peer group, so he wouldn't be one of those who'd sit on the sidelines. (Participant 7)

Development of self-awareness

The respondents noted that in addition to the process of choice they experienced and the effort to control different aspects of their lives, their deviation from conventional conduct in terms of education and in other ways and the need to examine each decision and question the choices customarily accepted by the majority of the population promoted their development of self-awareness and awareness in general.

> You are in a constant process. If you do something everyone else does, you don't stop and think whether it is right for you. You are already into something, part of a herd that walks forward in a given direction. But when you choose your own way, you have to constantly think about whether it's the right path. You constantly check whether it's right for you. Whatever happens to the children, you suddenly think perhaps that's not right. I think this is very good, because it develops awareness and self-awareness about things in general. (Participant 1)

Moreover, Participant 3 said, "It's infinite learning; I really love it, it appeals to me and I discover a lot about myself through it. There were times when I really felt stuck."

In this respect it is also interesting that the parents referred to the principle of developing self-awareness and self-knowing when they spoke about their children's education: "We enable them and encourage them to ask themselves such questions and to connect to themselves" (Participant 15).

Change in lifestyle

Some of the respondents noted that the choice of homeschooling had paved their way to other choices, which changed their lifestyle. For them, the step of leaving the education system was significant and subsequently led them to other changes in other realms of their lives.

For the parents, the act of questioning a practice that is so widely accepted in society—sending one's children to school—and their success in developing an alternative led to the questioning of other practices that they had previously taken for granted. Thus, for example, they reexamined the issue of nutrition and began eating healthier food than they had in the past, reconsidered the subject of feeding infants and chose to breastfeed rather than use formula, and also redefined the meaning of career for themselves in ways that were not necessarily consistent with the accepted perception of the concept but were suitable for them personally.

> Since then our world has been completely different. There's no comparison. It's a completely different world. It's as though we said we'd start with one change and now it is never ending. Things change all the time. It's really like that, as though the moment we thought about something so significant as the education of our children, the mandatory education law, what most people do and so forth ... from

the moment we questioned this and survived it, everything became open for questioning. (Participant 28)

It was the sort of thing that we then also began to eat healthier food and become aware of the whole issue of nutrition in quite an extreme way—what we wouldn't eat at all and what we would—things we hadn't thought about much. It came together, our entire life changed radically. (Participant 8)

Slowing down the pace of life

For some of the respondents, homeschooling was a way to slow down the pace of life for them and the other members of the family. These parents described their lifestyle before they began homeschooling as stressful and fast moving and spoke positively about the slower pace of life and reduction of stress that accompanied their choice to educate the children at home.

They noted that unlike in the past, the morning hours had become calm hours when there was no obligation to get up at a set time and hurry to get the children to school. The slower pace was also notable at other times of the day, when it was now unnecessary, for instance, to rush to get home from work before the children and prepare their lunch or tidy the house in the evening and go to bed on time in order to get up early the next morning, and so forth and so on. For example, "Life is much more relaxed than having to get up in the morning, get the kids organized …" (Participant 13) and "So my life was much more intensive before. What happened to me was that suddenly I had the opportunity to slow down the pace" (Participant 1).

> Stopping the race of getting the kids to school at seven, the earliest possible for the preschool, rushing to work in order to get back 1 minute before having to pick them up, coming home and managing to get everything necessary done with the children and tidy the house—and all that in the little time that remained—and then going to bed thinking about what you had to do tomorrow, stopping that crazy pace. (Participant 11)

Finally, Participant 4 said, "In most cases, you don't have to set out at eight in order to get to an activity. The earliest is nine, and we try to make it later. So our entire life is much more relaxed."

Slowing down the pace enabled the parents to be more relaxed and calm and to devote more and higher quality time to the children. It also enabled the children to learn at their own pace, not the one dictated by others; the respondents considered this a more correct way of learning. The underlying assumption of this view is that learning occurs when the learner is "available"; thus, learning at the student's pace is effective because it takes place when he or she is receptive—at the right time, place, and manner for the individual. Participant 9 said, "First of all, I am much more thoughtful and calm and take things much easier. Sometimes I just watch the children discover, find, and learn to understand all sorts of things by themselves." Another participant said,

> There's learning that is incidental. In other words, in school it is very selective. I think that when children are available to absorb what they are taught, they learn, and when they aren't, they don't. At home things are more open, more open to the children's pace. (Participant 24)

Living in the present

Some of the respondents said that for them, the transition to homeschooling was actually a shift to living in the present rather than the future, that is, dealing with things occurring now and not just planning ahead.

> At this point in time I'm not constantly thinking about the future. On the one hand, I am looking ahead; but on the other hand, I'm living my life in the present, and I tell the children it's great to live in the present with the difficulties, because that's our situation right now. (Participant 2)

Moreover, Participant 23 said, "The thing is that we live as though it's mainly about what's happening here."

Rectifying past experiences of school

For some of the respondents, homeschooling represented an effort to rectify their own past experiences with school. These experiences included, among others, being forced to study material that they were not ready for, a daily schedule dictated by the school that was not suitable for them, and a sense that the school "looked right through them."

As a result of these negative experiences, which one of the respondents even defined as a "trauma," the parents took action to protect their children from such experiences by educating them at home.

> I know that the age of readiness for reading and writing is up to age 9. That means it ranges from age 5 to age 9, and there are some children, like [name withheld], who are interested and some like [name withheld], who knows all the letters and can read but even now doesn't enjoy it. It doesn't interest her enough for her to sit down and learn, so I don't push her. I know it will come one day when she's ready. The day will come. As a child I suffered terribly from this and I said I would never force my children. I sort of knew there wasn't any alternative, but then I discovered there was one. (Participant 1)
>
> It bothered me terribly that I had to study for a test and I had to hand in papers and I had to get up in the morning—all that obligation. I didn't live near the school; every day I had to get on a bus terribly early, and the whole thing was so difficult for me ... so actually we began the homeschooling as a result of our pain and our past. (Participant 8)

Table 1. Focuses of meanings.

Super-Theme	Themes
Control (14)	Responsibility (9), choice (3), and control (5)
Family (5)	Sense of family (5)
Child (6)	The child in the center (6)
Lifestyle (15)	Development of self-awareness (4), general change in lifestyle (3), slowing down the pace (10), living in the present (3), and rectifying past experiences of school (3)

Note. Numbers in parentheses represent the number of interviewees who mentioned each theme or super-theme.

Table 1 presents the themes that arose from the interviews divided into four super-themes. The numbers in parentheses represent the number of interviewees who mentioned each theme or super-theme. As can be seen, more parents referred to the super-themes of control and lifestyle than to those of family and child. All of the themes and super-themes describe holistic aspects of homeschooling, that is what homeschooling meant to the parents in terms of control, family, children, and lifestyle.

Conclusions and discussion

As noted in the introduction to this article, much research has examined homeschooling as a pedagogical practice intended to replace the conventional school system. Accordingly, it has focused on different pedagogical aspects of homeschooling, such as the curriculum, the learning process, scholastic achievements, teaching methods, teaching materials, and others.

However, the findings of the present research indicate that for the interviewees, homeschooling was much more than a pedagogical choice and was associated with diverse aspects of their daily lives.

It is therefore important to understand the significance of the parents' choice of homeschooling beyond the pedagogical aspect. For some homeschoolers, the choice of schooling at home is a life-changing decision (on this, see also Lees, 2014). Therefore, it is important to understand the significance of homeschooling for families not only from an educational and pedagogical perspective but from a holistic one as well.

Focuses of meaning

Homeschooling can be considered through the focuses of meaning attributed to this practice. The most common focus—that of pedagogy—involves various aspects of the educational process. From this point of view, one might consider homeschooling as the ultimate form of parents' involvement in the education of their children (Authors, 2013).

However, an investigation of the meaning of homeschooling practice from a holistic perspective, as presented in this article, reveals additional focuses of meaning that may deepen our understanding of our question in the present research: "When you say *homeschooling*, what do you mean?" According to our research findings, the main focuses of meaning attributed to home-schooling are control (responsibility, choice, and control), lifestyle (development of self-awareness, change in lifestyle, slowing down the pace, living in the present, and rectifying past experiences of school), family (sense of family), and child (the child in the center).

Control and lifestyle seem to be more important to the interviewees than family or child, as more parents mentioned them (see Table 1). This may indicate that the aspects associated with lifestyle and parents' need for control are central in their choice of homeschooling and in many cases even more important than family and other aspects. It might suggest that homeschooling can be seen as part of broader social changes currently under way that also serve as the foundation for other changes in the field of education in general. In other words, the changes in lifestyle in the postmodern era and the greater control of individuals over their lives constitute the core of a change being expressed in numerous social and educational processes, of which homeschooling is only one.

The finding that home education is largely about lifestyle and control is consistent with the conclusions of earlier research in an American context (Stevens, 2001). In the following, we discuss the findings in order of their importance, beginning with control and lifestyle, followed by family and child.

Examination of homeschooling in terms of control and choice highlights these aspects of the lives of homeschoolers. It draws our attention to questions involving the relevance of the issue of control to other aspects of the lives of homeschoolers, the extent to which homeschoolers implement the principle of choice in other realms, the degree of conflict between the two principles—control and choice (e.g., giving a child choice means diminishing some of the parent's control)—and so forth. It would be interesting to use psychological questionnaires to examine the behavioral aspects of the ability of self-direction and compare parents who homeschool with parents who send their children to school.

Examination of homeschooling in terms of the lifestyle focus of meaning also highlights family life; it involves questions regarding the impact of choosing homeschooling on lifestyle, the pace of life, the relative speed and significance of the impact on different aspects of life, realms that are not affected by the choice of homeschooling, the cultural impact of homeschooling on lifestyle, and more.

The focuses on family and the role of the child are interrelated. Examination of the practice of homeschooling in terms of these focuses of meaning highlights the family life of the participants and gives rise to questions concerning the importance of family values in the lives of homeschoolers, the extent to which these values contradict those of socialization and culture, the role of the child in the family constellation, the resolution of contradictions between the values of family and of individuation that underlie the child-centered approach, and more. It would be interesting to conduct research on parents' views regarding the potential conflict between values of family and of individuation as well as how they try to resolve this contradiction in practice.

Mapping out homeschooling in terms of the focuses of meaning attributed to it (those presented here and others) could serve as a reflective tool for parents who educate their children at home. As such they could use it to examine the character of the homeschooling they practice in terms of the importance they ascribe to each of these focuses of meaning. They could also use this as a basis to trace their emphases on the different focuses of meaning from a historic perspective, from the period before they engaged in homeschooling (because they had no children or their children attended school) and other significant points in their family history to the present.

Such mapping might also serve as a planning tool: It could be used to determine goals for the future by examining the desired situation in terms of the relative importance of the different focuses of meaning.

Correspondingly, people outside of the family or group of homeschoolers, such as researchers and policymakers, might use such mapping to better understand the different families that engage in homeschooling based on the focuses of meaning they ascribe to the practice.

Historical development

As mentioned briefly earlier, education took place at home and was one of the aspects of daily life (education is life) throughout most of human history (Brubacher, 1947; Romi & Shmida, 2009). The Industrial Revolution created the necessity to separate education; it was organized to take place at set times in set places and was not connected to daily life.

Examination of the current trend of homeschooling as a pedagogical choice alone perpetuates this separation between life and education. From this point of view, the most significant difference between schooling and homeschooling is that in the latter, education takes place at home instead of school.

Examination of homeschooling from a holistic perspective reveals that it embodies a trend of returning to a practice of education as one of the aspects of daily life that accordingly takes place at home. The study of homeschooling as a pedagogical choice alone is liable to blur this important trend.

In comparison, research on homeschooling as a holistic practice may reveal the close relationship that has been reestablished between education and life. Even though the choice of the parents in the present research to educate their children at home might be considered a pedagogical one, for them homeschooling was more than that. It actually constituted a choice to restore the connection of aspects of learning and education with other aspects of life, such as issues of control, family, child, and lifestyle.

The separation of life from education was a characteristic of the modern period. However, the reconnection between life and education in present times represents a universal development occurring in many places in the Western world, including Israel. It is particularly important to consider this, as it reflects a dramatic change in the way children are being raised and educated. One sign of this is the steady increase over the past decades in the number of children being homeschooled in different countries throughout the Western world.

Figure 1 is a schematic description of our view of the development of the relationship between education and the home. Point A represents the period in which life and education were connected (most of history). Point B signifies the time of the Industrial Revolution, when education and instruction were separated from daily life and became the realm of the school. Point C represents a view of contemporary homeschooling as a purely pedagogical practice, an alternative to education at school. Point D illustrates the result of a holistic view of homeschooling, which reveals it as an attempt to return to the premodern period and reconnect home and education.

Naturally, in modern times (represented in the figure by Point B), there were situations when life and education were connected (as reflected in Dewey's theory of life and education). However, the prevailing trend was one in which education took place detached from life, both physically (in a different place, namely, the school) and in terms of content.

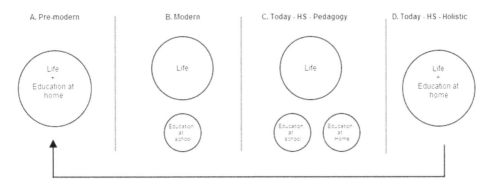

Figure 1. Schematic description of our view of the development of the relationship between education and the home. HS = homeschooling.

Limitations

In considering the conclusions of the present research, some limitations should be taken into account. Some researchers divide homeschooling into two streams: structured and unstructured homeschooling, also referred to as homeschooling and unschooling, respectively. This division is grounded in different pedagogical approaches, and the research described here did not examine the difference between parents who hold different pedagogical approaches. It would be interesting to conduct research from a holistic perspective that examines the differences between these two perspectives and the relevant focuses of meaning that each group respectively attributes to homeschooling.

It is reasonable to assume that the focuses of meaning identified among homeschoolers are associated with the length of time the families have engaged in this practice. For example, we would expect families that have educated their children at home for a long time to mention more aspects of lifestyle compared with newer homeschoolers. It might be interesting to design a follow-up study regarding the correspondence of the focuses of meaning attributed to homeschooling and the length of the participants' experience with homeschooling.

Home education is primarily a decision made by parents regarding their children, and therefore the current research explored the way in which parents perceive home education. It would be very interesting in future research to examine the same research question among homeschooled children.

The present research was based on the declarative level of information; the parents presented their attitudes and perceptions in response to questions about what homeschooling meant to them. The results of such research contribute interesting insights into the worldview of parents as expressed on the declarative level; however, they are still limited to the realm of perceptions and attitudes.

Further research should examine how this declarative level is expressed in practice, particularly with regard to the focuses of meaning that arose here. For example, it would be interesting to investigate the extent to which the principle of choice or the principle of child-centeredness is expressed in homeschoolers' lives.

In addition, the findings of the present research indicate that parents perceive homeschooling not only as a pedagogical act but as a holistic practice that affects many different aspects of their lives. This study was conducted using a qualitative methodology. It would be interesting to try to validate these findings using quantitative research methods by means of questionnaires. Our search did not reveal any questionnaires of this type; therefore, it would be interesting in further research to create such instruments. An investigation of that type would enable examination of the correlations between different items as well as their relative weights and perhaps help to construct a psychometric scale for interviews related to homeschooling.

It is important to consider the effect of mothers' characteristics on their views. Variables such as level of education, number of children, and degree of religiosity could have an impact on perceptions. In the present research, the sample size precluded examination of these aspects. It would be interesting in further research to study the way in which they affect the attitudes examined here.

Summary

The present research was intended to expand the set of concepts used in reference to homeschooling (also known as elective home education) and to support the argument that a holistic approach would reveal additional focuses of meaning to that of pedagogy. The study of homeschooling from a broader conceptual perspective may further the understanding of this practice, serve as a reflective tool, provide a planning instrument for homeschoolers, and reveal contemporary homeschooling as a return to earlier times when education and life were interwoven and took place primarily at home.

The present article is another step toward a growing understanding of the factors that underlie the rapidly increasing practice of homeschooling. This research may contribute to a broader perspective on homeschooling.

Exploring homeschooling beyond its pedagogical aspect enables us to look at it as part of much broader social trends and in the overall context of human existence in terms of life and education—its connection to our past, what it means in the present, and perhaps also how it might help shape our future.

Acknowledgments

Ari Neuman and Oz Guterman contributed equally to this article.

Funding

This research was conducted with assistance from the Center for Literacy at Western Galilee Academic College.

References

Aurini, J., & Davies, S. (2005). Choice without markets: Homeschooling in the context of private education. *British Journal of Sociology of Education*, 26(4), 461–474. doi:10.1080/01425690500199834

Avner, J. A. (1989). Home schoolers: A forgotten clientele? *School Library Journal, 35*(11), 29–33.

Bagwell, J. N. (2010). *The academic success of homeschooled students in a South Carolina technical college.* Lincoln: University of Nebraska.

Barratt-Peacock, J. (2003). Australian home education: A model. *Evaluation and Research in Education, 17*(2–3), 101–111. doi:10.1080/09500790308668295

Bates, V. L. (1991). Lobbying for the lord: The new Christian right homeschooling movement and grassroots lobbying. *Review of Religious Research, 33,* 3–17. doi:10.2307/3511257

Bertozzi, V. (2006). *Unschooling media: Participatory practices among progressive homeschoolers* (Doctoral dissertation). Retrieved from http://arvindguptatoys.com/arvindgupta/home schoolerssix.pdf

Bleicher, J., & Bleicher, J. (1980). *Contemporary hermeneutics: Hermeneutics as method, philosophy and critique.* London, UK: Routledge & Kegan Paul.

Blok, H., & Karsten, S. (2011). Inspection of home education in European countries. *European Journal of Education, 46*(1), 138–152. doi:10.1111/ejed.2011.46.issue-1

Brubacher, J. S. (1947). *A history of the problems of education.* New York, NY: McGraw-Hill.

Cai, Y., Reeve, J., & Robinson, D. (2002). Home schooling and teaching style: Comparing the motivating styles of home school and public school teachers. *Journal of Educational Psychology, 94*(2), 372–380. doi:10.1037/0022-0663.94.2.372

Central Bureau of Statistics. (2016a). *Collection of data on the occasion of International Women's Day 2015.* Retrieved from http://www.cbs.gov.il/reader/

Central Bureau of Statistics. (2016b). *Families in Israel: Data on the occasion of Family Day.* Retrieved from http://www.cbs.gov.il/reader/

Coleman, R. E. (2010). *Ideologues, pedagogues, pragmatics: A case study of the homeschool community* in *Delaware County* (Unpublished master's thesis). Ball State University, Muncie, IN.

Creswell, J. W. (1995). *Qualitative inquiry and research design: Choosing among five traditions.* London, UK: Sage.

Davis, A. (2006). Evolution of homeschooling. *Distance Learning, 8*(2), 29–36.

Dewey, J. (1986). Experience and education. *The Educational Forum, 50*(3), 241–252. doi:10.1080/00131728609335764

Dewey, J. (1997). *How we think.* New York, NY: Dover.

Evangelisti, S. (2013). Learning from home: Discourses on education and domestic visual culture in early modern Italy. *History, 98*(333), 663–679. doi:10.1111/hist.2013.98.issue-333

Gaither, M. (2008). *Homeschool: An American history.* New York, NY: Palgrave Macmillan.

Gaither, M. (2009). Homeschooling in the USA: Past, present and future. *Theory and Research in Education, 7*(3), 331–346. doi:10.1177/1477878509343741

Glense, C., & Peshkin, A. (1992). *Becoming a qualitative researcher: An introduction.* New York, NY: Longman.

Hiatt, D. B. (1994). Parent involvement in American public schools: An historical perspective 1642–1994. *School Community Journal, 4*(2), 27–38.

Jorgensen, D. L. (1989). *Participant observation: A methodology for human studies.* London, UK: Sage.

Kunzman, R., & Gaither, M. (2013). Homeschooling: A comprehensive survey of the research. *Other Education, 2*(1), 4–59.

Lees, H. E. (2014). *Education without schools: Discovering alternatives.* Bristol, UK: Policy.

Lincoln, Y. S., & Guba, E. G. (1986). But is it rigorous? Trustworthiness and authenticity in naturalistic evaluation. *New Directions for Program Evaluation, 1986*(30), 73–84. doi:10.1002/(ISSN)1551-2371

Marchant, G. J., & MacDonald, S. C. (1994). Homeschooling parents: An analysis of choices. *People and Education*, *2*, 65–82.

Maykut, P., & Morehouse, R. (1997). *Beginning qualitative research: A philosophic and practical guide*. London, UK: Falmer.

Meighan, R. (1997). *The next learning system and why home-schoolers are trailblazers*. London, UK: Education Heretic.

Ministry of Education. (2009). *Director general's circular*. Retrieved from http://cms.educa tion.gov.il/educationcms/applications/mankal/etsmedorim/3/3-1/horaotkeva/k-2009-8a-3-1-37.htm

Neuman, A., and R., Aviram. (2003). Home schooling as a fundamental change in lifestyle. *Evaluation and Research in Education 17*(2-3): 132–143.

Neuman, A., and O., Guterman. (2013). *Home schooling - the ultimate form of parental involvement in their children's education*. Paper presented at the 1st international confer-ence on Family, Education and Media in a Diverse Society, January 2013, in Jerusalem, Israel.

Neuman, A., and Guterman, O. (2016). Structured and unstructured homeschooling: a proposal for broadening the taxonomy. *Cambridge Journal of Education*, 1–17.

Ray, B. D. (2011). *2.04 million homeschool students in the United States in 2010*. Retrieved from http://www.nheri.org/HomeschoolPopulationReport2010.html

Ray, B. D. (2013). Homeschooling associated with beneficial learner and societal outcomes but educators do not promote it. *Peabody Journal of Education*, *88*(3), 324–341. doi:10.1080/0161956X.2013.798508

Ray, B., & Warez, J. (1991). The academic achievement and affective development of home-schooled children. In J. Van Galen & M. Pitman (Eds.), *Homeschooling: Political, historical and pedagogical perspectives* (pp. 43–61). Norwood, NJ: Ablex.

Romi, S., & Shmida, M. (2009). Non-formal education: A major educational force in the postmodern era. *Cambridge Journal of Education*, *39*(2), 257–273. doi:10.1080/03057640902904472

Rothermel, P. (2002). *Home-education: Rationales, practices and outcomes* (Unpublished doctoral dissertation). Durham, UK: University of Durham.

Rothermel, P. (2004). Home-education: Comparison of home-and school-educated children on PIPS baseline assessments. *Journal of Early Childhood Research*, *2*(3), 273–299. doi:10.1177/1476718X04046650

Rothermel, P. (2005). Can we classify motives for home education? *Evaluation and Research in Education*, *17*(2), 74–89. doi:10.1080/09500790308668293

Shkedi, A. (2011). המשמעות מאחורי המילים [*The meaning behind the words*]. Tel Aviv, Israel: Ramot.

Snyder, M. (2013). An evaluative study of the academic achievement of homeschooled students versus traditionally schooled students attending a Catholic university. *Catholic Education*, *16*(2), 288–308.

Stevens, M. (2001). *Kingdom of children: Culture and controversy in the homeschooling movement*. Princeton, NJ: Princeton University Press.

Tyack, D. B. (1980). *The one best system: A history of American urban education*. Cambridge, MA: Harvard University Press.

Wilhelm, G. M., & Firmin, M. W. (2009). Historical and contemporary developments in home school education. *Journal of Research on Christian Education*, *18*(3), 303–315. doi:10.1080/10656210903333442

Willis, G. (1991). Phenomenological inquiry: Life world perception. In E. C. Short (Ed.), *Forms of curriculum inquiry* (pp. 173–186). Albany: State University of New York.

Homeschool Parents and Satisfaction with Special Education Services

Albert Cheng, Sivan Tuchman, and Patrick J. Wolf

ABSTRACT

Homeschooling is controversial for a variety of reasons. One concern is whether families are sufficiently equipped to serve students with disabilities. We investigate this issue by assessing parental satisfaction with the special education services that their child is receiving in various educational sectors (e.g., homeschool, traditional public, public charter, and private). Using a nationally representative sample of U.S. households from the National Household Education Survey, we find that parents who homeschool are more satisfied than parents of children in traditional public schools and a variety of private schools with the special education services that they are receiving. Despite obvious selection bias in our sample, we view parental satisfaction as one of many important indicators for the quality of special education services. The results from this study suggest that homeschooling is a potentially beneficial option for serving students with disabilities, though additional research examining other student outcomes would be invaluable.

Participation in homeschooling and other forms of school choice have recently expanded. The population of children homeschooled, in particular, has approximately doubled from 1 to 2 million in the last decade, according to the U.S. Department of Education (2015). One reason for the expansion of school choice is to provide better educational opportunities for specific types of students, among them students with disabilities (Lake, 2010). School choice also disentangles a student's schooling options from their residential location, which may lead to inequalities in educational opportunities (Goldhaber, Lavery, & Theobald, 2015; Sass, Hannaway, Xu, Figlio, & Feng, 2012). Students with disabilities have historically only been placed in schools that offer specialized programs, limiting the schooling options that are available to them. For example, private schools are often viewed as a means to improve educational outcomes for students from disadvantaged backgrounds, yet just approximately 3% of students with disabilities attend them (U.S. Department of Education, 2015).

The potentially innovative nature and individualized attention students might receive in schools of choice, homeschool[1] being one such option, make them prime opportunities to improve outcomes for students with disabilities (Van Kuren, 2000). Currently, 18 different private school choice programs (e.g. vouchers, tax-credit scholarships, and education savings accounts) exist specifically for students with disabilities. Four of these programs are educational savings accounts, which allocate public dollars to parents who may then select educational services and materials, and are popular among many homeschooling families (The Friedman Foundation for Educational Choice, 2015). Moreover, students with disabilities are increasingly finding schools of choice through charters and open enrollment to better match students with educational environments and offerings.

Despite the potential promise for students with disabilities, school choice remains controversial. One source of concern is that schools of choice will not be able to accommodate and adequately educate these types of students. Most private school choice programs do not require that schools maintain Individualized Education Programs (IEP), which outline educational goals and services as well as other federal civil rights statutes, for their students (The Friedman Foundation for Educational Choice, 2015). Other critics suggest that parents who choose to homeschool are ill-equipped to provide necessary services for students with a disability (Van Kuren, 2000). Similarly, homeschool settings, private schools, and charter schools may not have the economies of scale that exist in traditional public school districts to accommodate the diverse needs of students with disabilities (Lake & Gross, 2012). There are also concerns over the potential for schools of choice to discriminate against students with disabilities during the enrollment process despite evidence that enrollment disparities may not be solely due to discriminatory practices (Setren, 2015; Winters, 2013, 2014; Zimmer & Guarino, 2013). Lastly, there is little research and knowledge about the effectiveness of various school choice options for students with disabilities, primarily due to data limitations. This limitation may preclude parents from making the most informed decisions about all available schooling options for their students with special needs.

There are additional points of contention regarding the ability for homeschooling to effectively serve students with disabilities. Due to the individualized instruction in a personalized setting that it offers, homeschooling may provide academic benefits for students with disabilities. Being highly familiar with their own children, parents can potentially implement curriculum and instruction that suits unique learning needs and produces greater educational gains. Still, it is not clear that homeschooling always provides benefits to students with disabilities. Parents may be ill prepared to implement pedagogical practices designed to improve outcomes for students with disabilities.

Without an interdisciplinary team made up of various educators, service providers, and parents like an IEP team, parents may struggle to make certain decisions about how to best educate their child. Given the little that is known about whether students with disabilities are amply served by home-schooling arrangements, Cook, Bennet, Lane, and Mataras (2013) issue a call for researchers to more rigorously examine the issue:

> Considering the limited research on the efficacy of homeschool for students with disabilities—physical disabilities, in particular—there is a need for further study on the effects of homeschooling on the academic, social, and quality of life of students with disabilities. Although there may be challenges to conducting true experimental research, more research using systematic and tightly controlled quasi-experimental designs is warranted. (p. 99)

It is in the spirit of this call that we conduct our analysis. We examine satisfaction with publicly provided special education services for parents with children in homeschooling arrangements, comparing those ratings with ratings of parents who receive special education services through traditional public, public charter, and private schools. We use a nationally representative sample of nearly 2,000 U.S. families who have children with special needs. To our knowledge, this is the first study to explore satisfaction with special education services across various school sectors while also doing so at scale and with a systematic sample.

Relevant literature

Serving students with disabilities

The focus on supporting the unique needs of students with disabilities in schools has continued to grow since the passage of Section 504 of the Rehabilitation Act of 1973, prohibiting discrimination against individuals and ensuring civil rights on the basis of disability. The legal protections for students with disabilities have grown out of the passage of the Education of All Handicapped Children Act (EAHCA) of 1975, the Americans with Disabilities Act (ADA) of 1990, and the Individuals with Disabilities Education Act (IDEA) in 1997, which was renewed in 2004. These federal laws entitled students with disabilities to a free and appropriate public education (FAPE), nondiscrimination, and equal access to public facilities and institutions. IDEA currently stipulates that students with disabilities be educated in the least restrictive environment, so that they may be educated, to the highest extent possible, with their nondisabled peers and still receive FAPE. The specifications for each individual student's educational goals, set of services, and learning environment are detailed in an IEP and are updated yearly by an IEP team composed of the student's family and school staff. As of the 2012–2013 school year, of the over 6.4 million students with an IEP, comprising 12.9% of the student population ages 3–21, 61% were educated in the general education classroom at least 80% of the time (U.S. Department of Education, 2015).

While IDEA clearly states the requirement that local education agencies (LEAs) "identify, locate, and evaluate" students with disabilities in private schools, as part of their child-find process,[2] there is no specific language in the law for students who are homeschooled by parental choice. Federal guidance regarding students who are homeschooled stipulates that state law determines whether homeschooled students with disabilities are considered to be in a parentally placed private school or not. This legal language does not guarantee an individual's right to services or entitlement to funds but does create a mechanism for parents who homeschool to have their student evaluated for and possibly receive some support for services.[3]

IDEA has increased funding and arguably improved services for students with disabilities in traditional public schools, but increased costs and rates of identification have not been followed with clear evidence that students have been better served over time. As various types of school choice (e.g., vouchers, charters, virtual schooling, and homeschooling) have expanded, the potential of school choice to improve services to students with disabilities has become more prevalent (Butcher & Bedrick, 2013; Cullen & Rivkin, 2003; Greene & Buck, 2010; Greene & Forster, 2003; Lindberg, 2016). By introducing mechanisms such as competition and improved student-school matches, private schools, homeschooling, and public charter schools may be positioned to improve services for students with disabilities (Greene, 2007). School choice offers students and parents various options for schooling based on their specific desires and needs. This premise is similar to that of special education, which aims to individualize student learning experiences in order to enable students to meet their unique academic, social–emotional, and postsecondary IEP goals. These two ideals meet when school choice programs enable students with disabilities and their families to choose the school that they think will best meet their educational needs (Lake, 2010).

School choice may also provide students with disabilities an opportunity to be fully included in the general education population at their schools. Private and charter schools often provide students with disabilities this opportunity because these schools lack the scale to provide self-contained special-education programs; some religious private schools do so due to their convictions about equity and inclusivity (Bryk, Lee, & Holland, 1993; Scanlan, 2008; Setren, 2015). Public schools have been legally required to place students with disabilities in the least restrictive environment since the EAHCA of 1975. Presumably, integrating students with disabilities into general education classrooms is beneficial, though research studying the effects of inclusion on academic achievement is limited (Cosier, Causton-Theoharis, & Theoharis,

2013; Daniel & King, 1997; Klingner, Vaughn, Hughes, Schumm, & Elbaum, 1998; Mills, Cole, Jenkins, & Dale, 1998; Rea, McLaughlin, & Walther-Thomas, 2002; Waldron & McLeskey, 1998). The biggest challenges to studying inclusive practices is the variation in the definition of inclusion as well as the continued issue in special education research of small sample size (Kalambouka, Farrell, Dyson, & Kaplan, 2005). Nevertheless, systematic reviews conclude that inclusive practices are at least as effective as less inclusive settings in improving academic achievement, particularly for younger students with disabilities. Gains in social and emotional skills are less consistently positive, however, in many of these studies (Freeman & Alkin, 2000; Kalambouka et al., 2005; Lindsey, 2007; Salend & Duhaney, 1999).

Homeschooling students with disabilities

In contrast, homeschooling often provides individualization without the inclusiveness that IDEA aims to achieve. The extant literature pertaining to students with disabilities who are homeschooled is extremely small and primarily relies on small samples of convenience and case studies. Even the most basic statistics about the true number of students with disabilities who are homeschooled, aside from those in homebound care, are difficult to ascertain given the challenge in assessing the number of students who are homeschooled on top of the various factors that influence the identification of students with disabilities (Dhuey & Lipscomb, 2011; Duffey, 2002).

Despite this research challenge, many studies document the reasons why parents opt to homeschool their child with disabilities. These parents elected to homeschool primarily because they were unsatisfied with the services and care that their previous school was providing or wished to shield their child from bullying, stigma, and other negative school interactions. These reasons are consistent both throughout the United States (Beck, Egalite, & Maranto, 2014; Duffey, 2002; Gaither, 2009; Hurlbutt, 2011; Shifrer, 2013; Westling, 1996), and in other countries (Arora, 2006; Kidd & Kaczmarek, 2010; Parsons & Lewis, 2010; Reilly, 2004; Reilly, Chapman, & O'Donoghue, 2002).

However, less is known about the effectiveness of special education services provided in homeschooling contexts. Unique features of homeschooling provide reasons that it is an effective means for serving students with disabilities. The low student-to-teacher ratio enables students to learn at their own pace. Meanwhile, the instructor, typically the parent, is able to carefully design an instructional program, to structure the schedule of the school day, and to use pedagogical methods that are most suitable for the student. This is not to mention that parents who select into homeschooling are highly motivated and may also be most familiar with the child's unique needs. In a homeschool context, students may also be educated in an inclusive environment and yet be shielded from labels that induce negative stigma and lowered expectations—factors that may hinder educational success (Kidd & Kaczmarek, 2010; Shifrer, 2013; Shifrer, Callahan, & Muller, 2013; Van Kuren, 2000).

On the other hand, critics charge that homeschooled students have fewer opportunities for social interaction relative to other students who attend traditional public or other types of schools (Evans, 2003; Gutmann, 1987; but see Medlin, 2000; 2013). Other critics point out that homeschool parents are typically uncertified and untrained teachers and question whether they have the preparation to instruct their children as effectively as professionals (Van Kuren, 2000). Some critics additionally mention that homeschool parents instruct their children in a particular worldview or teach in prescriptive ways, limiting the student's ability to be self-determining and prepared for civic life (Cai, Reeve, & Robinson, 2002; Gutmann, 1987; Reich, 2002, 2005). Although these criticisms broadly apply to homeschooling, they possess particular relevance for students with disabilities. Failing to adequately educate, socialize, and prepare these students for civic life is a more acute problem for this more vulnerable segment of the population.

The effectiveness of homeschooling for students with disabilities can be examined empirically. A handful of studies have explored how homeschool instructors teach students with disabilities and whether their management strategies lead to desirable student outcomes (Duvall, 2005; Duvall, Delquadri, Elliot, & Hall, 1992; Duvall, Delquadri, & Ward, 2004; Duvall, Ward, Delquadri, & Greenwood, 1997). Though these studies utilize small convenience samples, the authors conclude that instructional environments provided in homeschools are at least as conducive as environments provided in traditional public schools for improving achievement and maintaining engagement for students with basic learning disabilities or even more significant needs such as attention-deficit disorder. According to these studies, students in homeschooling environments were engaged in their learning more often than students in traditional public schools and realized greater gains in math and reading achievement.

Although studies by Duvall (2005), Duvall and colleagues (1997), and Duvall and colleagues (2004) are valuable and suggest that homeschooling arrangements sufficiently serve students with disabilities, more research is warranted. The samples in these studies sometimes included as few as four homeschool students from a nonrandom sample, making it difficult to generalize findings. Moreover, causal claims about homeschooling certainly cannot be made based upon this research. These limitations also characterize homeschooling research outside the United States (Arora, 2003). Although we cannot address the ability to make causal claims, we aim to address sampling limitations by using a larger, nationally representative sample of U.S. families.

Parental satisfaction with special education

Beyond the research on students with disabilities who are homeschooled, other studies use measures of parental satisfaction to assess the quality of special-education services provided by private schools. Parents of students with disabilities are involved in their students' educational environment due to IEP meetings and advocacy, which may make them particularly helpful in rating service quality. Parents participating in Florida's McKay program, which provides vouchers for students with disabilities to attend private schools, are generally more satisfied with special-education services, reported smaller class sizes, and indicated fewer behavioral issues than parents of students with disabilities in traditional public schools (Greene & Forster, 2003; Weidner & Herrington, 2006).

Other research of cyber charter schools, which provide most or all of their educational services online, suggests parents and their children with disabilities are more satisfied with the cyber charter school than their prior traditional public school (Beck et al., 2014; Beck, Maranto, & Lo, 2013). Despite these results on parental satisfaction, one large-scale study of online charter schools showed much lower learning gains for students, particularly those with disabilities, relative to their counterparts in traditional public schools (Woodworth et al., 2015). It is possible that a parent reports higher satisfaction with cyber charter schools for reasons other than their ability to improve student achievement—a proposition that requires more investigation. In general, these results for cyber charters may be insightful for homeschooling research as many homeschooling families are now using the services of cyber charters. Whether students with disabilities are well-served by homeschooling in conjunction with cyber-charters is unclear.

Finally, some scholars have explored satisfaction with publicly provided special education services provided specifically in a homeschool context. This work suggests that homeschooling parents are generally satisfied with these services. However, much of the work lacks a counterfactual. Such research relies on either (a) qualitative interviews where homeschool parents report being satisfied with their current arrangements or (b) surveys of homeschool parents from which a percentage of satisfied families can be calculated (Arora, 2006; Westling, 1996). From these studies, one cannot ascertain if homeschool families are more or less satisfied than families who select other schooling arrangements for their child with disabilities. One study compared satisfaction levels for homeschool or traditional public school parents who have children with disabilities and finds higher satisfaction levels among homeschool parents. Again, however, the comparison is limited to a small sample of convenience (Delaney, 2014).

In this study, we shed additional light regarding whether homeschooling can be a viable means for providing adequate special education services.

Specifically, we compare levels of parental satisfaction with special education services for families who homeschool their children to families who send their children to traditional public schools, public charter schools, Catholic private schools, other religious private schools, or nonreligious private schools.

Methods

Data

Data for our analysis come from the National Household Education Survey. This data set is regularly collected by the U.S. Department of Education and comprises a nationally representative sample of over 17,000 U.S. households. In our analysis, we examine approximately 2,000 households that have children with disabilities. The proportion of households associated with each school sector is shown in Table 1. For instance, about 1% of U.S. households that have children with disabilities opt to homeschool those children. Almost 90% of these households send their children with disabilities to traditional public schools. To further describe our sample, Table 2 displays the percentage of students with disabilities in each school sector. For example, 11.3 percent of all homeschooled children are classified as having a learning disability.

Parents responded to a series of survey questions in 2012, including whether they have a student with disabilities and in which school sector the child receives his or her education. Parents also responded to Likert-type items to indicate, on a scale of 1 through 4, their satisfaction level with various dimensions of the special education services their child is receiving. Higher values signify greater satisfaction levels.

It is possible that many homeschooling parents deliver special education services on their own to their children. If so, then satisfaction ratings provided by homeschool families would lack face validity as such ratings would be self-evaluations. It is for this reason that we only include families that report receiving services through a formal IEP from a local school district, another local government health or social agency, or other health care provider. Table 2 also allows us to feel confident that our sample is not

Table 1. Proportion of households in each school sector.

Sector	Percentage (%)
Homeschool	1.0
Traditional public school	90.5
Public charter school	5.5
Catholic private school	1.0
Religious, non-Catholic private school	1.1
Nonreligious private school	0.9

Note. Sample is limited to households with students with disabilities.

Table 2. Sample statistics of the distribution of disabilities across sectors.

Type of disability	Homeschool	Traditional public school	Public charter school	Catholic private school	Religious, non-Catholic private school	Non-religious private school
			Percentage (%)			
Learning disability	11.3	9.4	8.4	0.6	6.4	10.4
intellectual disability/ cognitive impairment	1.3	1.7	1.3	0.9	1.0	2.2
Speech or language impairment	5.8	6.1	6.0	4.7	3.7	5.3
Serious emotional disturbance	4.0	2.7	4.1	0.9	1.0	3.9
Deafness or other hearing impairment	0.8	1.3	1.6	1.0	1.5	1.4
Blindness of other visual impairment	1.5	1.3	1.5	1.6	1.4	1.4
Orthopedic impairment	2.3	2.3	2.5	1.6	2.1	2.2
Autism	2.3	1.9	2.1	1.1	1.5	1.7
Pervasive developmental disorder	1.5	1.0	0.7	0.9	1.4	2.7
Attention deficit disorder	9.8	10.7	10.9	8.0	9.3	12.3
Developmental delay	5.5	3.8	2.8	2.4	2.7	4.3
Traumatic brain injury	0.8	0.5	0.8	0.7	0.6	0.5
Other health impairment	0.7	4.1	3.2	3.2	3.7	5.1

Note. Source: Author's calculations. Some individuals report multiple disabilities, hence percentages do not add up to the total percentage of individuals with a disability within each school sector.

Table 3. Summary statistics for satisfaction variables.

	Mean	Standard deviation	Range
Satisfaction with provider's communication with family	3.32	0.87	1–4
Satisfaction with special needs teacher or therapist	3.47	0.77	1–4
Satisfaction with provider's ability to accommodate child's needs	3.33	0.86	1–4
Satisfaction with provider's commitment to help the child	3.39	0.85	1–4
Overall satisfaction	3.35	0.77	1–4

Note. Higher numbers indicate greater levels of satisfaction.

comprised of homebound students with disabilities as the distribution of types of disabilities is relatively stable across sectors. As it turns out, over 90% of homeschooling families in our data receive services from one of these entities. We thus assume that homeschool parents are not self-evaluating, lending more credence to our measures of satisfaction.

We specifically assess parental satisfaction with the publicly provided service provider's (a) communication with the family, (b) teacher or therapist assigned to the student, (c) ability to accommodate the child's needs, and (d) commitment. We also average ratings on these four individual items to construct an overall satisfaction measure. Table 3 shows summary statistics for responses to these four items as well as our measure of overall satisfaction.

Empirical strategy

We use ordinary least squares regression analysis to estimate a series of models where the dependent variable is one of the five measures of satisfaction with special-education services.[4] Our key independent variables of interest are indicators for the school sector in which the special-needs child is receiving his or her education. Our coefficient estimates describe differences in satisfaction ratings for parents across the different school sectors. Our data allow us to additionally control for a host of background demographic variables. In particular, we control for parent's educational attainment and household income as well as the child's race, gender, age, type of disability, and family structure. All estimations include sampling weights and standard error corrections so that our results are nationally representative.

Results

Our results indicate that parents who homeschool their children with disabilities are more satisfied with special education services than parents who send their students to public or Catholic private schools. Complete results are shown in Table 4.

In columns 1 through 4, we compare parental satisfaction levels for various aspects of the special education services that students receive. Estimates in Table 4 depict differences in satisfaction levels between parents in a given school sector relative to homeschooling parents. Negative coefficients indicate that parents in the given school sector are less satisfied with that particular service than homeschooling families are. For instance, column 1 shows comparisons of satisfaction with the communication parents receive from their providers. Parents who homeschool their children with disabilities are 0.16 scale points more satisfied than similar parents in public charter schools with the communication they receive from their respective service providers. These homeschooling parents are also 0.25 and 0.40 scale points more satisfied with the communication that they receive relative to parents in traditional public and Catholic schools, respectively. However, parents who have students with disabilities in religious, non-Catholic private schools are 0.08 scale points more satisfied with the communication that they receive than their homeschooling counterparts. All differences are statistically significant at the 0.01 level. There also does not appear to be differences in satisfaction with the service provider's communication between homeschooling parents and parents who send their children with disabilities to non-religious private schools.

In column 2, we observe similar patterns regarding parental satisfaction with the teacher or therapist providing special education services.

Table 4. Results.

	(1) Satisfaction with provider's communication with family	(2) Satisfaction with special-needs teacher or therapist	(3) Satisfaction with provider's ability to accommodate child's needs	(4) Satisfaction with provider's commitment to help the child	(5) Overall satisfaction
School Sector					
Public charter	−0.160***	−0.292***	−0.088***	−0.098***	−0.112***
	(0.018)	(0.024)	(0.025)	(0.026)	(0.017)
Traditional	−0.252***	−0.324***	−0.198***	−0.315***	−0.256***
public	(0.016)	(0.023)	(0.022)	(0.024)	(0.016)
Catholic private	−0.403***	−0.487***	−0.410***	−0.442***	−0.411***
	−0.037	−0.032	−0.03	−0.046	(0.030)
Religious, non-	0.084***	−0.036	0.072**	0.164***	0.135***
Catholic	(0.021)	(0.026)	(0.028)	(0.023)	(0.017)
private					
Non-religious	0.012	0.021	0.212***	−0.016	−0.003
private	(0.022)	(0.028)	(0.033)	(0.030)	(0.026)
Observations	1,843	1,656	1,769	1,838	1,910
R^2	0.055	0.059	0.074	0.068	0.062

Note. Omitted category is homeschooling families. All models control for parent's educational attainment, household income, child's race, child's gender, child's disability, whether child come from a two-parent home. Standard errors in parenthesis.
***$p < 0.01$. **$p < 0.05$. *$p < 0.1$.

Homeschool parents are more satisfied with this aspect of their special education services than parents whose children attend public charter, traditional public, or Catholic private schools. Differences in satisfaction on this dimension of special education services between homeschool parents and these other parents range from 0.3 to 0.5 scale points ($p < 0.01$). However, homeschooling parents appear as satisfied with their teacher or therapist providing special education services as parents whose children with disabilities attend nonreligious and non-Catholic, religious private schools.

Relative to parents who send their child to public charter schools, traditional public schools, and Catholic schools, homeschooling parents are also more satisfied with their provider's ability to accommodate the needs of their child with disabilities by about 0.1, 0.2, and 0.4 scale points respectively ($p < 0.01$). These estimates are shown in column 3. Conversely, parents who send their child to religious, non-Catholic private schools or nonreligious private schools are more satisfied than homeschooling parents with the ability of their special education provider to accommodate their child's needs by approximately 0.1 ($p < 0.05$) and 0.2 ($p < 0.01$) scale points.

Turning to column 4 of Table 4, we see the aforementioned patterns persist when considering satisfaction with the service provider's commitment to help their students with disabilities. Homeschool families are more satisfied than families who have selected public charter schools, traditional public schools, and Catholic schools for their child. However, homeschool parents are less satisfied with their provider's commitment to help their students with disabilities than families who have selected religious, non-Catholic private schools. Note, too, that the range of differences in this dimension of parental satisfaction are similar in magnitude to the estimates for other dimensions of parental satisfaction. Lastly, there is no statistically significant difference in satisfaction with the provider's commitment between homeschool families and families who have selected nonreligious private schools.

Overall, as shown in column 5, parents who homeschool their children with disabilities are more satisfied with their special-needs services than their counterparts who send their children to public charter, traditional public, and Catholic schools. These differences range from 0.10 to 0.40 scale points. In terms of effect sizes, these differences are about 14%–53% of a standard deviation in satisfaction ratings. In contrast, these homeschooling parents are generally less satisfied than parents who send their children with disabilities to religious, non-Catholic private schools.

Discussion and conclusions

The aim of our analysis was to describe parents' satisfaction with the special education services that they receive for their students with disabilities. We pay particular attention to comparing these satisfaction levels between parents who homeschool and those who opt for other schooling arrangements. In a nationally representative sample of nearly 2,000 U.S. families, we find that homeschool parents are more satisfied than parents who send their student with a disability to public and Catholic schools with the special education services that they receive.[5] On the other hand, homeschool parents are less satisfied than parents who send their child to religious, non-Catholic private schools with those services.

Assuming that parental satisfaction is some indication of quality, the results suggest publicly provided special education services offered to parents who homeschool are not worse than services offered to parents in a variety of school settings. Nonetheless, we caution that satisfaction ratings must be interpreted with care. Considering an example mentioned earlier, research on cyber charters finds high levels of parental satisfaction despite other work suggesting that cyber charters are not effective at improving student achievement. Such a finding may cast doubt on the legitimacy of a satisfaction rating. That being said, research of other school choice programs often finds greater parental satisfaction tied to improved student outcomes (Kisida & Wolf, 2015; Peterson et al., 1999; Wolf et al., 2013). In general, however, we maintain that parental satisfaction ratings should not be discounted even if results are not commensurate with outcomes such as student achievement because parents may choose particular schooling arrangements for a variety of other legitimate reasons (Kelly & Scafidi, 2013). Indeed, homeschooling families often remove their children with special needs from institutional schooling environments to shield them from bullying or negative stigma (Beck et al., 2014; Parsons & Lewis, 2010; Shifrer, 2013). Satisfaction ratings could capture the efficacy of alternative schooling arrangements to address a variety of relevant needs. While researchers often evaluate educational interventions and policy based upon student achievement outcomes, the role of parent perceptions of school quality can be valuable in assessing other relevant dimensions of schooling that are not captured by test scores (e.g., school safety, social–emotional development). In fact, the use of academic outcomes for students with disabilities may not be the most relevant metric if the goals of special education are outside the scope of what a standardized test can measure.

Additional limitations to our analysis are worth mentioning. For example, our work cannot ascertain why homeschool parents exhibit higher satisfaction levels. Teske and Schneider (2001) point out that based upon virtually all research of parental satisfaction with schools, parents who exercise school choice report higher levels of satisfaction than parents who do not choose. Variation in parental satisfaction ratings could simply reflect ex-post rationalizations of their choice instead of marked differences in quality. On the other hand, our results demonstrated lower satisfaction ratings among a key group of parents who exercised school choice, namely, parents selecting Catholic schools. This result may be evidence that satisfaction ratings are not simply post hoc rationalizations of making a selection or simply a reflection of the ability to choose. Catholic schools typically espouse egalitarian values, which may mean that all students—those with disabilities included—receive the same curriculum and are held to the same standards. Indeed, Catholic schools are known not to provide separate academic tracks for students with varying abilities (Bryk et al., 1993; Cheng, Trivitt, & Wolf, 2016; Coleman & Hoffer, 1987; Trivitt & Wolf, 2011). This educational approach may not be what parents expect or desire for their student with disabilities.

There are other sources of bias that may stem from asking individuals to self-report satisfaction levels. Reference-group bias, in particular, is most salient. This source of bias arises when individuals have unequal internal standards for assessing what it means to be satisfied (King, Murray, Salomon, & Tandon, 2004). In our work, if internal standards differ between parents who receive special education services in different school sectors, then satisfaction ratings are no longer comparable. For instance, suppose homeschool parents systematically have lower standards and thresholds for satisfaction than other parents. If so, our research would overstate the homeschool parents' levels of satisfaction because they would self-report greater satisfaction with their special education services than other types of parents who receive the same services. It is unclear whether reference group bias is present in self-reported satisfaction ratings, and researchers currently lack the methods to correct for it in this context. Ultimately, obtaining a fuller picture of the quality of special education services requires evaluating student outcomes along with other indicators such as parental satisfaction. Undertaking this task is a topic for future research, which has rarely been done, even among traditional public schools, because data on students with disabilities is difficult to obtain.

Finally, our research cannot speak to homeschool families who are the sole provider of special education services to their children with disabilities. Our analysis only includes families who receive services from a local school district, another government agency, or a formal health care provider. Thus, the results, at best, indicate that homeschool families who receive special education services from these types of providers are more satisfied with these services than families who receive similar services in most other types of school settings. Nonetheless, our findings are consistent with prior research demonstrating that homeschooling can be more effective when homeschool families partner with or receive training from tutors, public school teachers, and other professionals (Duvall et al., 1992; Hook & DuPaul, 1999). Our findings also lend credence toward the calls for collaboration and partnerships between different types of schooling arrangements and institutions to improve services for children with disabilities (Arora, 2006; Delaney, 2014; Van Kuren, 2000).

Although much more research must be done to better understand homeschooling and special education, our findings give reason for pause regarding the concerns that homeschooling is not a viable means to serve students with disabilities. The results are also consistent with prior research which finds that students with disabilities are at least as effectively served in a homeschool setting as in a traditional public school setting (Duvall, 2005; Duvall et al., 2004, 1997). This study additionally bolsters these prior research findings, which have limited external validity due to small samples of convenience, by making comparisons across a nationally representative sample of families. Taken together, this work and prior research seem to suggest that homeschooling can be a valuable option for students with disabilities, especially if services are provided in partnership and collaboration with other institutions and professionals.

In closing, this study likely raises more questions than it answers. With what, exactly, are parents satisfied and why? To what extent is satisfaction an accurate and reasonable proxy for special education quality? That is, how is satisfaction tied with student outcomes if at all? What is the nature of services being offered across different school sectors? How are these services similar or different? We hope our work will spur additional inquiry into these and other related questions so that scholars, policymakers, and practitioners can better serve students with disabilities.

Notes

1. Our use of the term homeschooling does not apply to students who are homebound due to their disability.
2. 34 CFR § 300.131 (2004).
3. 34 CFR § 300.137 (2004).
4. We estimate linear regression models for all of our dependent variables. Although the only continuous dependent variable in our models is a measure of overall satisfaction, ordered logit estimation of the other discrete variables yielded similar results as the linear regression models. Hence for ease of interpretation, we report linear regression coefficients.
5. One might worry that the sample sizes for homeschool and private-school families is low, given that they collectively make up only about 5% of the sample. These small sample sizes should not bias our estimates but only make it more difficult to detect statistically significant results. Thus, we can be even more confident that the differences that we have detected across these sectors is material and not due to random chance.

References

Arora, T. C. (2003). School-aged children who are educated at home by their parents: Is there a role for educational psychologists? *Educational Psychology in Practice, 19*(2), 103–112. doi:10.1080/02667360303237

Arora, T. C. (2006). Elective home education and special educational needs. *Journal of Research in Special Educational Needs, 6*(1), 55–66. doi:10.1111/j.1471-3802.2006.00059.x

Beck, D., Egalite, A. J., & Maranto, R. A. (2014). Why they choose and how it goes: Comparing special education and general education cyber student perceptions. *Computers & Education, 76*, 70–79. doi:10.1016/j.compedu.2014.03.011

Beck, D., Maranto, R. A., & Lo, W. (2013). Determinants of student and parent satisfaction at a cyber charter school. *The Journal of Educational Research, 107*(3), 209–216. doi:10.1080/00220671.2013.807494

Bryk, A. S., Lee, V. E., & Holland, P. B. (1993). *Catholic schools and the common good.* Cambridge, MA: Harvard University Press.

Butcher, J., & Bedrick, J. (2013, October). *Schooling satisfaction: Arizona parents' opinions on using education savings accounts.* Indianapolis, IN: The Friedman Foundation for Education Choice.

Cai, Y., Reeve, J., & Robinson, D. T. (2002). Home schooling and teaching style: Comparing the motivating styles of home school and public school teachers. *Journal of Educational Psychology, 94*(2), 372–380. doi:10.1037/0022-0663.94.2.372

Cheng, A., Trivitt, J. R., & Wolf, P. J. (2016). School choice and the branding of Milwaukee private schools. *Social Science Quarterly, 97*(2), 362–375.

Coleman, J. S., & Hoffer, T. (1987). *Public and private high schools: The impact of communities.* New York, NY: Basic Books.

Cook, K. B., Bennet, K., Lane, J. D., & Mataras, T. K. (2013). Beyond the brick walls: Homeschooling students with special needs. *Physical Disabilities: Education and Related Services, 32*(2), 90–103.

Cosier, M., Causton-Theoharis, J., & Theoharis, G. (2013). Does access matter? Time in general education and achievement for students with disabilities. *Remedial and Special Education, 34*(6), 323–332. doi:10.1177/0741932513485448

Cullen, J. B., & Rivkin, S. G. (2003). The role of special education in school choice. In *The economics of school choice* (pp. 67–106). Chicago, IL: University of Chicago Press.

Daniel, L. G., & King, D. A. (1997). Impact of inclusion education on academic achievement, student behavior and self-esteem, and parental attitudes. *The Journal of Educational Research, 91*(2), 67–80. doi:10.1080/00220679709597524

Delaney, A. M. (2014). Perspectives of parents of students with disabilities toward public and homeschool learning environments (Doctoral dissertation). Walden University, Minneapolis, MN.

Dhuey, E., & Lipscomb, S. (2011). Funding special education by capitation: Evidence from state finance reforms. *Education Finance and Policy, 6*(2), 168–201. doi:10.1162/EDFP_a_00031

Duffey, J. (2002). Home schooling children with special needs. *Journal of Special Education Leadership, 15*(1), 25–32.

Duvall, S. (2005). The effectiveness of homeschooling students with special needs. In B. S. Cooper (Ed.), *Homeschooling in full view: A reader* (pp. 151–166). Greenwich, CT: Information Age Publishing.

Duvall, S., Delquadri, J. C., & Ward, L. D. (2004). A preliminary investigation of the effectiveness of homeschool instructional environments for students with attention-deficit/hyperactivity disorder. *Social Psychology, 33*(1), 140–158.

Duvall, S., Ward, L. D., Delquadri, J. C., & Greenwood, C. R. (1997). An exploratory study of home school instructional environments and their effects on the basic skills of students with learning disabilities. *Education and Treatment of Children, 20*(2), 150–173.

Duvall, S. F., Delquadri, J. C., Elliot, M., & Hall, R. V. (1992). Parent-tutoring procedures: Experimental analysis and validation of generalization in oral reading across passages, settings, and time. *Journal of Behavioral Education, 2*(3), 281–303. doi:10.1007/BF00948819

Evans, D. L. (2003, September 2). Home is no place for school. *USA Today.* Retrieved from http://usatoday30.usatoday.com/news/opinion/editorials/2003-09-02-oppose_x.htm

Freeman, S. F. N., & Alkin, M. C. (2000). Academic and social attainments of children with mental retardation in general education and special education settings. *Remedial and Special Education, 21*(1), 3–26. doi:10.1177/074193250002100102

The Friedman Foundation for Educational Choice. (2015). *The ABCs of school choice: The comprehensive guide to every private school choice program in America.* Indianapolis, IN: The Friedman Foundation for Educational Choice.

Gaither, M. (2009). Homeschooling goes mainstream. *Education Next, 9*(1), 10–19.

Goldhaber, D., Lavery, L., & Theobald, R. (2015). Uneven playing field? Assessing the teacher quality gap between advantaged and disadvantaged students. *Educational Researcher, 44,* 293–307. doi:10.3102/0013189X15592622

Greene, J. P. (2007). Fixing special education. *Peabody Journal of Education, 82*(4), 703–723. doi:10.1080/01619560701603213

Greene, J. P., & Buck, S. (2010). The case for special education vouchers. *Education Next, 10,* 1.

Greene, J. P., & Forster, G. (2003). *Vouchers for special education students: An evaluation of Florida's McKay Scholarship Program.* New York, NY: Manhattan Institute for Policy Research.

Gutmann, A. (1987). *Democratic Education.* Princeton, NJ: Princeton University Press.

Hook, C. L., & DuPaul, G. (1999). Parent tutoring for students with attention/hyperactivity disorder. Effects on reading performance at home and school. *School Psychology Review, 28* (1), 60–75.

Hurlbutt, K. S. (2011). Experiences of parents who homeschool their children with autism spectrum disorders. *Focus on Autism and Other Developmental Disabilities, 26*(4), 239–249. doi:10.1177/1088357611421170

Kalambouka, A., Farrell, P., Dyson, A., & Kaplan, I. (2005). *The impact of population inclusivity in schools on student outcomes.* London, UK: University of London, Centre for Evidence-Informed Policy and Practice in Education.

Kelly, J., & Scafidi, B. (2013). *More than scores: An analysis of why parents choose private schools.* Indianapolis, IN: The Friedman Foundation for Educational Choice.

Kidd, T., & Kaczmarek, E. (2010). The experiences of mothers home educating their children with autism spectrum disorder. *Issues in Education Research, 20*(3), 257–275.

King, G., Murray, C., Salomon, J. A., & Tandon, A. (2004). Enhancing the validity and cross-cultural comparability of measurement in survey research. *American Political Science Review, 98*, 191–205. doi:10.1017/S000305540400108X

Kisida, B., & Wolf, P. J. (2015). Customer satisfaction and educational outcomes: Experimental impacts of the market-based delivery of public education. *International Public Management Journal, 18*(2), 265–285.

Klingner, J. K., Vaughn, S., Hughes, M. T., Schumm, J. S., & Elbaum, B. (1998). Outcomes for students with and without learning disabilities in inclusive classrooms. *Learning Disabilities Research & Practice, 13*(3), 153–161.

Lake, R. J. (2010). *Unique schools serving unique students: Charter schools and children with special needs.* Seattle, WA: Center for Reinventing Public Education.

Lake, R. J., & Gross, B. (2012). Making choice work for students with special needs. In R. Lake & B. Gross (Eds.), *Hopes, fears, & reality* (pp. 43–53). Seattle, WA: Center for Reinventing Public Education.

Lindberg, M. (2016). *Special education school vouchers: A look at southern states.* Atlanta, GA: The Southern Office of the Council of State Governments.

Lindsey, G. (2007). Educational psychology and the effectiveness of inclusive education/ mainstreaming. *British Journal of Educational Psychology, 77*(1), 1–24. doi:10.1348/000709906X156881

Medlin, R. (2000). Homeschooling and the question of socialization. *Peabody Journal of Education, 75*(1/2), 107–123. doi:10.1080/0161956X.2000.9681937

Medlin, R. (2013). Homeschooling and the question of socialization revisited. *Peabody Journal of Education, 88*(3), 284–297. doi:10.1080/0161956X.2013.796825

Mills, P. E., Cole, K. N., Jenkins, J. R., & Dale, P. S. (1998). Effects of differing levels of inclusion on preschoolers with disabilities. *Exceptional Children, 65*(1), 79.

Parsons, S., & Lewis, A. (2010). The home-education of children with special needs or disabilities in the UK: Views of parents from an online survey. *International Journal of Inclusive Education, 14*(1), 67–86. doi:10.1080/13603110802504135

Peterson, P. E., Howell, W. G., & Greene, J. P. (1999). *An Evaluation of the Cleveland Voucher Program after Two Years.* Cambridge, MA: Harvard University, Program on Education Policy and Governance.

Rea, P. J., McLaughlin, V. L., & Walther-Thomas, C. (2002). Outcomes for students with learning disabilities in inclusive and pullout programs. *Exceptional Children, 68*(2), 203–222.

Reich, R. (2002). The civic perils of homeschooling. *Educational Leadership, 59*(7), 56–59.

Reich, R. (2005). Why home schooling should be regulated. In B. S. Cooper (Ed.), *Homeschooling in full view: A reader* (pp. 109–120). Greenwich, CT: Information Age Publishing.

Reilly, L. (2004). *How Western Australian parents manage the home schooling of their children with disabilities.* Paper presented at the AARE Annual Conference, Melbourne, Australia.

Reilly, L., Chapman, A., & O'Donoghue, T. (2002). Home schooling of children with disabilities. *Queensland Journal of Educational Research, 18*(1), 38–61.

Salend, S. J., & Duhaney, L. M. G. (1999). The impact of inclusion on students with and without disabilities and their educators. *Remedial and Special Education*, 20(2), 114–126. doi:10.1177/074193259902000209

Sass, T. R., Hannaway, J., Xu, Z., Figlio, D. N., & Feng, L. (2012). Value added of teachers in high-poverty schools and lower poverty schools. *Journal of Urban Economics*, 72(2), 104–122. doi:10.1016/j.jue.2012.04.004

Scanlan, M. (2008). The grammar of Catholic schooling and radically "Catholic" schools. *Catholic Education: A Journal of Inquiry and Practice*, 12(1), 25–54.

Setren, E. (2015). *Special education and English language learner student in Boston Charter schools: Impact and classification*. Cambridge, MA: MIT Department of Economics.

Shifrer, D. (2013). Stigma of a label educational expectations for high school students labeled with learning disabilities. *Journal of Health and Social Behavior*, 54(4), 462–480. doi:10.1177/0022146513503346

Shifrer, D., Callahan, R. M., & Muller, C. (2013). Equity or marginalization? The high school course-taking of students labeled with a learning disability. *American Educational Research Journal*, 40(4), 656–682. doi:10.3102/0002831213479439

Teske, P., & Schneider, M. (2001). What research can tell policymakers about school choice. *Journal of Policy Analysis and Management*, 20(4), 609–631. doi:10.1002/(ISSN)1520-6688

Trivitt, J. R., & Wolf, P. J. (2011). School choice and the branding of Catholic schools. *Education Finance and Policy*, 6(2), 202–245. doi:10.1162/EDFP_a_00032

U.S. Department of Education. (2015). *Digest of education statistics 2013*. Washington, DC: National Center for Education Statistics, Institute of Education Sciences.

Van Kuren, L. (2000). Home schooling: A viable alternative for students with special needs. *CEC Today*, 7(1), 1–9.

Waldron, N. L., & McLeskey, J. (1998). The effects of an inclusive school program on students with mild and severe learning disabilities. *Exceptional Children*, 64(3), 395–405.

Weidner, V. R., & Herrington, C. D. (2006). Are parents informed consumers: Evidence from the Florida McKay scholarship program. *Peabody Journal of Education*, 81(1), 27–56. doi:10.1207/S15327930pje8101_3

Westling, D. L. (1996). What do parents of children with moderate and severe mental disabilities want? *Education and Training in Mental Retardation*, 31, 85–114.

Winters, M. (2013). *Why the gap? Special education and New York City charter schools*. Seattle, WA: Center for Reinventing Public Education.

Winters, M. (2014). *Understanding the charter school special education gap: Evidence from Denver, CO*. Seattle, WA: Center for Reinventing Public Education.

Wolf, P. J., Kisida, B., Gutmann, B., Puma, M., Eissa, N., & Rizzo, L. (2013). School vouchers and student outcomes: Experimental evidence from Washington, DC. *Journal of Policy Analysis and Management*, 32(2), 246–270.

Woodworth, J. L., Raymond, M. E., Chirbas, K., Gonzalez, M., Negassi, Y., Snow, W., & Van Donge, C. (2015). *Online charter school study*. Stanford, CA: Center for Research on Education Outcomes.

Zimmer, R., & Guarino, C. (2013). Is there empirical evidence that charter schools "push out" low-performing students? *Educational Evaluation and Policy Analysis*, 35(4), 461–480. doi:10.3102/0162373713498465

Are Homeschoolers Prepared for College Calculus?

CHRISTIAN P. WILKENS and CAROL H. WADE

GERHARD SONNERT and PHILIP M. SADLER

Homeschooling in the United States has grown considerably over the past several decades. This article presents findings from the Factors Influencing College Success in Mathematics (FICSMath) survey, a national study of 10,492 students enrolled in tertiary calculus, including 190 students who reported homeschooling for a majority of their high school years. The authors found that, compared with students who received other types of secondary schooling, students who homeschooled: (a) were demographically similar to their peers, (b) earned similar SAT Math scores, and (c) earned higher tertiary calculus grades.

The education of students who homeschool has attracted growing interest over the past decade, not least because the number of such students appears to have reached considerable proportions. While we lack current data (and, for that matter, cannot conduct an accurate headcount) because many states and localities do not require families to report homeschooling (HSLDA, 2014), the National Center for Education Statistics (NCES, 2007), in 2007, estimated the number of students who homeschooled at about 1.5 million students, or 2.9% of the school-age population (Bielick, 2008; estimates were generated using National Household Education Survey [NHES] sample data). Since that time, the current population of homeschooled students is thought to have increased to over 2 million students (as of 2013–2014), or more than 4% of the school-age population (Basham, Merrifield, & Hepburn, 2007; Boschee & Boschee, 2011; Kunzman & Gaither, 2013). Homeschooling, therefore, involves a larger number of students than do charter schools, which have attracted far more public interest and a larger share of systematic scholarly attention (NCES, 2013a; nationwide charter school enrollment of ~1.8 million students [2010–2011]; Kafer, 2009).

With the growing proportion of newly graduated homeschooled students knocking on the door of admission to colleges and universities across the United States, there has been particular interest among scholars on the academic performance of students who homeschool (Gloeckner & Jones, 2013). Specifically, scholars have focused on the extent to which homeschooling "works," for whom, and under what conditions. Belfield (2005) characterized the overarching research interests of the field as including both "the absolute performance of homeschoolers [and] the treatment effect of homeschooling" (p. 170). To date, we know surprisingly little about either domain. Work on the performance of homeschoolers—to which this article seeks to contribute—has remained largely anecdotal, subject to bias, and highly politicized (including experimental or quasi-experimental work; for a good review of approaches and examples, see Murnane & Willett, 2011). A survey of literature revealed mixed findings when college level grade point average was compared between traditionally prepared students and homeschooled students (Gloeckner & Jones, 2013). Little work has been capable of shedding light on the treatment effect of homeschooling (including experimental or quasi-experimental work; for a good review of approaches and examples, see Murnane & Willett, 2011).

CHALLENGES OF HOMESCHOOL RESEARCH

Why is our knowledge base so thin? A persistent challenge of studying homeschooling has been that students who homeschool do so beyond the institutional structures of traditional schools, and across widely varying political landscapes. The business of assembling representative datasets capable of accurately characterizing the experiences and performance of homeschooled students has historically proven to be close to impossible (Kunzman & Gaither, 2013). We have, therefore, been forced to make estimates about homeschoolers from small samples. The most recent 2007 National Household Education Survey (National Center for Education Statistics, 2009), and perhaps the most credible portrait of homeschooling nationwide, estimated characteristics of the national homeschooling population from a sample of 290 students.

A second factor complicating any homeschool research has been defining the scope and scale of the treatment. Belfield (2005) and Jones-Sanpei (2008) both pointed out that homeschooling is often not an either–or proposition. While some families pursue comprehensive at-home approaches, many homeschooling students participate in school-based distance learning programs, or attend a local school for part of the day. The 2007 Parent and Family Involvement in Education survey (Herrold & O'Donnell, 2008) reported 16% of homeschoolers as "[e]nrolled in school part time." Moreover, it is a rare student who exclusively homeschools over the entire K–12 grade span. Though (again) data are thin, Isenberg (2002) estimated a mean homeschooling duration of just two years—and later noted high attrition (63%) after the first year of homeschooling (Isenberg, 2007). At the moment, we can make few claims about what homeschooling is, or what common experiences students who homeschool share.

A third and ongoing challenge is that research on homeschooling in the modern era has been intensely politicized. A great deal of the available scholarship has been conducted or published by advocacy organizations, or by scholars with explicit agendas to promote or criticize homeschooling (for a good review, see Gaither, 2008). Advocates have claimed that homeschooling promotes flexibility, individualization, and improved academic performance of students, including those with "special learning needs" (Ray, 2010; Rudner, 1999). Critics have worried about homeschooling's potential for unreported abuse, psychological harm, and uneven academic rigor (West, 2009). Contrast, for example, one recent claim made by Brian Ray (2009), a researcher sponsored by the advocacy group Home School Legal Defense Association (HSLDA): "Homeschoolers are still achieving well beyond their public school counterparts . . ." (p. 3) with a counterclaim by Robin West (2009) of the Georgetown University Law Center:

> There is indeed no credible evidence that homeschoolers as a group do worse on standardized tests, but contrary to their [i.e., the advocates'] claims, there is also no credible evidence that they do better. There is no credible evidence of accomplishment here at all. (p. 10)

Such work has generated considerable noise without consensus. As Kunzman and Gaither (2013) summarize: ". . . unfortunately most of this work contains serious design flaws that limit its generalizability and reliability" (p. 16).

HOMESCHOOLERS AND ACADEMIC PERFORMANCE

Two exceptions to this are studies by Belfield (2005), who found that homeschoolers taking the SAT scored slightly better than expected on the SAT verbal section, and slightly lower than expected on the SAT math section, and Qaqish (2007), who found that homeschoolers taking the ACT scored slightly lower than expected on the mathematics section. Belfield's data, which encompassed the 2001 cohort of SAT takers, contained 6,033 students identified as homeschoolers. They also included a range of self-reported demographic controls. Belfield's analysis clearly addressed the challenges presented by the self-selected cohort of students taking the SAT and attempted to correct for selection effects (e.g., relatively low pro-portions of homeschoolers take the SAT) and family background controls (e.g., homeschoolers were found to be advantaged, on average, in terms of family wealth and educational background). Belfield concluded, with a range of caveats, that the slightly higher SAT verbal scores he reported "may reflect greater parental competence" in reading/writing than in math-ematics (p. 173). Qaqish's data included 1,477 homeschooled students and 1,477 nonhomeschoolers taking the ACT mathematics test prior to March 2003. Qaqish's design constructed matched groups of homeschoolers and nonhomeschoolers by gender, grade, race/ethnicity, and family income, and used these groups to calculate mean scores for each test item, along with total ACT mathematics raw scores—and found that mean scores for non-homeschooled students were slightly higher than those of homeschooled students.

Belfield (2005) also explored the course taking and academic per-formance of homeschoolers as a group, and found that homeschoolers demonstrated divergent proficiency across content areas, in comparison with students who experienced a range of other types of schooling. Belfield's (2005) work is unique in that it avoided the use of a self-selected sample (e.g., of SAT- or ACT-takers), reported on the courses homeschoolers took while in high school and college, and did not rely on post hoc controls for selection bias or demography.

RESEARCH QUESTION

With the previous results representing the extent of our reliable infor-mation, there appears to be a dire need to augment and improve the knowledge base. Our study intends to make a contribution to knowledge about the preparation of homeschoolers for—and success in—tertiary cal-culus courses. In this research, tertiary calculus is referred to as the first single variable calculus course taken at the college level. We analyze data from the 2009–2010 Factors Influencing College Success in Mathematics (FICSMath) survey, a nationally representative study of 10,492 students who completed the FICSMath survey at the beginning of their tertiary calcu-lus course. The group of 190 homeschool students in the FICSMath study affords the unique opportunity of gaining nationally representative insight into homeschooling. We address the following tripartite research question: Among college calculus students, to what extent do homeschoolers differ from their nonhomeschooled peers in (a) demographic and socioeconomic background characteristics, (b) secondary mathematics preparation, and (c) performance in tertiary calculus?

DATA AND METHODS

The FICSMath survey project, conducted at the Science Education Department of the Harvard-Smithsonian Center for Astrophysics, with funding from the National Science Foundation (NSF Award # 0813702) is among the few—and certainly the most recent—national-level studies of students' mathematics course taking, instructional experiences, and performance in tertiary calculus. The FICSMath research emerged from previous research—the Factors Influencing College Science Success (FICSS) study—that identified secondary mathematics as the only significant positive predictor of performance across all three freshman college science courses of biology, chemistry, and physics (Tai & Sadler, 2007). FICSMath institution recruitment, sample selection, item generation, pilot testing, and instrument validity and reliability are capably described elsewhere (Barnett, Sonnert, & Sadler, 2012; Wade, 2011).

The FICSMath dataset includes a large sample of college students who were enrolled in tertiary calculus at a broad range of institutions, from community colleges to Research I universities. A stratified random sample of the institutions of higher education contained in the National Center for Education Statistics (NCES) Integrated Postsecondary Education Data System as of 2007, was drawn: The institutions were first stratified by type (2-year versus 4-year), and each of the resulting two bins was then subdivided into three by size (small, medium, and large). Surveys were received from students in 134 participant institutions across the United States. Students took the FICSMath survey near the beginning of the 2009 Fall semester. Professors then held the surveys until after the completion of the course, at which time they recorded the students' grades earned in the course. The main dependent variable is student performance in tertiary calculus. In the end, there were 10,492 surveys returned to Harvard University, with no student identifiers.

For this article, we have tried not to rely heavily on student perception (e.g., whether they worked hard in high school), but only on relatively concrete aspects of tertiary calculus students' recalled experiences (such as course taking). The accuracy and reliability of self-report depends primarily on context, relevance, and survey clarity (Bradburn, 2000; Niemi & Smith, 2003; Pace, Barahona, & Kaplan, 1985). In particular, self-reports of course taking, grades earned, and standardized test scores made by college students tend to be highly accurate when compared to transcript records (Anaya,

1999; Baird, 1976). In a recent review of existing research on self-report, Kuncel, Credé, and Thomas (2005) concluded that self-report may be characterized as particularly accurate in samples where the surveys address issues relevant to the respondents. In this case, students completed the FICSMath survey in tertiary calculus during the beginning of their fall semester, which is when reflection upon students' prior experience is commonplace. To gauge reliability, we conducted a test–retest study in which 174 students from three different colleges took the survey twice, 2 weeks apart. Our analysis found that, for groups of 100, less than a 0.04% chance of reversal existed.

Our analysis excludes students who attended high schools outside of the United States ($n = 838$, or 8.0% of the dataset) and the small number of students who reported attending specialty "all-male" or "all-female" high schools, "vocational" high schools, "International Baccalaureate (IB)" schools, and "Magnet schools." These latter exclusions ($n = 577$ students in total, or 5.6% of the dataset) were made to avoid analytic uncertainty. The FICSMath survey question about high school type (Q2: What type of high school did you go to?) allowed students to select multiple options— confounding interpretation of responses from some students who selected more than one high school type. Students who reported attending both a "Public" school and a "Public Charter" school ($n = 22$) are similarly excluded from this analysis.

These exclusions, while a relatively small percentage of the dataset, present a risk of mischaracterizing students who attended Parochial schools, many of which are single-gender (Spielhagen, using 2011–2012 National Catholic Education Association data, reported that 31.5% of Catholic high schools were single gender [2013, p. 69]). These exclusions also present a risk of mischaracterizing students who attended private, non-Parochial or charter schools, an unknown percentage of which are single gender. Readers are cautioned that our reporting on "private, Parochial," "private non-Parochial," and "charter" schools, while of policy interest to many (and therefore included despite such cautions), does not include students who attended single-gender, vocational, magnet, or IB variants.

RESULTS

The vast majority of students who completed the FICSMath survey attended public high schools ($n = 7,803$, or 86.0%), while a relatively small percent of respondents reported homeschooling for a majority of high school ($n = 190$, or 2.1%). This percentage appears similar to the (2007) NCES estimate of 2.9% of the school-aged population, and somewhat smaller than Ray's (2011) estimate of 3.5%–4.7% (although Ray's methodology and advocacy leave us more comfortable relying on the NCES study, despite its age). That the sample of students who homeschooled in the FICSMath dataset appears quite similar to a national estimate of the percentage homeschooling during the K–12 school years is, we think, a strong argument against the existence of any extreme selection bias. Not all students who graduated from high school (homeschooled or otherwise) attended college in 2010, and neither did all homeschooled students who attended college in 2010 take the FICSMath survey. We believe the 2.1% homeschooling rate to be a representative sample of the population, which will contribute to the importance of the findings we describe as follows. Additionally, the FICSMath data set of homeschoolers includes variables unavailable through the 2007 National Household Education Survey, which made national-level estimates from a sample size of 290 homeschoolers. Using the somewhat smaller sample available in FICSMath survey, we provide new information about the path homeschooled students take to college-level (tertiary) calculus.

Table 1 shows the type of high school that has been included in our analysis and the gender of the respondents. Excluded from the data in Table 1 are 78 respondents, or 0.9% of the data, who did not disclose the type of high school attended. The 190 students who reported homeschooling will be the main focus of our analysis and subsequent discussion. A notable feature of the FICSMath sample is that, across school types, college students taking single-variable calculus are disproportionately male (56%–62%), compared with the overall gender composition of college undergraduates. Data from the 2012 Current Population Survey (CPS) indicate that just 44.0% of undergraduate students were male (U.S. Census Bureau, 2012, Table 5).

Table 2 shows that students in the FICSMath sample were predominantly White (65%–83%), and non-Hispanic (81%–90%), and that most students used English while at home (84%–92%). Among those students who reported homeschooling in high school, Table 2 indicates that those who homeschooled were likewise predominantly White (78%), with single-digit percentages of other racial backgrounds, and predominantly non-Hispanic (86%). Most homeschoolers (92%) used English while at home.

Readers surprised by the above descriptors should note that the K–12 and undergraduate populations in the United States differ in a number

TABLE 1 Reported Type of High School Where a Majority of High School Education Was Received Among Tertiary Calculus Students Responding to the FICSMath Survey, 2009 ($N = 8,999$)

| High School Type | Gender | | | |
	Male (%)	Female (%)	NR (%)	Number (%)
Homeschool	111 (58)	68 (36)	11 (6)	190 (2.1)
Public	4,819 (62)	2,575 (33)	409 (5)	7,803 (86.0)
Private, Parochial	340 (56)	237 (39)	29 (5)	606 (6.7)
Private, Non-Parochial	204 (61)	107 (32)	21 (6)	332 (3.7)
Public Charter	40 (59)	23 (34)	5 (7)	68 (0.8)

Note. NR = No Response.

TABLE 2 Demographic Background of Tertiary Calculus Students Responding to the FICSMath Survey by Type of High School Where a Majority of High School Education Was Received ($N = 8,999$)

	School Type				
Variables	Home School (%)	Public (%)	Private, Parochial (%)	Private, Non-Parochial (%)	Public Charter (%)
Race					
White	148 (78)	5,723 (73)	505 (83)	254 (77)	44 (65)
Black	3 (2)	325 (4)	16 (3)	12 (4)	9 (13)
Asian	9 (5)	651 (8)	25 (4)	23 (7)	2 (3)
PI	1 (1)	65 (1)	4 (1)	0 (0)	0 (0)
AI/AN	5 (3)	99 (1)	6 (1)	6 (2)	1 (1)
Other	13 (7)	587 (8)	32 (5)	23 (7)	7 (10)
Not Reported	11 (6)	353 (5)	18 (3)	14 (4)	5 (7)
Ethnicity					
Non-Hispanic	163 (86)	6,816 (87)	545 (90)	299 (90)	55 (81)
Hispanic	15 (8)	682 (9)	49 (8)	17 (5)	8 (12)
Not reported	12 (6)	305 (4)	12 (2)	16 (5)	5 (7)
Home Language					
English	174 (92)	6,541 (84)	560 (92)	288 (87)	58 (85)
Not English	5 (3)	1,004 (13)	36 (6)	30 (9)	7 (10)
Not reported	11 (6)	258 (3)	10 (2)	14 (4)	3 (4)

Note. PI = Pacific Islander; AI/AN = American Indian or Alaska Native.

of ways. U.S. Census data indicate that the current K–12 population is much more diverse than the undergraduate population. As of the 2010–2011 school year, just 54% of current K–12 students identified as "White alone" (compared with 70% of undergraduates), and 77% of current K–12 students identified as non-Hispanic (compared with 90% of undergraduates; NCES, 2012b, Indicator 6).

Such racial and ethnic differences between the undergraduate and K–12 populations are likely the result of a large racial and ethnic matriculation gaps in the United States. Readers are cautioned against leaping beyond the data reported here to conclusions about the path of students in high schools generally, keeping in mind the limits of what we can and cannot report. These data are representative of college undergraduates taking single-variable calculus only, and it is clear that such students are—compared with other college students—disproportionately male and—compared with K–12 students generally—disproportionately White and non-Hispanic. Additionally, the FICSMath survey reports on parent education and support for mathematics at home, both incomplete but helpful indicators of family socioeconomic status (NCES, 2012c).

Figure 1 presents the highest education levels of parents or guardians reported by students in the FICSMath sample. Here, for ease of modeling, we have converted ordinal survey responses (students selected from options: "Did not finish high school," "High school," "Some college," "Four years of

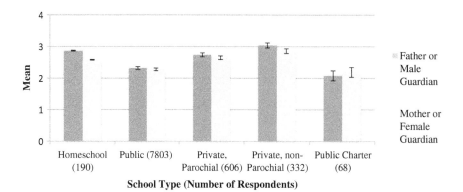

FIGURE 1 Level of father or male guardian's highest level of education and mother or female guardian's highest level of education by type of high school, with the number of calculus students responding to the FICSMath survey ($N = 8{,}999$ total).

Note. Scale: 0 = *did not finish high school*; 1 = *high school*; 2 = *some college*; 3 = *four years of college*; 4 = *graduate school*. Error bars indicate 1 standard error.

college," and "Graduate school") to an interval variable (0–4) as a rough indicator of parent attainment throughout our sample. The distribution of parent educational attainment demonstrated broad overlap, with slightly higher levels of parent/guardian educational attainment among those who were homeschooled or who attended private schools (Parochial or non-Parochial), compared with those who attended public or charter schools. Because the distribution of parent education levels violated the normality assumption of analysis of variance (ANOVA) modeling, nonparametric Kruskal-Wallis tests were performed. These tests indicated that these reported parental education differences by school type were significant for both male parent/guardians ($H = 218.7$, $p < .0001$) and female parent/guardians ($H = 153.8$, $p < .0001$). However, such significance should be viewed with caution, given skew differences across school types (see Fagerland & Sandvik, 2009), and the results should be interpreted as exploratory only.

What about home support for mathematics? Figure 2 presents the self-reported "degree to which home environment was supportive of math" among students in the FICSMath sample. As with parent education, the distribution of home support for mathematics demonstrated broad overlap. Mean self-reported home support among students who attended public schools was 3.8 (rating scale 0–5; 0 = *not supportive at all*, 5 = *very supportive*), with slightly higher home support among students who homeschooled (4.2), and slightly lower levels of support among students in charter schools (3.4). Given that the distribution of home support violated the normality assumption of ANOVA, a nonparametric Kruskal-Wallis test was performed and indicated that these differences were significant ($H = 43.8$, $p < .0001$). These distributions did not violate test assumptions.

An additional background characteristic of ongoing interest among homeschool researchers—and worth investigating as a student background

170

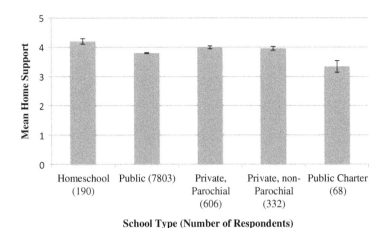

FIGURE 2 Mean of the degree to which home environment was supportive of math by high school type and number of students responding on the FICSMath survey ($N = 8,999$ total).

Note. Rating scale 0–5; 0 = *not supportive at all*, 5 = *very supportive.*

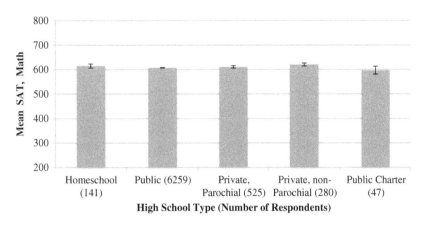

FIGURE 3 SAT Mathematics score of students responding to FICSMath survey, 2009, by type of high school ($N = 7,252$ total). Math scores of students who took the ACT converted to SAT math scores per ACT-SAT concordance table (Dorans, 1999).

characteristic in this study—is academic achievement on standardized tests during the high school years. For all their limitations, the SAT and the ACT provide standardized measures of the mathematics skills of students while in high school—and can help characterize the extent to which various high school paths have been successful in preparing students for college calculus. Figure 3 reports the SAT scores of students in the FICSMath dataset by high school type; the scores of students who took the ACT are included in this table using a concordance table provided by Dorans (1999, p. 9); the overall sample mean on the SAT Math section was 608.6 (scale: 200–800).

TABLE 3 Average Grades in College-Level Calculus Among Students Responding to FICSMath Survey by Type of High School Where a Majority of High School Education Was Received ($N = 5,526$)

High school type	n	Median grade	Mean grade	SE
Homeschool	100	92.0	87.2***	1.219
Public	4,752	84.5	80.6	.202
Private, Parochial	418	84.5	82.3	.610
Private, Non-Parochial	227	84.5	81.9	.891
Public Charter	29	82.0	78.9	3.090

Note. Final course grades reported by college professors. This table excludes students repeating college-level calculus, or who took college-level precalculus. Grades reported on 0–100 point scale. Significance testing via Tukey post-hoc pairwise comparisons, reference category "public."
***$p < .001$.

Most students across school types reported taking either the SAT or the ACT. For students in traditional public schools, the completion rate was 80.2% ($n = 6,259$); for homeschoolers the completion rate was 74.3% ($n = 141$). Distributions of SAT Math scores were generally similar in range and shape but violated normality assumptions,[1] ruling out straight ANOVA tests for significance. Post-hoc Tukey pairwise comparisons of mean SAT Math scores indicated no significant differences by school type, with one exception: the mean score difference between students attending private, non-Parochial schools (624.7) and those attending traditional public schools (607.6) was significant at the $\alpha = 0.05$ level.

In Table 3 we report final course grades for single-variable college calculus by high school type. For this analysis, we excluded students repeating college calculus, or who took bridge mathematics courses after high school (e.g., college-level precalculus), as we were most interested in gaining insight into tertiary calculus performance from students taking different high school paths. This explains the change in homeschool numbers from more than 100 in all previous tables to exactly 100.

Distributions of final course grades in single-variable college calculus were generally similar in range and shape but violated normality assumptions,[2] ruling out straight ANOVA tests for significance. Post-hoc Tukey pairwise comparisons indicated that the difference between mean final course grades of students who homeschooled (87.2 out of 100) and those who attended traditional public schools (80.6 out of 100) was significant at the $\alpha = 0.05$ level.

Among first-time coursetakers, students who attended public, charter, and private schools during high school earned similar final grades in college calculus. Students who homeschooled during high school, however, earned significantly higher grades than students who attended traditional public schools ($\alpha = 0.05$). Even though the homeschoolers had the highest average grade, their advantage over students from school types other than

TABLE 4 Full Linear Regression Model of Average Grades in College-Level Calculus Among Students Responding to FICSMath Survey by Type of High School Where a Majority of High School Education Was Received and Background Characteristics ($N = 5,701$)

Student background characteristics	B	SE B	β
Intercept	55.212	2.304	–
Homeschool	4.357	1.710	.042*
Public	−1.262	1.457	−.031
Private, Parochial	.087	1.474	.002
Private, Non-Parochial	−1.260	1.555	−.019
Public Charter	−.432	2.826	−.002
Gender	−3.664	.409	−.131***
White	1.822	1.175	.048
Black	−.441	1.399	−.006
Asian	.849	1.206	.017
Pacific Islander	2.900	2.185	.020
American Indian/Alaska Native	−2.068	1.677	−.018
Other race	.625	1.443	.010
Hispanic origin	−.500	1.146	−.008
English primary home language	−1.979	.868	−.042*
Highest education, male parent/guardian	.245	.205	.021
Highest education, female parent/guardian	.052	.223	.004
Home support for math	.878	.171	.077***
SAT/ACT Math scores	.041	.002	.281***

Note. This table excludes students repeating college-level calculus, or who took college-level precalculus. School type, race, ethnicity, and home language coded as 0 = no, 1 = yes. Gender coded as 0 = female; 1 = male. Math scores of students who took the ACT converted to SAT math scores per ACT-SAT concordance table (Dorans, 1999). "Home support for math" coded on a 0–5 rating scale; 0 = *not supportive at all*, 5 = *very supportive*.
*$p < .05$; ***$p < .001$.

public schools did not reach significance. This may be due in part to the relatively low numbers in this school type—and accordingly low statistical power.

Finally, we predicted student performance in tertiary calculus from school type in multivariate linear regression models. All predictors discussed above (school type, gender, race, ethnicity, home language, parental education, home support for mathematics, and SAT/ACT math scores) were included in an initial multivariate model. This full model is presented in Table 4, with predictors grouped by conceptual area.

Notably, just five predictors in the initial (full) model appeared to demonstrate significance—homeschooling, gender, English as the primary home language, home support for mathematics, and SAT/ACT mathematics score. None of the other school types appeared likely to contribute to a final (reduced) model.

A final (reduced) model was generated from this initial model by stepwise regression, wherein nonsignificant predictors were deleted one at a time until only statistically significant items remained (criterion for model entry: $\alpha = 0.25$; criterion for retention: $\alpha = 0.05$). The final model included

TABLE 5 Final Linear Regression Model of Average Grades in College-Level Calculus Among Students Responding to FICSMath Survey by Type of High School Where a Majority of High School Education Was Received ($N = 5,701$)

Student background characteristics	B	SE B	β
Intercept	54.220	1.369	—
SAT/ACT Math scores	.041	.002	.280
Gender	−3.652	.405	−.130
Home support for math	.962	.164	.085
Homeschool	5.186	1.460	.050

Note. All predictors significant at $p < .001$ and ranked by β. This table excludes students repeating college-level calculus, or who took college-level precalculus. Math scores of students who took the ACT converted to SAT math scores per ACT-SAT concordance table (Dorans, 1999). Gender coded as $0 =$ female; $1 =$ male. "Home support for math" coded on a 0–5 rating scale; $0 = $ *not supportive at all*, $5 = $ *very supportive*. "Homeschool" coded as $0 = $ no, $1 = $ yes.

four of the predictors identified in the initial model (homeschool status, gender, home support for mathematics, and SAT/ACT mathematics score). The final model also saw one predictor demonstrating significance in the initial model removed (English as the primary home language). The final (reduced) model is presented in Table 5. The number of homeschool students in the final model was 100. No other high school types survived in the model, thus they are not shown in Table 5.

The most powerful predictor of final college calculus course grades appeared to be SAT/ACT math scores. The parameter estimate for SAT/ACT math scores (scale of 200–800 points) may be interpreted as "An SAT/ACT math score increase of 1 point predicted a final college calculus grade increase of .041 points." An increase in SAT/ACT math scores of 1 standard deviation (here, 100.1 points), would therefore predict a final college calculus grade increase of 4.1 points.

Being female, reporting supportive home environments for mathematics, and homeschooling were also found to be successful predictors of higher final college calculus grades. For homeschooling, the parameter estimate of 5.2 may be interpreted as "Homeschooling (versus enrollment in a traditional school type) predicted a final college calculus grade increase of 5.2 points." The variability captured from the FICSMath dataset was 10.42% and 0.24% for the controls and the added homeschool variable, respectively. The total variability captured was 10.66%. While the homeschool variable captured a comparatively small percentage of the variability, it is important to recognize that no other school type survived the model.

LIMITATIONS

Importantly, the nature of the dataset restricts its generalizability to *only* those students who made the leap from high school mathematics to tertiary calculus, with an obvious selection bias toward the upper reaches of mathematics ability and affinity, vis-à-vis the general high school population. This limitation also applies to the groups of homeschoolers. Readers are warned not to draw broad conclusions from this work about "all students who homeschool." *How restricted are generalizations made from this work?* With respect to high school graduation, NCES estimated that the national Averaged Freshman Graduation Rate for 2009–2010 (most recent data; includes those who homeschooled) was 78.2% (Stillwell & Sable, 2013, p. 4). College matriculation has been estimated at 68.2% of high school graduates (2-year average [2010 & 2011]; includes 2- and 4-year colleges; NCES, 2012a, Table 236). And the most recent examination of college course taking indicated that roughly 32.5% of bachelor's degree recipients in 2007–2008 earned credit for college calculus (NCES 2013b, Table 12). So the students included in the FICSMath dataset and reported here are a subset of those who attended high school, certainly not a majority. Yet there is still some use in these estimates, and it is worth considering what these estimates may capture. If it is reasonable to characterize students who graduated from high school, went to college, and enrolled in calculus as "successful" in the domain of mathematics achievement—then the group of students included in the FICSMath dataset represent something of an upper limit. These students are the ones who have done well in mathematics. Likewise, it seems reasonable to think that those not in the dataset—who did not take calculus, who did not go to college, or who did not graduate from high school—are the ones who have been (as a group) less successful in mathematics. The findings we present may shed some light on the achievement of students who have done well in mathematics, but are likely silent on the achievement of the majority who have not.

A second limitation is that the FICSMath dataset is predominantly based on student surveys (with the exception of professor-provided final course grades), so the findings here include limitations all surveys face: What students retrospectively report about parent education levels or home support, for example, may not align precisely with the same data parents themselves would provide.

DISCUSSION

The title of this article asks a single question: *Are homeschoolers prepared for college calculus?* While a complete answer this question remains elusive, the evidence from the FICSMath survey presented above is worth considering in some detail.

First, the racial and ethnic backgrounds of students in the FICSMath sample appear comparable to undergraduates nationwide. Majorities of students in the FICSMath dataset (currently taking single-variable college calculus)—homeschooled or otherwise—were male, White, non-Hispanic, and used

English while at home during the high school years. The most recent available U.S. Census data (for the 2010–2011 school year) appear similar: 70% of U.S undergraduates identified as "White alone" (70%), and 90% identified as non-Hispanic (NCES, 2012b, Indicator 10); we do not have reliable data about previous home language use among college students. The 190 students in the FICSMath sample who reported homeschooling for a majority of high school also appear to be demographically comparable to students who attended other types of high schools by gender, race, ethnicity, or home language; we found no evidence of differential selection into homeschooling by these factors.

Second, we examined parent/guardian education and home support for mathematics while in high school. Parents of homeschoolers appearing in the FICSMath dataset appear to have had about as much education as parents of students who attended Parochial or non-Parochial private schools (averaging approximately "four years" of college), and more education than those whose children attended public or charter schools (averaging "some" college). Homeschoolers also reported higher scores for "degree to which home environment was supportive of math," (averaging 4.2 on a 5-point scale) compared to all other school types (averaging between 3.4 and 4.0 on a 5-point scale). While both findings may make some amount of intuitive sense, we cannot overemphasize that we do not have evidence of a causal relationship in these data; a range of mechanisms are possible.

Third, in Figure 3 we examined SAT Math scores (and concordant ACT Math scores). We found no significant differences between mean SAT Math scores of students who reported homeschooling and those who attended other types of high schools (mean scores ranged between 596–618), with the exception of students who attended private, non-Parochial schools, whose SAT Math score average (625) was significantly higher than that of students who attended traditional public schools. Such a "no difference" finding comparing students who homeschooled to students from other types of schools appears slightly more positive than the findings of Belfield (2005) and Qaqish (2007), who reported slightly lower SAT Math and ACT Math scores among homeschoolers, respectively.

Fourth, in Table 3 we examined final course grades in single-variable college calculus. We found that, among first-time calculus students who had not taken college precalculus, students who homeschooled earned significantly higher final grades (Mean: 87.2 out of 100) than students who attended all other school types (Means ranged from 78.9–82.3 out of 100). We were intrigued by this finding, as it raises a number of questions. The demographic backgrounds of students who homeschooled appear similar to students who attended other types of high schools, including academic achievement in mathematics, yet they appear to earn higher college calculus grades. Why? Are we just seeing an artifact of differential selection into—or out of—college calculus, based on previous coursework, confidence, or other factors? Or is there some sort of beneficial "treatment effect" of homeschooling during high school that may carry over into college mathematics coursework? Again, we are unable to speak to these questions with the FICSMath dataset, but they highlight the need for further examination of homeschooling during the precollegiate years and the transition into college and careers.

Fifth, and finally, we examined the extent to which any of the predictors discussed throughout this article could successfully contribute to a model predicting final grades in single-variable college calculus. Our initial (full) model in Table 4 affirmed that homeschooling did show an effect that was significant and positive with all of the discussed controls included. We were somewhat surprised to see controls such as race, Hispanic origin, and parent education levels contribute little to the initial model—particularly given that parent education levels could conceivably contribute to a homeschooled student's experiences in mathematics. Yet it appears that "home support for mathematics" is a better (positive and significant) predictor of college calculus grades—yielding some evidence that parental support for mathematics matters more than parental education. The final (reduced) model, presented in Table 5, affirms a range of predictors determined significant, though the magnitude of each varied considerably. Most powerful were SAT/ACT math scores (our proxy measure for mathematics skills during high school), along with gender and home support for mathematics. Interestingly, although the FICSMath sample was found to be disproportionately (63%) male, we found that being male predicted lower final college calculus course grades (a drop of −3.7 points with a Y chromosome).

Our main interest in this article was the path of students by high school type—particularly those students who reported homeschooling. Homeschooling demonstrated significance as a predictor and is included in the final model (no other school type demonstrated significance), and the magnitude of the effect of homeschooling (versus not) appears to be considerable. A predicted final college calculus score gain of more than 5 points, or roughly half a grade, is certainly meaningful for students and worth consideration in future work.

There remains much work to be done in the area of homeschool research. For example, *Why do the students who homeschooled earn higher average college calculus grades than others?* Is this due to the impact of homeschooling as a treatment during the high school years? Are we seeing evidence of distinct student traits (e.g., if students who homeschooled were more likely than others to seek academic supports in college, ultimately earning higher grades)? Selection effects into or out of college calculus? Is in-school learning so bad that homeschoolers benefit from staying away? FICSMath is designed to explore some aspects of the mathematics experiences of students while in high school—but as we have noted above, the precise nature and average duration of, and course taking experiences during, homeschooling remain unknown, and what we have reported here indicates the worth of expanded attention in the future.

FUNDING

This research was supported by Grant No. 0813702 from the National Science Foundation. Any opinions, findings, and conclusions in this article are the authors' and do not necessarily reflect the views of the National Science Foundation.

NOTES

1. Via Kolmogorov-Smirnov test for large-n public schools, Shapiro-Wilk for other school types.
2. See Note 1.

REFERENCES

Anaya, G. (1999). Accuracy of self-reported test scores. *College and University, 75*(2), 13–19.

Baird, L. (1976). *Using self-reports to predict student performance* (Research Monograph No. 7). New York, NY: College Entrance Examination Board.

Barnett, M., Sonnert, G., & Sadler, P. (2012). More like us: The effect of immigrant generation on college success in mathematics. *International Migration Review, 46*(4), 891–918. doi:10.2307/41804867

Basham, P., Merrifield, J., & Hepburn, C. (2007). *Home schooling: From the extreme to the mainstream* (2nd ed.). Vancouver, BC: Frasier Institute. Retrieved from http://www.fraserinstitute.org/publicationdisplay.aspx?id=13089

Belfield, C. (2005). Home-schoolers' performance on the SAT. In B. Cooper (Ed.), *Home schooling in full view* (pp. 167–177). Charlotte, NC: Information Age Publishing.

Bielick, S. (2008). *1.5 million homeschooled students in the United States in 2007.* U.S. Department of Education (NCES 2009-030). Retrieved from http://www.nces.ed.gov/pubs2009/2009030.pdf

Boschee, B., & Boschee, F. (2011). A profile of homeschooling in South Dakota. *Journal of School Choice: International Research and Reform, 5*(3), 281–299. doi:10.1080/15582159.2011.604982

Bradburn, N. (2000). Temporal representation and event dating. In A. A. Stone, J. S. Turkan, C. A. Bachrach, J. B. Jobe, H. S. Kurtzman, & V. S. Cain (Eds.), *The science of self-report* (pp. 49–61). Mahwah, NJ: Lawrence Erlbaum Associates.

Dorans, N. (1999). *Correspondences between ACT and SAT I scores.* New York, NY: College Board. Retrieved from http://www.ets.org/Media/Research/pdf/RR-99-02-Dorans.pdf

Fagerland, M., & Sandvik, L. (2009), The Wilcoxon–Mann–Whitney test under scrutiny. *Statistics in Medicine, 28,* 1487–1497. doi:10.1002/sim.3561

Gaither, M. (2008). *Homeschool: An American history*. Hampshire, UK: Palgrave Macmillan.

Gloeckner, G., & Jones, P. (2013). Reflections on a decade of changes in homeschooling and the homeschooled into higher education. *Peabody Journal of Education, 88*(3), 309–323.

Herrold, K., & O'Donnell, K. (2008). Parent and family involvement in education, 2006–07 school year (NCES 2008-050). Washington, DC: National Center for Education Statistics. Retrieved from http://nces.ed.gov/pubs2008/2008050.pdf

Home School Legal Defense Association (HSLDA). (2014). *State laws*. Purcelville, VA: Author. Retrieved from http://www.hslda.org/laws

Isenberg, E. (2002). *Home schooling: School choice and women's time use*. Occasional Paper Series, National Center for the Study of Privatization in Education, Teachers College. Retrieved from http://ncspe.org/publications_files/406_OP64.pdf

Isenberg, E. (2007). What have we learned about homeschooling? *Peabody Journal of Education, 82*(2–3), 387–409. doi:10.1080/01619560701312996

Jones-Sanpei, H. (2008). Practical school choice in the United States: A proposed taxonomy and estimates of use. *Journal of School Choice: International Research and Reform, 2*(3), 318–337. doi:10.1080/15582150802378676

Kafer, K. (2009). A chronology of school choice in the U.S. *Journal of School Choice: International Research and Reform, 3*(4), 415–416. doi:10.1080/15582150903489786

Kuncel, N., Credé, M., & Thomas, L. (2005). The validity of self-reported grade point averages, RICs, and test scores: A meta-analysis and review of the literature. *Review of Educational Research, 75*(1), 63–82. Retrieved from http://www.jstor.org/stable/3516080

Kunzman, R., & Gaither, M. (2013). Homeschooling: A comprehensive survey of the research. *Other Education: The Journal of Educational Alternatives, 2*(1), 4–59. Retrieved from http://www.othereducation.stir.ac.uk/index.php/OE/article/view/10/55

Murnane, R., & Willett, J. (2011). *Methods matter: Improving causal inference in educational and social science research*. Oxford, UK: Oxford University Press.

National Center for Education Statistics (NCES). (2009). *National Household Education Survey, 2007* [Data file]. Washington, DC: Author. Retrieved from http://nces.ed.gov/nhes/dataproducts.asp#2007dp

National Center for Education Statistics (NCES). (2012a). *Digest of education statistics, 2012*. Washington, DC: Author. Retrieved from http://nces.ed.gov/programs/digest/d12/

National Center for Education Statistics (NCES). (2012b). *Participation in education, 2012*. Washington, DC: Author. Retrieved from http://nces.ed.gov/pubs2012/2012045_2.pdf

National Center for Education Statistics (NCES). (2012c). *Improving the measurement of socioeconomic status for the National Assessment of Educational Progress: A theoretical foundation*. Washington, DC: Author. Retrieved from http://nces.ed.gov/nationsreportcard/pdf/researchcenter/socioeconomic_factors.pdf

National Center for Education Statistics (NCES). (2013a). *Charter school enrollment*. Washington, DC: Author. Retrieved from http://nces.ed.gov/programs/coe/pdf/coe_cgb.pdf

National Center for Education Statistics (NCES). (2013b). *Today's baccalaureate: The fields and courses that 2007-08 bachelor's degree recipients studied* (NCES 2013-755). Washington, DC: Author. Retrieved from http://nces.ed.gov/pubs2013/2013755.pdf

Niemi, R., & Smith, J. (2003). The accuracy of students' reports of course taking in the 1994 National Assessment of Educational Progress. *Educational Measurement: Issues and Practice, 22*(1), 15–21. doi:10.1111/j.1745-3992.2003.tb00112.x

Pace, C., Barahona, D., & Kaplan, D. (1985). *The credibility of student self-reports*. Los Angeles, CA: UCLA Center for the Study of Evaluation.

Qaqish, B. (2007). An analysis of homeschooled and non-homeschooled students' performance on an ACT mathematics achievement test. *Home School Researcher, 17*(2), 1–12.

Ray, B. (2009). Homeschool progress report 2009: Academic achievement and demographics. Purcelville, VA: Home School Legal Defense Association. Retrieved from http://www.hslda.org/docs/study/ray2009/

Ray, B. (2010). Academic achievement and demographic traits of homeschool students: A nationwide study. *Academic Leadership Journal, 8*(1), 1–40. Retrieved from http://contentcat.fhsu.edu/cdm/compoundobject/collection/p15732coll4/id/456/rec/1

Ray, B. (2011). *2.04 million homeschool students in the United States in 2010*. National Home Education Research Institute Report. Retrieved from http://www.nheri.org/HomeschoolPopulationReport2010.pdf

Rudner, E. (1999). Scholastic achievement and demographic characteristics of home school students in 1998. *Education Policy Analysis Archives, 7*(8), 1–33. Retrieved from epaa.asu.edu/ojs/article/view/543

Spielhagen, F. (2013). *Debating single-sex education: Separate and equal?* (2nd ed.). Lanham, MD: Rowman & Littlefield Education.

Stillwell, R., & Sable, J. (2013). *Public school graduates and dropouts from the common core of data: School year 2009–10: First Look* (Provisional Data) (NCES 2013-309rev). U.S. Department of Education. Washington, DC: National Center for Education Statistics. Retrieved from nces.ed.gov/pubs2013/2013309rev.pdf

Tai, R., & Sadler, P. (2007). High school chemistry instructional practices and their association with college chemistry grades. *Journal of Chemical Education, 84*(6), 1040–1046. Retrieved from http://www.cfa.harvard.edu/smg/ficss/research/articles/JCE_Instruction_Prac.pdf

United States Census Bureau. (2012). *Current Population Survey, 2012* [Data file]. Retrieved from http://www.census.gov/hhes/school/data/cps/2012/tables.html

Wade, C. (2011). *Secondary preparation for single variable college calculus: Significant pedagogies used to revise the four component instructional design model* (Unpublished doctoral dissertation). Clemson University, Clemson, SC.

West, R. (2009). The harms of homeschooling. *Philosophy and Public Policy Quarterly, 29*, 7–11. Retrieved from ippp.gmu.edu/QQ/Vol29_3-4.pdf

Does Homeschooling or Private Schooling Promote Political Intolerance? Evidence From a Christian University

ALBERT CHENG

Political tolerance is the willingness to extend civil liberties to people who hold views with which one disagrees. Some have claimed that private schooling and homeschooling are institutions that propagate political intolerance by fostering separatism and an unwillingness to consider alternative viewpoints. I empirically test this claim by measuring the political tolerance levels of undergraduate students attending an evangelical Christian university. Using ordinary least squares regression analysis, I find that for these students, greater exposure to private schooling instead of traditional public schooling is not associated with any more or less political tolerance, and greater exposure to homeschooling is associated with more political tolerance.

Since the inception of the American primary and secondary public school system in the 19th century, one of its aims has been to prepare children to be healthy participants in civil society. Accomplishing this aim requires inculcating several civic virtues into children. One of these virtues is political tolerance, defined as the willingness to extend basic civil liberties to political or social groups that hold views with which one disagrees.

The public school system instructs the vast majority of American children, but many children receive formal schooling through other means. For instance, the U.S. Department of Education estimates that 4.5 million students attended private schools during the 2011–2012 school year, 80% of whom attended private schools with a religious orientation (Broughman & Swaim, 2013). During the same time period, 1.8 million children were home-schooled, according to other data from the U.S. Department of Education. Though this figure only represents 3.4% of the school-age population, trends indicate that the number of homeschooled children continues to rapidly expand (Noel, Stark, Redford, & Zuckerberg, 2013).

Yet some political theorists and pundits have questioned whether private schooling, especially if it is religious in nature, and homeschooling are institutions that are capable of inculcating political tolerance as well as other virtues necessary for healthy civic life in a liberal democracy. Both religious private schooling and homeschooling have been viewed as institutions that propagate political intolerance by fostering separatism, religious fundamentalism, and an unwillingness to consider alternative worldviews or values (Apple, 2005; Balmer, 2006; Boston, 2011; Ross, 2010; Yurakco, 2008).

Critics of religious private schooling and homeschooling further contend that the traditional public school system has the comparative advantage in teaching children to be politically tolerant. These critics reason that a traditional public school takes all students and consequently exposes each of its students to different ideas and other people who come from a diverse set of backgrounds. Such exposure then creates opportunities for students to learn to be more open minded, prepared for democratic life, cooperative with those who hold different perspectives than they do, and enabled to overcome any prejudices that their parents may possess (Gutmann, 1987; Reich, 2005; West, 2009). Indeed, the founders of the U.S. public school system argued that providing all students with a common schooling experience would temper the religious fanaticism that threatens to fracture civil society (Glenn, 1988).

These claims regarding the impact of public schools, private schools, and homeschooling on political tolerance are theoretically plausible, but do they comport with the empirical evidence? This study tests these claims by analyzing the political tolerance levels of students who attend a private, evangelical Christian university (henceforth, referred to as "the university" to maintain anonymity) but have varying primary and secondary schooling backgrounds. In particular, I seek to answer the following research question: Are children who attended traditional public schools more politically tolerant than children who were homeschooled or attended private schools? The aim is to paint a descriptive picture of the relationship between schooling background and political tolerance. The results will bring empirical evidence to bear upon the claim that public schools are more effective than private schools and homeschooling at instilling political tolerance into students. Without such an investigation, we are left with generalizations and articles of faith about the nature of public schools, private schools, and homeschooling and their respective effects on political tolerance.

The remainder of this article is divided into four sections. What follows in the first section is a review of the previous research findings regarding educational background and political tolerance. Second, I describe the data set and methods that I use in this study. I present the results in the third section and conclude with a discussion of those results in the final section.

LITERATURE REVIEW

Private Schooling and Political Tolerance

OBSERVATIONAL EVIDENCE

Contrary to the widespread belief that public schools have the comparative advantage in instilling the virtue of political tolerance in children, empirical studies have generally concluded that children who attend private schools are at least as politically tolerant as children who attend public schools (Wolf, 2005). Several nationally representative studies provide evidence for this point. For instance, in a national survey of 3,400 Latinos, Greene, Giammo, and Mellow (1999) find that adults who have received some private schooling for their primary and secondary education are more politically tolerant than those who have only received traditional public schooling. Elsewhere, the National Household Education Survey (NHES) conducted by the U.S. Department of Education reveals that children who attend Catholic and secular private schools are more politically tolerant than children who attend public schools (Belfield, 2004; Campbell, 2002a).

Although the NHES data also demonstrate that children who attend religious, non-Catholic private schools are *less* politically tolerant than public-school children, this result is contrasted by several other studies that find students who attend evangelical-Christian schools exhibit as much if not more political tolerance than their counterparts who attend public schools (Godwin, Ausbrooks, & Martinez, 2001; Wolf, Greene, Kleitz, & Thalhammer, 2001). However, Godwin, Godwin, and Martinez-Ebers (2004) find mixed results for students in fundamentalist Christian high schools. Among 10th graders, students at the fundamentalist school were less politically tolerant than their public-school counterparts, but the difference becomes statistically insignificant when controlling for various background characteristics. On the other hand, 12th graders at the fundamentalist school exhibited greater political tolerance than the 12th graders in public schools.

Notably, Godwin and colleagues (2004) also found that 10th-graders in the fundamentalist school more strongly disliked groups that advocated for more homosexual and women's rights.[1] This result, however, is not indicative of political tolerance. To reiterate, political tolerance is defined as the willingness to extend civil liberties to groups who hold views with which one disagrees. As Sullivan, Piereson, and Marcus (1982) and Thiessen (2001) have argued, one can dislike particular groups and disapprove of their beliefs but still tolerate them.

EXPERIMENTAL EVIDENCE

Studies of private-school vouchers bring an additional body of evidence to bear upon the ability of public and private schools to instill political tolerance in their respective students. Because the vouchers are randomly awarded by lottery, these studies are able to utilize an experimental design to determine the causal effects of attending a private school. Outcomes of students who have applied for and been awarded a voucher to attend a private school (the treatment group) are compared with students who have applied for but not been awarded a voucher (the control group). These studies report that voucher students are at least as politically tolerant as those who did not receive a voucher (Campbell, 2002b; Howell, Peterson, Wolf, & Campbell, 2002; Wolf, Peterson, & West, 2001). These experimental studies allow one to infer that greater political tolerance among private-school students is caused by private schooling instead of other factors that may have influenced these students to select into private schools absent a lottery.

Overall, the empirical evidence demonstrates that the belief that private schools instill illiberal and intolerant attitudes is mistaken. Rather, private schools are as able and, in several cases, more effective than public schools at inculcating political tolerance in students. Nonetheless, the issue remains salient today. Critics of school choice programs, for example, still worry that religious private schools will engage in religious indoctrination, teaching students extreme views and fostering closed-mindedness (Tabachnick, 2011; Wing, 2012).

Homeschooling and Political Tolerance

On the other hand, little empirical inquiry has been conducted regarding the political tolerance levels of homeschooled children. In a rich, narrative study of six conservative Christian homeschooling families, Kunzman (2009) asked parents whether they would approve of government regulations to restrict other homeschooling parents from teaching religious views or other ideologies with which they disagreed. In each case, the parents generally disapproved of such regulations, despite their convictions against those opposing religions or ideologies. Kunzman further observed that homeschooled children were more politically tolerant than their parents. But because the study only focused on homeschooling families, it contains no comparisons of political tolerance between homeschooled children and children who attend public or private schools.

Other studies of homeschooling have investigated other civic outcomes besides political tolerance. In one analysis, Smith and Sikkink (1999) use the 1996 NHES data set and find that parents of homeschooled children are more involved in civic activities (e.g., voting, attending public meetings, volunteering for community service, or contacting their public officials) than parents of public-school children. Elsewhere, a survey of over 7,000 adults in the United States who were homeschooled as children demonstrates that they are more involved in their communities and engaged in civic affairs than other U.S. adults (Ray, 2004). Summarizing the research on homeschooling and civic engagement and participation, Medlin (2000) writes:

> Home-schooled children are taking part in the daily routines of their communities. They are certainly not isolated; in fact, they associated with—and feel close to—all sorts of people. . . . They may be more socially mature and have better leadership skills than other children as well. And they appear to be functioning effectively as members of adult society. (p. 119)

This conclusion is consistent with Medlin's (2013) more recent review of the homeschooling research and contradicts the theory that homeschooling diminishes a child's sense of civic engagement and participation (Apple, 2005; Lubienski, 2000; Reich, 2002).

Although none of these studies specifically compare the political tolerance levels of children with different schooling backgrounds, they may help to form theories. For instance, it is not unreasonable to expect that those who are more community minded tend to form more associations with others from different cultural backgrounds or hold different viewpoints, even without attending public schools. Thus, an increase in community mindedness may be associated with an increase in political tolerance, a conclusion with some empirical support (Cigler & Joslyn, 2002). However, greater community mindedness does not necessarily lead to exposure to a greater diversity of groups as many individuals may have rich associations but only with others who are like them. Putnam (2000) differentiates between *bonding* and *bridging* social capital. The former helps to "reinforce exclusive identities and homogenous groups"; the latter is "outward looking," helping individuals to establish relationships with others "across diverse social cleavages" and to form heterogeneous group associations (p. 22). So given limited research evidence that homeschooled students are more community minded than other students, it is sensible to predict that homeschooled students will also be more politically tolerant while recognizing that it is equally reasonable to suspect that home schooling will be less politically tolerant. More empirical work linking community mindedness and political tolerance would be helpful.

A second reason to suspect that homeschooled students are more politically tolerant is related to the degree of self-actualization that they have experienced. Sullivan and colleagues (1982) theorized and empirically verified that individuals who have a stronger sense of their personal identity tend to exhibit more political tolerance. Greene (2005) explains:

> A Catholic (for example) who is secure in his own identity as a Catholic will find it easier to accept that others are not Catholic, and thus to accept their right not to be Catholic, whereas a Catholic who is not secure in his own Catholicness may seek to prove (to others and himself) that he really is Catholic by denigrating non-Catholics and refusing to respect their rights. (p. 194)

Individuals who are less secure in their identity tend to feel more threatened when their views are challenged. Hence, they wish to control or even quell these threats and ultimately are more uncompromising in their actions and outlook. Because homeschooling is a highly personalized educational arrangement and usually constitutes holistically introducing students to a particular worldview and way of life, homeschooled students typically attain a higher degree of self-actualization (Medlin, 2013; Sheffer, 1997). Consequently, homeschooled students may be more politically tolerant than those who attend a traditional public school. In fact, traditional public schools may be an institution that stunts self-actualization for some of its students because it threatens those students' sense of self by endorsing a worldview that clashes with the one held by those students (Kunzman, 2010).

Indeed, data from the U.S. Department of Education show that parents most often choose to homeschool their children because they "desire to provide religious or moral instruction" (Planty et al., 2009, p. 14). Critics of homeschooling charge that this desire is precisely the problem: Instilling a single worldview into children causes them to be more narrow minded and intolerant. However, other empirical work suggests that this may not be the case; rather, religious values are consistent with values necessary for a liberal democracy. For instance, Eisenstein (2006) has documented that Christians largely agree that the principles of their faith require them to be tolerant of others who hold views with which they disagree. Thus, homeschooling that places an emphasis on religious and moral instruction may actually help to foster political tolerance. At the very least, Christian families engaging in homeschooling for religious and moral reasons may value others' right to religious freedom and exhibit more tolerance simply because they recognize that their ability to homeschool is founded upon that same right.

CONTRIBUTION OF THIS PRESENT STUDY

Homeschooling is a controversial public policy issue and the subject of spirited debate. In particular, there are reasons to believe that homeschooling may lead to greater political tolerance or diminish it, yet there are no empirical studies testing these reasons (Ray, 2013). This present study is intended to begin filling this gap in the literature about homeschooling as well as to add to the empirical literature that compares the political tolerance levels of students who attend private and public schools—an issue that until recently has less often been empirically investigated.

Scholars have also become increasingly interested in comparing students across all schooling types (i.e., public school, religious and nonreligious private schools, and homeschooling). Data to conduct such inquiry have been rare but are becoming more widely available. The National Study on Youth and Religion, for example, is a nationally-representative, longitudinal survey of adolescents that has generated numerous research opportunities, including an investigation into the influence of school type on student religiosity (Uecker, 2008). Similarly, the Cardus Education Survey enables researchers to examine academic, spiritual, and cultural outcomes of U.S. and Canadian adults who have attended different types of schools (Van Pelt, Sikkink, Pennings, & Seel, 2012). In this present study, I follow these efforts to make comparisons across school types by analyzing political tolerance outcomes—a related outcome but one not yet investigated using the two aforementioned data sets—for undergraduate students with diverse schooling experiences. The data and the methods used in this study are the topics of the next section.

DATA AND METHODS

Measuring Political Tolerance

An individual's level of political tolerance is measured by a widely-used instrument developed by Sullivan and colleagues (1982), who have also shown the instrument to possess a high degree of validity and reliability. The instrument, called the *content-controlled political tolerance scale*, consists of two parts. In the first part, the political tolerance scale provides the respondent with a list of popular social and political groups, such as Republicans, gay-rights activists, or fundamentalist Christians. The respondent is asked to select the group with beliefs that he opposes the most; this group is called his *least-liked group*. If there is an unlisted group that the respondent opposes even more, he is given the option to write down the name of that group.

The second part of the political tolerance scale measures the respondent's willingness to extend basic civil liberties to members of his least-liked group. The respondent is presented with a series of statements about his least-liked group and is asked to indicate his level of agreement with those statements. For instance, one statement proposes, "Members of your [least-liked group] should be allowed to make a public speech." The respondent then selects one of five answer choices in reply to that statement: strongly disagree, disagree, neutral, agree, or strongly agree. Agreeing would be the more tolerant answer for this specific statement, whereas disagreeing may be considered more tolerant for other reverse-coded questions. The responses to each statement are coded and combined to create an overall measure of political tolerance for the respondent.

Study Sample

The study sample consists of 304 out of the approximately 4,000 undergraduates at the university—a private, Christian university in the western United States. I collected data using a survey with the content-controlled political tolerance scale and several questions asking about the study participants' demographic and ideological background characteristics. Study participants also indicated the type of school (i.e., traditional public school, private school, homeschool) that they attended for each year throughout their 13 years of primary and secondary education. A stratified sampling method was used to create a representative sample of the university's student body. Specifically, because all students either (a) live in one of the many campus dormitories or (b) live off-campus and commute, the student population was stratified by place of residence. The university's administrative office provided data detailing the number of students who lived in each dormitory and the number of students who commuted. The research team then randomly sampled students within each stratum, administering the surveys face-to-face. The data that the research team collected were ultimately weighted by strata to make the study sample reflective of the student population at the university. Descriptive statistics of the sample are displayed in Table 1.

There are three reasons why the university's student body provides a useful population to explore this study's research question. First, the university was founded upon and continues to operate according to a more fundamentalist Christian tradition. In fact, one of its missions is to provide a biblically-based education, and all undergraduate students must agree to a doctrinal statement in order to apply for admission and regularly attend chapels throughout the school week. At minimum, describing the political tolerance levels of students who selected into this type of university will be valuable, especially because critics of private schooling and homeschooling contend that students who have greater exposure to religiously conservative environments do not learn to tolerate alternative viewpoints. Indeed, the students at the university who attended private schools or were homeschooled for their primary or secondary education likely did so for religious or moral reasons.

Second, students at the university have experienced different amounts of public schooling, private schooling, or homeschooling. Not only have many students received their formal education in only one of the three

TABLE 1 Sample Statistics

	Percent
Gender	
Female	60.86
Male	39.14
Age	20.21[a]
Year in School	
Freshman	22.11
Sophomore	27.39
Junior	27.06
Senior	20.46
Fifth-year or more	2.97
Major	
Humanities	31.91
Life Sciences	24.01
Business	10.20
Social Sciences	8.22
Education	10.53
Technical Sciences or Engineering	12.50
Undeclared	2.63
Racial or Ethnic Background	
American Indian or Alaskan Native	0.66
Asian or Pacific Islander	20.93
Black	1.00
Hispanic or Latino	12.96
White	60.80
Mixed-Race	3.65
Years of Homeschooling[b]	
0 years (No homeschooling)	78.95
1−6 years	8.56
7−12 years	7.57
13 years (Only homeschooling)	4.93
Years of Private Schooling[b]	
0 years (No private schooling)	50.00
1−6 years	24.67
7−12 years	15.46
13 years (Only private schooling)	9.87
Years of Public Schooling[b]	
0 years (No public schooling)	21.05
1−6 years	18.08
7−12 years	20.07
13 years (Only public schooling)	40.79

Note. $N = 304$.
[a]Denotes a sample average; all other numbers are percentages.
[b]Students were asked to indicate whether they received private schooling, public schooling, or homeschooling for each of their 13 years of primary and secondary education; for purposes of brevity, figures presented in the table are aggregated into the four categories (a) no years, (b) 1−6 years, (c) 7−12 years, and (d) 13 years.

schooling sectors but also many others have received their formal education in more than one of these sectors. For instance, some students attended public primary schools but then attended private secondary schools. Others were homeschooled before attending public or private schools. This variation enables me to answer the original research question by using ordinary least squares regression analysis to estimate the relationship between amount of schooling in a particular school sector and political tolerance. It is rare to conduct such an analysis because of the difficulty in finding populations that include substantial proportions of homeschooled students while being easily accessible for data collection.

Third, though the students differ in schooling background, they have all self-selected to attend the university. Thus, they are similar on many observable and unobservable characteristics (e.g., religiosity, academic achievement) that may have led to this selection. This homogeneity naturally acts as a way to control for many background characteristics, helping to isolate the explanatory power of schooling background on political tolerance. Of course, the sample is not perfectly homogenous, so I still control for various observable background characteristics in my empirical model when possible.

Empirical Model and Analyses

In particular, I estimate the following model:

$$y_i = \beta_0 + \beta_1 H_i + \beta_2 P_i + \boldsymbol{\beta_3 X_i} + \mu_i,$$

where y_i is the political tolerance score for student i and $\mathbf{X_i}$ is a vector of variables that control for ideological and demographic background characteristics; u_i is the error term. P_i and H_i are the variables of interest and are equal to the number of years of private schooling and homeschooling that student i received, respectively. As mentioned earlier, I weighted the observations by sampling strata (the place of residence) in order to correct for any discrepancies between the study sample and the population of undergraduates at the university.

I also cluster my standard errors by sampling strata. Clustering is necessary because unobserved variation between students who live in the same place of residence may be correlated. For example, each residence hall community may develop its own distinct identity and eccentricities, which then influence all students who live there. Thus, students living in the same residence hall cannot be considered independent observations. Absent clustering, standard errors would typically be understated, consequently distorting the results by producing type I errors.

Note that years of public schooling is not included as a covariate. All students indicated the type of school they attended for each of the 13 years of primary and secondary schooling, so once the number of years of homeschooling and private schooling are determined, the number of years of public schooling is also determined. Thus, the estimate of β_1 in the regression model is interpreted as the partial effect on political tolerance that results from replacing one year of public schooling with one year of homeschooling. Likewise, the estimate of β_2 is interpreted as the partial effect on political tolerance that results from replacing one year of public schooling with one year of private schooling. I present the results in the following section.

RESULTS

Survey Responses

Table 2 lists the least-liked group that study participants have selected as well as the proportion of them who have chosen that group. It is unsurprising that most study participants have chosen atheists, pro-choicers (people who support abortion), and gay-rights activists as their least-liked group, given that they attend an evangelical-Christian, and hence more religiously conservative, university.

But the choice of a least-liked group is not an indication of political tolerance. Measuring levels of political tolerance requires analyzing the study participants' willingness to extend various civil liberties to members of their least-liked group, whatever it might be. Table 3 lists the eight Likert-scale items aimed at capturing this willingness and shows how the study participants responded to each statement. For example, about half of the respondents strongly disagreed that the government should be able to tap the phones of their least-liked group.

The last item in Table 3, "I feel that [the least-liked group] is dangerous," is not intended to capture political tolerance and hence is not included in the derivation of the political tolerance measure. Rather, that question is a measure of perceived threat. Studies have shown perceived threat is an important determinant of political tolerance, so it is included as an independent covariate in the regression models to distinguish its effect on political tolerance from the effects of other predictors of political tolerance (Eisenstein, 2006; Greene, Mellow, & Giammo, 1999; Sullivan et al., 1982; Wolf Greene, Kleitz, & Thalhammer, 2001).

TABLE 2 Least-Liked Group Selection

Group	Percentage
Atheists	36.18
Pro-choicers (people who support abortion)	29.61
Gay-rights activists	12.83
Muslims	7.24
Conservative Christians	6.25
Democrats	2.96
Other	1.65
Pro-lifers (people who oppose abortion)	1.64
Republicans	1.64

TABLE 3 Responses on the Tolerance Scale

	Response (Percentages)				
Likert-Scale Items	Strongly Disagree	Disagree	Neutral	Agree	Strongly Agree
The government should be able to tap the phones of [the least-liked group].	49.34	32.57	14.47	2.63	0.99
Members of [the least-liked group] should be allowed to teach in public schools.	7.26	12.21	20.79	36.30	23.43
Members of [the least-liked group] should be allowed to make a public speech.	3.62	7.57	15.46	42.43	30.92
Members of [the least-liked group] should be able to run for president or other elected office.	7.95	14.24	17.88	33.11	26.82
Members of [the least-liked group] should be able to hold public demonstrations or rallies.	5.2	14.14	22.37	33.55	24.01
Books that are written by members of the [the least-liked group] should be banned from the public library.	40.40	34.11	14.57	8.61	2.32
I would allow members of [the least-liked group] to live in my neighborhood.	0.66	4.98	8.97	43.19	42.19
[The least-liked group] should be outlawed.	40.53	26.58	15.95	9.97	7.97
I feel that [the least-liked group] is dangerous.	19.41	22.70	21.71	24.67	11.51

Note. $N = 304$. Scale comprised of the first 8 items. Cronbach's alpha $= 0.87$.

TABLE 4 Relative Frequency Table of Political Tolerance Levels

Score	Frequency (%)
−2.00 to −1.50	0.0
−1.51 to −1.00	2.0
−1.01 to −0.50	4.6
−0.49 to 0.00	8.9
0.01 to 0.50	19.4
0.51 to 1.00	25.0
1.01 to 1.50	18.1
1.51 to 2.00	22.0

Note. Average political tolerance score $= 0.860$. Standard deviation of political tolerance scores $= 0.790$. Political tolerance scores are derived by coding responses to each Likert-scale item and averaging them. Political tolerance scores can possibly range from −2 to 2. Higher scores mean that the individual is more tolerant. $N = 304$.

I code responses on the eight Likert-scale items on a scale of −2 to 2, with the higher numbers indicating the more politically tolerant answer. I then average the responses to the statements to generate a continuous measure of each study participant's political tolerance level. As mentioned in Table 4, the average political tolerance level is 0.860 with a standard deviation of 0.790. Political tolerance levels also range from slightly less than −1 to 2.

Results of Regression Analysis

Table 5 displays the results from various specifications of the model that I use to estimate the relationship between political tolerance and educational background. The first column is a rudimentary specification in which political tolerance scores are regressed on years of homeschooling and years of private schooling without any demographic or ideological control variables. This specification suggests that replacing a year of public schooling with homeschooling is associated with an increase in political tolerance by about 0.04 scale points (about 5% of a standard deviation in political tolerance). This result is significant at the level of $p < 0.01$. On the other hand, replacing one year of public schooling with one year of private schooling is associated with a decrease in political tolerance by about 0.01 scale points, a result that is only marginally significant ($p < 0.1$).

However, background demographic characteristics such as gender, race, or socioeconomic status have been shown to be important predictors of political tolerance (Campbell, 2002a; Wolf, Greene, et al., 2001). And even though the study sample consists of students at a conservative Christian university, political leanings and denominational affiliations may still vary. Because these demographic and ideological background characteristics are also predictors of political tolerance, it is essential to explicitly control for them in my analysis to avoid omitted variable bias (Eisenstein, 2006; Sullivan et al., 1982).

As shown in columns 2 and 3 of Table 5, adding only the demographic variables or both the demographic and ideological variables substantively changes the results. The decrease in political tolerance that is associated with private schooling is no longer statistically significant, and the positive relationship between homeschooling and political tolerance remains robust to these additional control variables.

It is worthwhile to mention that coefficient estimates of the control variables generally point in the expected direction. For instance, students who come from racial or ethnic minority backgrounds exhibit less political tolerance relative to White students. This result is consistent with the theory that a greater sense of perceived threat—a sense more common to individuals from racial or ethnic minority backgrounds—is associated with less political tolerance. This theory also explains why coefficient estimates for males is positive and statistically significant. That is, males perceive less threat than females. The coefficient estimate for the variable capturing political ideology is not statistically different from zero but is positive as expected; those who hold a more liberal ideology are more politically tolerant. Likewise, individuals who voted in the most recent election, an indication of civic mindedness, are more politically tolerant than those who did not. Finally, 4th-year students who probably have experienced a greater degree of self-actualization exhibit more political tolerance relative to first-year students.

TABLE 5 Regression Results

Independent Variables	Dependent Variable: Political Tolerance		
	(1)	(2)	(3)
Years of homeschooling	0.040***	0.028***	0.026***
	(0.009)	(0.007)	(0.008)
Years of private schooling	−0.010*	−0.006	−0.006
	(0.006)	(0.010)	(0.013)
Perceived threat	−0.205***	−0.213***	−0.219***
	(0.033)	(0.023)	(0.028)
Demographic controls			
Male		0.204*	0.186*
		(0.097)	(0.098)
Age		−0.0164	−0.0208
		(0.042)	(0.042)
Year in school[a]			
2nd year		0.0502	0.0379
		(0.161)	(0.156)
3rd year		−0.0385	−0.0277
		(0.140)	(0.135)
4th year		0.331*	0.336*
		(0.181)	(0.182)
5th year or more		−0.130	−0.113
		(0.217)	(0.228)
Racial or ethnic background[b]			
American Indian or Alaskan Native		−0.179	−0.234
		(0.328)	(0.320)
Asian or Pacific Islander		−0.294***	−0.271**
		(0.096)	(0.108)
Black or African American		−1.210	−1.208*
		(0.740)	(0.680)
Latino or non-White Hispanic		−0.249**	−0.227**
		(0.092)	(0.077)
More than one race		−0.0250	−0.00730
		(0.141)	(0.120)
Mother's educational attainment[c]			
High school graduate/GED		−0.337	−0.329*
		(0.207)	(0.178)
2-year college graduate		−0.692***	−0.676***
		(0.173)	(0.172)
4-year college graduate		−0.607*	−0.594**
		(0.295)	(0.250)
Master's degree		−0.327*	−0.315**
		(0.155)	(0.141)
Doctoral or professional (MD, JD) Degree		−0.331*	−0.318
		(0.181)	(0.241)
Father's educational attainment[c]			
High school graduate/GED		0.0216	0.0292
		(0.248)	(0.237)
2-year college graduate		0.206	0.226
		(0.254)	(0.255)
4-year college graduate		0.154	0.177
		(0.251)	(0.237)
Master's degree		0.406	0.417
		(0.363)	(0.371)
Doctoral or professional (MD, JD) degree		0.0213	0.0481
		(0.338)	(0.348)

194

(Continued)

TABLE 5 (*Continued*)

	Dependent Variable: Political Tolerance		
Independent Variables	(1)	(2)	(3)
Annual household income ($)[d]			
25,000 to 49,999		0.128	0.121
		(0.118)	(0.125)
50,000 to 74,999		0.270	0.268
		(0.156)	(0.165)
75,000 to 99,999		0.0637	0.0806
		(0.182)	(0.181)
100,000 to 149,000		0.269	0.272
		(0.215)	(0.206)
Over 150,000		0.0691	0.0635
		(0.214)	(0.216)
Two parent household		−0.160	−0.158
		(0.157)	(0.150)
Ideological controls			
Evangelical denomination			0.0329
			(0.201)
Religion influences behavior			0.0726
			(0.106)
Ascribes to a liberal ideology			0.0340
			(0.109)
Voted in last election			0.104
			(0.0726)
Constant	0.802***	1.419	0.982
	(0.0351)	(0.892)	(1.352)
R^2	0.153	0.304	0.308

[a]Omitted category is first-year student.
[b]Omitted category is "White."
[c]Omitted category is parent with less than a high school education.
[d]Omitted category is family with less than $25,000 in annual household income.
*$p < 0.10$; **$p < 0.05$; ***$p < 0.01$.

In general, the direction of the coefficient estimates point to what previous studies have found and theory predicts, lending confidence to the validity of the analysis (Marcus, Sullivan, Theiss-Morse, & Wood, 1995; Sullivan et al., 1982; Wolf, Greene, et al., 2001).

DISCUSSION AND CONCLUSION

This study brings two contributions to the existing research on schooling and political tolerance. First, the finding that increased exposure to private schooling does not decrease political tolerance comports with and adds to the empirical evidence that students who attend private schools are at least as tolerant as students who attend public schools (Wolf, 2005). Second, this study adds new insight into the political tolerance outcomes of homeschooled children—a topic that, to the best of my knowledge, has not been empirically investigated until now. Specifically, among a relatively homogenous group of undergraduates, all of whom attend an evangelical Christian university, those with more exposure to homeschooling relative to public schooling tend to be more politically tolerant.

Both of the results conflict with the belief that a common system of public schools is essential not only for all students but particularly for religiously conservative students to learn political tolerance. Instead of decreasing political tolerance among students who are more conservative in their religious beliefs, homeschooling is associated with greater political tolerance, and private schooling is not associated with any less tolerance. In other words, members of the very group for which public schooling is believed to be most essential for inculcating political tolerance (i.e., those who are more strongly committed to a particular worldview and value system) actually exhibit at least as much or more tolerance when they are exposed to less public schooling.

On the other hand, this study is unable to provide insight into how students at the university compare with others who do not attend the university. So it is unclear to what the extent the two conclusions that (a) homeschooled students exhibit greater political tolerance and (b) private-schooled students do not exhibit less political tolerance than public-school students are generalizable to other populations. More importantly, the findings of this study would be undermined by selection bias if the university disproportionately attracts particularly tolerant students who happen to have more years of homeschooling or private schooling while simultaneously attracting particularly intolerant students who happen to have more years of public schooling. Although it is not obvious that such selection is occurring, it will be useful to conduct similar analyses using different samples from other contexts to investigate the generalizability of this study's findings.

It is also important to note that this study is not sufficient to establish any causal relationships. It is unclear whether an increase in political tolerance is due to the exposure to homeschooling or because of selection: It is possible that unobservable factors that lead students to choose homeschooling may also lead students to be more politically tolerant. For example, those who ascribe to a more libertarian ideology may choose to exercise their liberties by schooling their children at home rather than in a public school. At the same time, those who ascribe to a more libertarian ideology may tend to recognize others' right to freedom of conscience and hence, be more politically tolerant (Kunzman, 2009). If true, a causal link between homeschooling and political tolerance cannot be established.

Two theories for why homeschooling may cause an increase in political tolerance were suggested earlier. First, students who are homeschooled may attain a greater degree of self-actualization because homeschooling is highly conducive to personalized instruction and enables students to be taught a consistent worldview. Second, the religious values taught in a homeschooling environment as well as in many religious private schools are consistent with political tolerance and other values necessary for a liberal democracy. Verifying these theories requires showing that homeschooling (a) does indeed lead to a greater degree of self-actualization, which Sullivan and colleagues (1982) have shown to lead to greater political tolerance, and (b) is more conducive to inculcating religious values that are consistent with and help to develop political tolerance. Such additional investigation is outside the purview of this study but doing so in the future may help to better identify and understand the factors that lead to different levels of political tolerance for students with varying schooling backgrounds.

Until then, the results of this descriptive study remain valuable: Among a relatively homogenous group of students that have chosen to attend a religiously conservative, evangelical-Christian university, more exposure to private schooling is not associated with greater political intolerance as is commonly believed. And in this same context, more exposure to homeschooling is associated with greater political tolerance.

ACKNOWLEDGEMENTS

I would like to thank Patrick Wolf and the reviewers of the *Journal of School Choice* for providing feedback on earlier drafts of this article.

NOTE

1. Compared to 12th-grade public-school students, 12th graders at the fundamentalist school also exhibited greater dislike of groups advocating for more homosexual or women's rights. But after controlling for background characteristics, the difference became statistically indistinguishable.

REFERENCES

Apple, M. W. (2005). Away with all teachers: The cultural politics of homeschooling. In B. S. Cooper (Ed.), *Homeschooling in full view: A reader* (pp. 75–95). Greenwich, CT: Information Age.

Balmer, R. (2006). *Thy kingdom come: How the Religious Right distorts the faith and threatens America*. New York, NY: Basic Books.

Belfield, C. R. (2004). Democratic education across school types: Evidence for the U.S. from NHES99. *Education Policy Analysis Archives, 12*(43). Retrieved from http://epaa.asu.edu/epaa/v12n43/

Boston, R. (2011, November 10). *Government support for religious intolerance: A bad idea at home and abroad* [Web log post]. Retrieved from https://www.

au.org/blogs/wall-of-separation/government-support-for-religious-intolerance-a-bad-idea-at-home-and-abroad

Broughman, S. P., & Swaim, N. L. (2013). *Characteristics of private schools in the United States: Results from the 2011-12 private school universe survey* (NCES 2013-316). Retrieved from http://nces.ed.gov/pubs2013/2013316.pdf

Campbell, D. E. (2002a). Making democratic education work. In P. E. Peterson & D. E. Campbell (Eds.), *Charters, vouchers, and public education* (pp. 241–267). Washington, DC: Brookings Institution Press.

Campbell, D. E. (2002b). *The civic side of school reform: How do school vouchers affect civic education?* (Center for the Study of Democratic Politics Working Paper). Retrieved from http://www.princeton.edu/csdp/events/Campbell041702/campbell2.pdf

Cigler, A., & Joslyn, M. R. (2002). The extensiveness of group membership and social capital: The impact on political tolerance attitudes. *Political research quarterly*, *55*(1), 7–25.

Eisenstein, M. A. (2006). Rethinking the relationship between religion and political tolerance in the US. *Political Behavior*, *28*(4), 327–348.

Glenn, C. (1988). *The myth of the common school*. Amherst, MA: The University of Massachusetts Press.

Godwin, R. K, Ausbrooks, C., & Martinez, V. (2001). Teaching tolerance in public and private schools. *The Phi Delta Kappa International*, *82*(7), 542–546.

Godwin, R. K, Godwin, J. W., & Martinez-Ebers, V. (2004). Civic socialization in public and fundamentalist schools. *Social Science Quarterly*, *85*(5), 1097–1111.

Greene, J. P. (2005). *Education myths: What special-interest groups want you to believe about our schools and why it isn't so*. New York, NY: Rowman and Littlefield Publishers, Inc.

Greene, J. P., Giammo, J., & Mellow, N. (1999). The effect of private education on political participation, social capital and tolerance: An examination of the Latino National Political Survey. *Georgetown Public Policy Review*, *5*(1), 53–67.

Greene, J. P., Mellow, N., & Giammo, J. (1999). Private schools and the public good: The effect of private education on political tolerance in the Texas poll. *Catholic Education: A Journal of Inquiry and Practice*, *2*(4), 429–443.

Gutmann, A. (1987). *Democratic education*. Princeton, NJ: Princeton University Press.

Howell, W., Peterson, P. E., Wolf, P. J., & Campbell, D. E. (2002). *The education gap: Vouchers and urban schools*. Washington, DC: Brookings Institution Press.

Kunzman, R. (2009). *Write these laws on your children: Inside the world of conservative Christian homeschooling*. Boston, MA: Beacon Press.

Kunzman, R. (2010). Homeschooling and religious fundamentalism. *International Electronic Journal of Elementary Education*, *3*(1), 17–28.

Lubienski, C. (2000). Whither the common good? A critique of home schooling. *Peabody Journal of Education*, *75*(1/2), 207–232.

Marcus, G. E., Sullivan, J. L., Theiss-Morse, E., & Wood, S. L. (1995). *With malice towards some: How some people make civil liberties judgments*. New York, NY: Cambridge University Press.

Medlin, R. (2000). Home schooling and the question of socialization. *Peabody Journal of Education*, *75*(1/2), 107–123.

Medlin, R. (2013). Homeschooling and the question of socialization revisited. *Peabody Journal of Education*, 88(3), 284–297.

Noel, A., Stark, P., Redford, J., & Zuckerberg, A. (2013). *Parent and family involvement in education, from the National Household Education Surveys Program of 2012* (NCES 2013-028). Retrieved from http://nces.ed.gov /pubs2013/2013028. pdf

Planty, M., Hussar, W., Snyder, T., Kena, G, Kewal-Ramani, A, Kemp, J., & Nachazel, T. (2009). *The condition of education 2009* (NCES 2009-081). Retrieved from http://nces.ed.gov/pubs2009 /2009081.pdf

Putnam, R. D. (2000). *Bowling alone: The collapse and revival of American community*. New York, NY: Simon and Schuster Paperbacks.

Ray, B. D. (2004). *Home educated and now adults: Their community and civic involvement, views about homeschooling and other traits*. Salem, OR: National Home Education Research Institute.

Ray, B. D. (2013). Homeschooling associated with beneficial learner and societal outcomes but educators do not promote it. *Peabody Journal of Education*, 88(3), 324–341.

Reich, R. (2002). The civic perils of homeschooling. *Educational Leadership*, 59(7), 56–59.

Reich, R. (2005). Why homeschooling should be regulated. In B. S. Cooper (Ed.), *Homeschooling in full view: A reader* (pp. 109–120). Greenwich, CT: Information Age.

Ross, C. J. (2010). Fundamentalist challenges to core democratic values: Exit and homeschooling. *William and Mary Bill of Rights Journal*, 18(4), 991–1014.

Sheffer, S. (1997). *A sense of self: Listening to homeschooled adolescent girls*. Portsmouth, NH: Boynton/Cook Publishers.

Smith, C., & Sikkink, D. (1999, April). Is private schooling privatizing? *First Things*, 92, 16–20.

Sullivan, J. L., Pierson, J., & Marcus, G. E. (1982). *Political tolerance and American democracy*. Chicago, IL: University of Chicago Press.

Tabachnick, R. (2011, May 23). The "Christian" dogma pushed by religious schools that are supported by your tax dollars. *AlterNet*. Retrieved from http://www. alternet.com

Thiessen, E. J. (2001). *In defence of religious schools and colleges*. Montreal, Canada: McGill-Queen's University Press.

Uecker, J. E. (2008). Alternative schooling strategies and the religious lives of American adolescents. *Journal for the Scientific Study of Religion*, 47(4), 563–584.

Van Pelt, D., Sikkink, D., Pennings, R., & Seel, J. (2012). Private religious protestant and Catholic schools in the United States and Canada: Introduction, Overview, and Policy Implications. *Journal of School Choice*, 6(1), 1–19.

West, R. L. (2009). The harms of homeschooling. *Philosophy and Public Policy Quarterly*, 29(3/4), 7–12.

Wing, N. (2012, August 8). Bobby Jindal school voucher system blasted as "destruction of education" by religious group. *The Huffington Post*. Retrieved from http://www.huffingtonpost.com

Wolf, P. J. (2005). School choice and civic values. In J. R. Betts & T. Loveless (Eds.), *Getting school choice right: Ensuring equity and efficiency in education policy*. Washington, DC: Brookings Institution Press.

Wolf, P. J., Greene, J. P., Kleitz, B., & Thalhammer, K. (2001). Private schooling and political tolerance. In P. E. Peterson & D. E. Campbell (Eds.), *Charters, vouchers, and public education* (pp. 268–290). Washington, DC: Brookings Institution Press.

Wolf, P. J., Peterson, P. E., & West, M. R. (2001). *Results of a school voucher experiment: The case of Washington, DC after two years* (John F. Kennedy School of Government Working Paper No. RWP02-022). Retrieved from http://papers.ssrn.com/sol3/papers.cfm?abstract _id=313822

Yuracko, K. A. (2008). Education off the grid: Constitutional constraints on homeschooling. *California Law Review, 96*, 123–184.

Index

Note: **Boldface** page numbers refer to tables & italic page numbers refer to figures. Page numbers followed by "n" refer to endnotes.

academic achievement 116–17; Black homeschool students 100, 108, 112, 116; definition 104; learning and 101–2; public school students 113
academic outcomes 8–9
academic performance, homeschoolers and 164–5
African American homeschool parents 9
African American homeschool parents, motivations for homeschooling: academic achievement 112–13, 116–17; ace/ethnicity 100; achievement scores variance 113–15; assumptions, limitations, and delimitations 108–9; characteristics of students and families 109; explanatory nonexperimental study 104–5; instruments, data, and data analysis 107–8; learning and academic achievement 101–2; population and sample 105–6; purpose and hypotheses 103–4; reasons for home education 100–1; reasons for homeschooling 109–12, **110**, **111**, 115; social, emotional, and psychological development 102; society in general and black community and culture 103
African Americans 99
American education 56; policy, factors 81; primary and secondary public school system 181
Americans with Disabilities Act (ADA) of 1990 146
Apple, M. W. 103
attendance laws and education 1
autonomous motivation 59
Aviram, R. 127

Belfield, C. 163–5
Bennet, K. 146
Black children: academic achievement 100; entrance to modern homeschool movement 99–100; establishing schools for 99; and White children 99

Black community and culture 103
Black homeschool students 109, **112**, **113**; academic achievement 108, 116; independent variables 116–17
Black homeschools 100, **107**; community 103–4; families 105, 106
Black public school 106, **107**, 113; *vs.* Black homeschool participants 107
blended learning 39
board of education 34
bricks-and-mortar schools, community role in 43–4
Brown v. Board of Education 44, 99
bundling 42–3

Campbell, D.E. 25
Catholic schools 35, 153–6
charter schools 10, 11, 37–9, 41, 42, 46, 145; cyber 9, 50, 51, 150; enrollment 94; public 50, 99, 147, *152*, 153, 154, 167; virtual 48
charters as desectorizing 37–9
Cheng, Albert 9, 25, 103
Cleveland school voucher program 45–6
Cogan, Melissa 12
college and career readiness 81, 84
Common Core State Standards 81
community: role in bricks-and-mortar schools 43; school as learning 43–4
content-controlled political tolerance scale 187, 188
conventional school system 125, 136
Cook, K. B. 146
cost per child, definition 105
Credé, M. 167
culture, Black community and 103
cybercharter 41, 42, 46, 51; school 9, 41, 46, 150
cyberschools 47, 48

democratic education 50
deschooling 2
desectorizing: charters as 37–9; virtuality as 39–42
digital education 45
digital learning 45

disabilities, students with 144, 146–9, **154**, 154–7; distribution of disabilities across sectors 151–2, **152**; empirical strategy 153
Duvall, S. 149
Dzehtsiarou, K. 28–9

ECAs 11, 14
ECHR *see* European Convention on Human Rights
ECtHR *see* European Court of Human Rights
education: attendance laws and 1; bureaucratization of 1; courses, technology-based distance 41; democratic 50; digital 45; online 50
education management organizations (EMOs) 52n3
Education of All Handicapped Children Act (EAHCA) of 1975 146
education savings accounts (ESAs) 11, 12
EFA *see* exploratory factor analysis
Eisenstein, M. A. 186
elective home education 30n2, 124, 141
EMOs *see* education management organizations
entrepreneurs, home education 1
Erickson, D. A. 118
ESAs *see* education savings accounts
ESSA *see* Every Student Succeeds Act
European Convention on Human Rights (ECHR) 21, 28, 30n2
European Court of Human Rights (ECtHR) 19–20, 22, 26, 28, 29, 30n2
Every Student Succeeds Act (ESSA) 7
exploratory factor analysis (EFA) 64

Factors Influencing College Success in Mathematics (FICSMath) survey 15; data and methods 166–7; funding 178; limitations 174–5; racial and ethnic backgrounds of students 175–6; research question 165–6; results 167–73, **168**, **169**, *170*, *171*, **172–4**
Fairfax campus's Web site 40
FAPE *see* free and appropriate public education
Farris, Michael 7
FICSMath survey *see* Factors Influencing College Success in Mathematics survey
Fields-Smith, C. 100–1
Florida: McKay program 150; virtual school 48, 84
formal instruction, definition 105
formal schooling 181; development 36; in United States 1
free and appropriate public education (FAPE) 146
full-time virtual schools 41, 42, 51

Gaither, M. 164
Garnett, N. S. 39
Gatto, John Taylor 2
gender, race and 9–10

Georgia: K–12 tuition tax credit program 95; Private School Tax Credit program 85; tax credit scholarships in 85; virtual schools in 41–2
German Constitutional Court (FCC) 20, 22–6, 28, 29, 30n2
German education policy 23
Germany's antihomeschooling policy 27
Glanzer, P. L. 25
Global Home Education Conference 7, 13
Godwin, R. K. 183
grade point average (GPA) 8
graduated homeschooled students 163
Greene, J. P. 186
Guba, E. G. 129
Gutmann, Amy 25

Hawthorne effect 108, 109
hegemonic public/private binary 33–7
hermeneutic phenomenological approach study, homeschooling 127–8
Hess, Rick 4
Hip Homeschool Moms 7
Holt, John 2
home education *see* homeschooling
home educators 2, 11–15, 51, 57, 101
Home School Legal Defense Association (HSLDA) 6, 7, 13, 164
homeschool/homeschooling: achievement scores variance 114–15; cost of 11; critics of 9, 10, 24, 103; efficacy for 62; entrepreneurs 1; growth in United States 3; impacts upon 48–51; as learning environments 57–8; legal in states 5; legal status 6–7; parent-led 99; political tolerance 25; and political tolerance 184–6; population in United States 82; quantitative researchers of 118; regulatory regimes for 33; research, empirical limitations 4–6; selection, reasons for 3; *see also* human right of home education
homeschool/homeschooling as pedagogical practice 124–7; analysis 129; change in lifestyle 133–4; child in center theme 130–1; focuses of meaning 136–8; historical development 138–9; limitations 140–1; living in the present 135; participants 128; procedure 128–9; rectifying past experiences of school 135–6; responsibility, choice, and control 131–2; self-awareness development 133; sense of family 130; slowing down pace of life 134–5
homeschool families 2, 3, 48–9, 106; family income for 6; financial support for 11–12
homeschool parents 2, 4, 6, 7, 12, 14, 56, 57, 59; African American 9; teaching practices 65
homeschool research, challenges of 163–4
homeschool student 2, 4–6, 8, 9, 13; definition 104; with disabilities 148–9; graduated 163; population 5, 163

homeschoolers 2–4, 35; and academic performance 164–5; advocacy efforts 6–7; Israeli 7; in Wisconsin 5
Hopkins, W. G. 108
households, in school sector 151, **151**
HSLDA *see* Home School Legal Defense Association
human right of home education 19–22; interference necessary 26–7; interference proportional 27–9; legitimate policy 23–5; policy for suitability 25–6; proportionality 22–3, 26
hybrid homeschool 3
hybrid homeschool, parents' reasons for selection 81–4, 87–91; demographic data for respondents 86–7; descriptive survey methods 85–6; family characteristics 93; funding 85; information and decision making 90–3; parents value 84–5; religious education 87, 95; respondents' stated reasons 89; sources of information 95; value of hybrid homeschool 94–5

ICCPR *see* International Covenant of Civil and Political Rights
ICESCR *see* International Covenant of Economic Social and Cultural Rights
IDEA *see* Individuals with Disabilities Education Act
Ideologues and Pedagogues (Galen) 7
IEP *see* Individualized Education Programs
Illich, Ivan 2
individualistic counterculture 2
Individualized Education Programs (IEP) 145
Individuals with Disabilities Education Act (IDEA) 146–8
Industrial Revolution 125, 138, 139
informal schooling 43
institutional private schools 33, 99
institutional public schools 99
institutional racism 99
International Covenant of Civil and Political Rights (ICCPR) 21
International Covenant of Economic Social and Cultural Rights (ICESCR) 21
Iowa Tests of Basic Skills (ITBS) 104–7
Isenberg, E.J. 5, 164
Israel: homeschoolers, Neuman and Guterman study 7; homeschooling 125
ITBS *see* Iowa Tests of Basic Skills

Jones-Sanpei, H. 164

K–12 education 42; online 41
K–12 grade-level school 105
K–6 school 47
K–12 tuition tax credit program, Georgia 95
Kelly, J. P. 86–8, 90, 93, 94

Kingdom of Children (Stevens) 2
Kisura, M. W. 100–1
Kuncel, N. 167
Kunzman, R. 164, 184

Lane, J. D. 146
Lastowska, Greg 44
learning: and academic achievement 101–2; blended 39; digital 45; online 41, 45; optimal 57; structured 105
learning environments, homeschools as 57–8
LEAs *see* local education agencies
least-liked group 187, 191, **191**, **192**
legal scholarship 34
legitimate policy 22–5
Lemon v. Kurtzman, 1971 50
liberal democracy 24, 25, 182, 186, 197
Lincoln, Y. S. 129
local education agencies (LEAs) 147
localism 44–8
Lubienski, C. 103
Lundy, G. 115

Martinez-Ebers, V. 183
Massachusetts Virtual Academy 47
Mataras, T. K. 146
Mazama, A. 115
Medlin, R. G. 102, 185
micro-schools 84
Milliken v. Bradley 44
modern homeschool movement, Black children entrance to 99–100
Moller, Kai 22, 26
motivation: autonomous 59; *see also* African American homeschool parents, motivations for homeschooling
motivation study, homeschools 57–9, 72–4; academic engagement 62; cluster analysis 66–9, 75n2; correlations among variables 65–7; data analysis 63–4; demographic characteristics 70–1; efficacy for homeschooling 62; measurement 60; need satisfaction 63; participant characteristics 59–60; procedure 63; satisfaction, efficacy, and academic engagement 69–70; support for autonomy 58, 61; support for competence 58, 61; support for relatedness 58, 62; teaching practices 63, 70
Muldowney, H. M. 83
Murphy, J. 20, 26, 83, 84, 94, 117

National Black Homeschoolers (NBH) 105
National Center for Education Statistics (NCES) 2, 3, 5, 7
National Home Education Research Institute (NHERI) 2, 7
National Household Education Survey (NHES) 5, 163, 168, 183

National Study on Youth and Religion 187
NBH *see* National Black Homeschoolers
NCES *see* National Center for Education Statistics
NCLB *see* No Child Left Behind
Neuman, A. 127
NHERI *see* National Home Education Research Institute
NHES *see* National Household Education Survey
No Child Left Behind (NCLB) 7, 46
North Carolina, virtual schools in 41–2
Nulty, D. D. 86

online course, modularity of 51
online education 50; K–12 41
online learning 41, 45
online school 52; state-sponsored 84
optimal learning 57

PALS *see* The Patterns of Adaptive Learning Survey
Parent and Family Involvement in Education survey 8, 164
parental satisfaction, with special education 150–1, **152**, 154–7
parental use of conditional negative regard (PCNR) 62
parental use of conditional positive regard (PCPR) 62
parent-educators 1, 10
parent-led home-based education 99
The Patterns of Adaptive Learning Survey (PALS) 61
PCNR *see* parental use of conditional negative regard
PCPR *see* parental use of conditional positive regard
PFI survey *see* Parent and Family Involvement in Education survey
Phillips, D. C. 118
Pierce v. Society of Sisters 13, 21, 33
pluralism 24, 25
political tolerance: empirical model and analyses 190–1; homeschooling and 184–6; levels **192**; measurement 187–8; regression analysis 193, **194–5**; scale responses **192**; study sample 188–90, **189**; survey responses 191–2
political tolerance, private schooling and: experimental evidence 184; observational evidence 183–4
polyphonic categorization of schools 49
Positive and Negative Conditional Regard Scale 62
Private School Tax Credit program, Georgia 85
private schooling and political tolerance: experimental evidence 184; observational evidence 183–4

private schools 34–5, 144, 147; choice programs 145; institutional 33, 99; parents 35; religious, critics of 182; voucher 184
The Problems in School Questionnaire (PIS) 61
public charter schools 50, 99, 147, *152*, 153, 154, 167
public schools 34, 147; achievement scores variance 114–15; *vs.* homeschool participants 107; student, definition 104; traditional 1–4, 8–9, 12–15, 37, 51, 87, 145, 147, 149, 150, *152*, 154, 157, 172, 176, 182, 183, 186
public/private binary, hegemonic 33–7
Putnam, R. D. 185

Qaqish, B. 165

race and gender 9–10
racial protectionism 9
racism, institutional 99
Ray, B. D. 7, 9, 57, 84, 87, 117
Reeve, J. 62
regulatory regimes, for homeschools 33
Rehabilitation Act of 1973 146
religious private schooling, critics of 182
Rendell-Baker v. Kohn. Rendell-Baker 36
Rudner, L. M. 116

Saiger, Aaron 3, 6, 13
SAT *see* scholastic aptitude test
Scafidi, B. 86–8, 90, 93, 94
Schaum v. Germany (2014) 22
Schneider, M. 156
scholarship 164; Georgia's HOPE Scholarship program 95; legal 34; tax credit 85–7
scholastic aptitude test (SAT) 8
school choice market, growth in 11–12
school sector, households in 151, **151**
school vouchers: Cleveland school voucher program 45; government-issued 37; private 184
SDT *see* self-determination theory
self-awareness development 133
self-determination theory (SDT) 57, 58–9; *see also* motivation study, homeschools
Sikkink, D. 184–5
Smith, C. 184–5
socialization 13, 50, 102, 138
special education, parental satisfaction with 150–1, **152**, 154–7
Spiegler, T. 20, 23, 29
SSOs *see* Student Scholarship Organizations
state-sponsored online schools 84
Stevens, Mitchell 7; *Kingdom of Children* 2
structured learning, definition 105
Student Scholarship Organizations (SSOs) 85
student's school-related problem 61

students with disabilities 144, 146–9, **154**, 154–7; distribution of disabilities across sectors 151–2, **152**; empirical strategy 153
Sullivan, J. L. 185, 187

tax credit scholarship 85–7
Taylor, V. 100
teaching practices: homeschool parents 65; motivational profiles 70; survey 79–80
Teske, P. 156
Thomas, L. 167
tony private academy 35
traditional classroom settings 81, 82
traditional public bureaucracies 1
traditional public school 1–4, 8, 9, 12–15, 37, 51, 87, 145, 147, 149, 150, *152*, 154, 157, 172, 176, 182, 183, 186

UMS *see* university model schools
United Nations Convention on the Rights of the Child (UNCRC) 28
United States: critics of home education 24; formal schooling in 1; homeschooling growth in 3; homeschooling population in 82; ideological "hegemony" in 34; NCES's Homeschooling in 6; subsidized faith-based schools 1
Universal Declaration of Human Rights (UDHR) 13, 21
university model schools (UMS) 81–3
unschooling 2, 49, 126, 140

Van Galen, J.A. 10
Virtual Academy 47, 48
virtual charter school 48
virtual education 39, 42, 43; impact of 48; programs 47–8
virtual schools 40, 43, 47; acceleration of 49; Florida 48, 84; full-time 41–2, 51; in Georgia and North Carolina 41–2
virtuality 43, 51; as desectorizing 39–42; long-run effect of 50

Wearne, Eric 3, 6
Wisconsin homeschool data 5, *5*
Wolf, P. J. 25

www.ingramcontent.com/pod-product-compliance
Ingram Content Group UK Ltd.
Pitfield, Milton Keynes, MK11 3LW, UK
UKHW010020280225
455677UK00023B/699